ANSWER
BACK

Culver Public Library

ANSWERING

BACK

Liberal Responses to Conservative Arguments

DAVID COATES

continuum

NEW YORK • LONDON

2010

The Continuum International Publishing Group Inc
80 Maiden Lane, New York, NY 10038

The Continuum International Publishing Group Ltd
The Tower Building, 11 York Road, London SE1 7NX

www.continuumbooks.com

Copyright © 2010 by David Coates

Answering Back by David Coates was originally published in hard cover by Praeger Press under the title *A Liberal Tool Kit*

http://www.greenwood.com/praeger

an imprint of Greenwood Publishing Group, Inc., Westport, CT.
Copyright © 2007 by David Coates.

This paperback edition by arrangement with Greenwood Publishing Group, Inc.

All rights reserved. No part of this book may be reproduced or transmitted in any form or by any means, electronic or mechanical, including photocopying, reprinting, or on any information storage or retrieval system, without permission in writing from Greenwood Publishing Group.

Library of Congress Cataloging-in-Publication Data
Coates, David, 1946–
Answering back : liberal responses to conservative arguments / by David Coates.
    p. cm.
Includes bibliographical references and index.
ISBN-13: 978-1-4411-2693-1 (pbk. : alk. paper)
ISBN-10: 1-4411-2693-7 (pbk. : alk. paper)
1. Liberalism–United States. 2. Conservatism–United States. 3. Right and left (Political science) 4. Political planning–United States. 5. United States–Politics and government. I. Title.

JC574.2.U6C63 2010
320.520973–dc22

2009017745

Typeset by Newgen Imaging Systems Pvt Ltd, Chennai, India
Printed in the United States of America

For Jonathan, with love,
at the start of his college career

Contents

Preface   ix

Chapter 1   A Call to Arms   1

Chapter 2   Clearing the Decks   13

Chapter 3   The Wonders of "Trickle-Down" Economics   34

Chapter 4   Cutting "Welfare" to Help the Poor   57

Chapter 5   Reforming Social Security   85

Chapter 6   Bringing Health to the Health Care System   106

Chapter 7   Immigration Control in a Land of Immigrants   138

Chapter 8   Is God Necessarily Conservative?   172

Chapter 9   The Wisdom of the War in Iraq?   201

Chapter 10 The Real Causes of the Financial Meltdown   230

Select Bibliography   273

Index   277

Preface

This book began life as another, as *A Liberal Tool Kit* published by Praeger-Greenwood in July 2007. Its aim then, as now, was to help build an informed and self-confident constituency for progressive social change. The task in 2007 was to support liberal candidates in the pursuit of power, and to roll back a string of conservative initiatives emanating from a Republican White House. The task in 2009 is fortunately different. It is now to defend, deepen and sustain a liberal beachhead established by Barack Obama and the Congressional Democrats in the wake of their election victory in November 2008. To that end, a set of changes has been made. The arguments and data have been updated. The focus of each chapter has been reset to address the issues faced by a new Democratic administration rather than by an old Republican one; and the chapter exploring whether "the economy was safe in Republican hands" has been replaced by one documenting the origins of the financial meltdown that rendered the original question mute.

The decision to revise and publish a new edition was a direct response to the new balance of political forces brought into play by the November 2008 election. Liberals may hail that as a resounding victory for their cause, but conservatives are not treating it as a resounding defeat for theirs. On the contrary, their opposition to progressive proposals on health care reform, social security, taxation and welfare, immigration and the war remains firmly intact. Right-wing think tanks continue to pitch their more conservative alternatives with the same degree of determination that they demonstrated before the election – actually pitching it in truth with slightly greater determination and stridency now because suddenly they have a liberal president to block as well as a liberal electoral coalition to undermine. So the debates which preceded the election are if anything *more* intense now that the election is over than they were in the run-up to it, and they are likely to become more intense still. The liberal case will therefore need to be made again, and made even more persuasively than before, not simply to blunt this reenergized conservative push-back but also to keep the pressure up on an administration which, though progressive in its instincts, might yet begin to retreat under that conservative onslaught unless the liberal voice is heard in the country, and heard loud and long. *Answering Back* was once vital to slow down a Republican majority taking this country to the right. Answering back is now vital to sustain a Democratic majority attempting to take it to the left.

In preparing what follows, I have gathered debts to a very special set of research assistants and friends. It was only through the dedicated efforts of Shannon Philmon, Grace Johnson, Kristin Olson, Nate Reister, Alison Duncan and Caitlin O'Connell that the writing and updating of this book was even possible. I am indebted to all of them for the quality of their research and for their willingness to tolerate lines of argument that so often diverged from their own. In addition to gathering much of the material upon which the manuscript was constructed, Caitlin, Shannon, Grace, Kristin and Nate read and commented upon parts of the argument as it emerged. So too did members of my immediate family, Eileen, Tom and Ed; and a number of my friends, Peter Siavelis, Joel Krieger, Michele Gillespie, Kevin Pittard, Neal Walls, Kathy Smith, and Greg Pollock. None of them are responsible for what follows, but all of them in their different ways helped to make what follows stronger. I thank them all.

For more detail than the notes can provide on the sources underpinning the arguments surveyed here, and for suggestions on further reading, please visit the sites associated with this book. You will find them at http://answeringbackdavidcoates.blogspot.com and at http://www.davidcoates.net.

I hope that you find what follows to be of value to you.

David Coates
Wake Forest University

CHAPTER 1

A Call to Arms

Democratic politics is largely a spectator sport. The crowd gets to play every now and then, but between elections, it is largely a matter of watching and listening. Most of us tire of that more quickly than we should, probably because – in a world of 24-hour news coverage – words flow in huge numbers, washing over us like summer rain. We get wet; and depending on the color of the rain, we either like it or we don't. In the years of the Bush presidency, given the predominant color of the water then falling in political America, those of a liberal persuasion did not enjoy the rain much at all. Now, with a different president and a more liberal agenda, it is conservatives who are suddenly getting very wet.

Political parties are the great rainmakers of the modern age. They package ideas. They put together programs. They organize blocs of voters. They tell us what is happening – what is going right and what is going wrong. They point a way forward; and they provide us with protection against the rain coming from the other side. When they are effective, they provide a narrative linking the private hopes of their supporters to some great national program of reform. They keep their own people dry by the quality of that narrative – by the ability of the arguments and images they deploy to act as an effective umbrella against narratives coming from their opponents. For at least

30 years after the New Deal, the biggest umbrella in American politics was a liberal one, constructed and held up by the Democrats. But that umbrella broke long ago, great holes torn in its canvas from the 1970s by the disintegration of the New Deal coalition and the rise of the Christian Right. For the last three decades – in one branch of government after another – a conservative umbrella has held sway, and Republicans have been the normal political beneficiaries of its canopy. The issue before us, as the Obama presidency begins, is whether that conservative canopy is itself now being replaced.

Right-wing forces in the United States clearly fear that it is. How else are we to understand the venom, outrage and even despair visible in much of the reaction by Republican politicians and their core supporters to the initial policy moves of the new administration? But one swallow does not make a summer, and though the election result in November 2008 was an important moment of realignment in American politics – as potentially important in its way as were the realignments of 1932 and 1980 – whether that potential can be realized is still to be determined. The big issue – of whether the United States will go to the left or to the right – is still in play; and though electoral fortunes are currently stacked in the Democrats' favor, the economic and military fortunes of the United States are not. The Obama presidency came into being in the midst of the worst economic downturn since the Great Depression and inherited the military and diplomatic legacy of what is arguably the worst foreign policy decision in the entire history of the Republic – the decision to invade Iraq in 2003 in pursuit of weapons of mass destruction that turned out not to be there. For the moment, Obama as president and the Democrats as legislators are the beneficiaries of a mess which they visibly inherited rather than created. Two months into the presidency, approval ratings for the new president were still in the high 60s and for his Republican opponents in the mid-20s,[1] with four Americans in five believing that the economic downturn was Bush's legacy rather than Obama's fault. But time will narrow those gaps. Conservative fortunes will rise again; and the Republican Party can be relied upon to do everything possible to slow liberal initiatives and to rewrite history in ways that place the blame for our contemporary ills on the politics of the center-left rather than on the politics of the center-right. That rewriting of history is already well under way, as we will see in later chapters that examine the arguments of conservative talk-show hosts and explanations of the US housing crisis.

So on one set of things at least we can be clear. If this liberal moment is to be consolidated, that consolidation will have to be won, and once won it will have to be defended. It will have to be won and defended by the adequacy of the policies emerging from the White House;[2] and it will have to be won and defended by the quality of the arguments used to deflate and deflect an inevitable and well-orchestrated conservative push-back. This book has been written explicitly to help in that deflation and deflection.

Answering back

R. H. Tawney once gave the British Labour Party a piece of advice that we could still use today. Crushed by a conservative landslide in 1931, reeling on the ropes of electoral defeat, there were plenty of people within that party ready to throw in the towel: but not R. H. Tawney. Do not panic in the face of resistance, he told the Party. Expect it. It is going to come anyway. Do not dodge the opposition by compromising principles and promising smooth things. "Support won by such methods is a reed shaken by every wind." Instead, get up and fight for what you believe in. You cannot negotiate on your knees. Explain your aims with complete openness and candor: and prepare for power by mobilizing behind you "a body of conviction as resolute and informed as the opposition" you face. Do not encourage your adherents "to ask what they will get from a [progressive] Government, as though a campaign were a picnic, all beer and sunshine." Ask them rather "what they will give." "Make them understand that [your return to power] is merely the first phase of a struggle, the issue of which depends on them."[3]

That was good advice in 1932, and it is good advice now, in the wake of the 2006 mid-term election and the 2008 presidential one. Those elections broke the Republican stranglehold on power in Washington. They gave the Democrats the ability to recapture the political agenda, and threw into stark relief the tensions currently dividing the Republican coalition. Election results in both 2006 and 2008 made clear that voters in general are more progressive than the conservative lobbyists in Washington would have us believe: certainly less overwhelmingly concerned with social issues than are the Christian Right; less willing to dismantle social security than are the libertarians; and more concerned with health care than with immigration. So there is a space – an opportunity again – for progressive politics. But "Obama's victory offers no guarantee of a re-alignment. It is only an opportunity to bring one about."[4] Political spaces always close, and close quickly, if they are not taken – particularly spaces like this one. Conservative forces have been shaken, but they will regroup. So if the progressive moment is not to be lost, liberals will need to respond as, long ago, Tawney did. The question is how: this way at least.

1. Calling the conservative bluff

If conservatives think that poverty and social injustice can be solved without government help, and that economic recovery requires only tax cuts and welfare reform, we should invite them to try it on a personal basis. We should invite them to settle in a run-down part of some northern city, deny themselves education, good social contacts and subsidized housing, take on the care of two or three small children and face a job market of unskilled low-paid work. Then we should invite them to go live the American Dream; and if they find that they cannot, then we should also invite them to admit that what they cannot do, others cannot be expected to do either. We should invite them to recognize that circumstances make people as well as people make circumstances, and that if we want people to prosper we must act on their circumstances also. The flourishing of individual rights, so important to American conservatives, requires a politics of equal starting points. There can be no genuine equality of rights, generation on generation, if vast income differences in one age-cohort produce huge inequalities in life chances for the next. Children cannot be held responsible for the poverty (or indeed affluence) into which they are born; and because they cannot, it is time to assert again the importance of level playing fields. It is time for liberals to say that when playing fields are as unequal as they are now, individual self-help and an active voluntary sector will never be enough to give everyone an equal chance. Level playing fields have to be built. Building them requires public programs. It requires a strong and assertive Liberalism.

The liberal voice need to be very clear too on some very basic points of political philosophy: clear on freedom, and clear on democracy. Freedom and license are not the same things, and formal freedoms have to have substance to be real. Proper political freedoms have to be matched by equivalent economic and social ones. Other advanced democracies know that. They even write basic social rights into their constitutions. We do not, but we are still subject to the same truth. If significant numbers of Americans cannot get proper health care, or face destitution if they lose their job, then their freedom is impaired, no matter how solid their right to vote is. That voting power too must be real as well as formal. Where is the real democracy when unregulated lobby money buys so much influence? Where is the real democracy when politicians are subject to vast no-go areas: no regulating companies, no giving American workers job protection, no managing markets? Conservatives are quick to tell us how much unnecessary taxation we pay. They are not so quick to tell us how much unnecessary expenditure we make to the private suppliers of our health care. But what is good for the goose is also good for the gander. We need to ask why people are "freer" if they hand over money to the private companies that they do not elect than to the politicians whom they do. We need to say that markets can be effective allocators of resources, can be genuinely sensitive to people's real preferences, but only if everyone operating freely within them has the same amount of purchasing power, the same amount of money to spend. To the degree that they do not – to the degree that incomes and property rights are significantly unequal – then to that degree too, unregulated markets become flawed. Markets in unequal societies respond to those with money. Democracies respond to people with votes. Everyone has a vote. Not everyone has money. It is time for the collective interests of the people with votes to prevail over the self-interest of the people with money.

2. Valuing intellectual endeavor

It is a striking feature of so much conservative commentary on the state of modern America these days that the sophistication of their problem specification is never matched by a parallel sophistication in the solutions canvassed. Conservative America is full of woes about our modern condition: too much regulation from the libertarians; too much moral decay from the Religious Right; too many immigrants; too many foreign wars . . . the list of woes is potentially endless. But not the solutions. They always come quick and short. Build a wall. Stop a gay marriage. Cut a tax. Get people off welfare. Leave it to the private sector. Set the people free. And if the problems persist, even when you have done all that freedom setting, blame liberals for their continued interference with the wonders of the free market, and then carry on much as before. Build a higher wall. Create a lower tax. Bring the limits on welfare even further forward; but whatever you do, do not pause and do not think. Just spot a problem, grab a cliché, and charge!

That cannot be the progressive way. We have to say that the social ills of contemporary America have such complex roots, and are so stacked one upon the other, that the last thing they will respond to are quick and simple solutions. In fact, so complex and intertwined are the issues here that conservatives often have a point: even well-intentioned progressive solutions can sometimes make things worse. Things are so interlocked and mutually reinforcing in the contemporary crisis of the American welfare state, for example, that movement forward on one front does often equate with movement back on another. Raising the age of retirement to ease the burden of payroll tax on the young may look desirable from one perspective, but not necessarily from all of them. It is great if you are white, young and affluent; but since on average the poor die younger than the rich, and a greater proportion of black Americans than white Americans are poor, not so great if you happen to be old, poor and African-American. Conundrums of that kind are always there for the advocates of free markets to exploit. Just leave everything to the interplay of supply and demand, they say. Do not interfere. If you move on one front, you will only make the other front worse. But how ludicrous is that? Complex and interlocking social problems are not solved by the quick fix of doing nothing. Interlocking social problems are only solved by joined-up policy initiatives that address each element of the conundrum simultaneously. This is not the moment for free-market economics 101. Advocating market solutions for every social problem is either lazy or self-indulgent. Unregulated markets reproduce and amplify inequalities. Well-regulated markets do not; and we should say so.

3. Recapturing the narrative

Political journeys are always long ones, and electoral coalitions are not just things to build. They are also things to sustain. I suspect that the real reason that the Republican Right rails so loudly against academia and the liberal media is that they know the importance of ideas and their dissemination, and they sense that a careful examination of many of their ideas can only expose their flaws. What is true for them is true for us also. Progressives have a powerful interest in the funding of extensive and rigorous social research. Facts can only help to demonstrate where policy is needed, and what that policy should be. And progressives have a huge interest in ensuring that awareness of their research is widely and effectively spread. The imbalance of resources between the think tanks of the Right and those of the Left is one of the great progressive weaknesses of the age. The paucity of liberal media outlets relative to conservative ones is the other great weakness. At least the shortage of center-left think tanks is now being corrected, if only incrementally and slowly, as liberals begin to grasp the nature of the conservative *movement* they face, and the need to match that movement by one of their own. That correction cannot come soon enough. In truth, it is long overdue and still inadequate in scale.[5]

The best way to build a movement is to play effective counter-hegemonic politics. That involves creating in the public mind both *a great divide* between what we stand for and what Republicans in practice offer, and a clear sense of the *principles* underpinning the progressive program on offer. Liberals will only create that sense of division if they talk openly and confidently again about morality and vision – emphasizing the importance of equality and justice, individual liberty based on positive rights, and real freedom rooted in economic and social security. The role of the Left as a moral force must be to make decency, compassion and care respectable again. We must talk not just about individualism and self-help, but also about responsibility to others; and we must insist that the trinity of equality, compassion and community constitutes *the* route to prosperity and progress, and not – as our political opponents would have it – prosperity's greatest barrier.[6]

If we are to answer back effectively against conservative orthodoxies that are as strongly held and widely disseminated as those facing us now, our liberal rebuttal will have to be powerful both in what it says and in how it is delivered. Creating arguments stronger than those we face requires of us that we learn from the way our political opponents build and disseminate their arguments, and that we set standards for ourselves that are higher than those common in conservative circles. To that end, the following guidelines seem appropriate, and will be followed in all the material developed here.

1. We need to deal with the alternative point of view in all its complexity
The first is this. It is no good deluding ourselves about the potency of our case by testing our arguments only against easy targets or straw men. What we have to do instead is build the conservative case in all its faces – putting its weak and strong components in their appropriate slots – and then respond to the case in its totality. We have to summarize conservative arguments with as much care as we can manage – leaving out as little as possible – and actually guide people to the places in which they can read those arguments more fully themselves. To do anything less would be both intellectually dishonest and politically self-defeating.

2. We need to balance complexity in argument with clarity in presentation
We then have to put the liberal response together in ways that make it accessible to the people who will use it. We have to make that response as strong and all-encompassing as it can be – and that means also making it as complex and internally coherent as it needs to be – but complexity in argument must not be matched by complexity in presentation and language. On the contrary, the prime skill we need to develop is one of saying complicated things in simple ways. Effective arguments are those that people can own. They cannot own what they cannot understand; and we will not persuade others if we cannot first persuade ourselves.

3. We need to design arguments that can run the gamut
  from sound bites to theses
Third, the liberal response needs to be constructed in such a way that it can be used differently for different audiences. Some audiences need long and complex conversations. In others, the long and complex would fall like concrete rain. All arguments are built out of separate

parts, and all good arguments move from the specific to the general, the simple to the complex, the visible to the underlying, the empirical to the theoretical and so on. Our answers have to be of that sophisticated kind, but they also have to be built from stand-alone parts that can be extracted for use in each specific case. We have to put the rebuttal together, that is, in such a way that people wanting to use it can easily cherry-pick the parts that are appropriate for the audience with which they happen to be dealing.

4. We have to anchor our case in solid and reliable evidence

If the exercise in which we are engaged here is to be more than one of assertion and counter-assertion, we also have to make sure that what we say is anchored in systematically gathered and high-quality data. That means that our case has to be firmly rooted in the best scholarship that is currently available. Conservative advocates tend not to read widely outside their comfort zone, but we have to; and as we do so, we have to make it possible for others to take the same journey themselves. Extensive footnotes (and in this case, also *academic Websites*[7]) are therefore vital to this purpose. People do not need to read the footnotes or visit the sites if they do not want to. Their very existence might be reassurance enough. But the underpinnings of what we say have to be part of how we answer back, because only if the underpinnings of our arguments exist (and are accessible) can we legitimately ask of our conservative opponents that they too demonstrate the foundations of theirs.

5. The problem specification has to be superior . . .

In addition to the quality of evidence, we will need to focus too on the way problems are framed and premises followed through. The Republican Right has long recognized the importance of how issues are "framed," and so too must we. Someone on welfare can be a "casualty," a "victim" or the "agent" of his/her own poverty: and which of those three notions prevails effectively fix the political responses thought appropriate. If welfare-recipients are victims they need help. If they are agents, they need strictures! So the policy implications of each problem specification have to be made clear, as does the evidence justifying the specification chosen. If the poor are victims, it has to be demonstrated. Equally, if they are not, their responsibility for their own plight has to be shown; and we need to see the showing.

6. . . . and the logic has to be tight
If that demonstration is to be effective, there can be no leaps in the logic that then carries us from problem specification to solution, and no treating of one issue in isolation from the rest. In the triangle of wages, employment and global competition, for example, the conservative argument we face is that raising the first (wages) in the context of the third (global competition) must adversely affect the second (jobs). If we do not like the low-wage policy which that argument generates, we will either have to challenge the logic of the conservative linkages, or change one of the variables in play. In this case, we are going to find that one of the variables has to go. We are going to find that we cannot have a viable wages policy without designing a trade policy that is consistent with it: because if we do not get those two things into some coherent and logical line, moderate and sensible people are just not going to be persuaded that our liberal alternative is even credible, let alone desirable. Our arguments, that is, will only persuade if they are genuinely superior and complete.

The great moving left show

So there are standards here that we have to meet as we answer back; and if we do so, two things should follow. The first is that the democratic character and quality of the debate should go up. We might not win every argument, but win or lose, knowledge of the issues and their solutions should be significantly enhanced. And anyway, more likely than not, if we hit these standards, we will win many of those arguments; and minds will slowly and imperceptibly change. Not the minds of the totally committed, of course. Those are already hermetically sealed by a catechism of clichés and half-truths that no dialogue can loosen. But if our arguments are strong and our procedures rigorous, we might reach other minds – more open minds, minds more liberal with a small "l" – minds of more independent Americans still keen to get to the bottom of the international and local ills that befall us.

Robert Reich once wrote a wonderful essay describing how the Republican Party had captured and colonized what he called the four great narratives of American political life – two hopeful, two fearful – that once had been the bedrock of support for progressive causes: "the triumphant individual," "the benevolent community," "the mobs at the gate" and "the rot at the top."[8] Twenty-five years earlier, in a different but related country, Margaret Thatcher had done the same thing to the Democratic Party's equivalent there – the British Labour Party. She had stolen their best tunes, drained them of their center-left content, and filled them with a conservatism of her own. She took their vocabulary – a vocabulary of freedom, justice and equality – and replaced its progressive content with a conservative one. She took the Left's main policy weapons and turned them upside down: telling the British people to think of the democratic management of a private economy as the main cause of that economy's poor performance rather than as the best route to its improvement. She effected what was known at the time as "the great moving right show."[9]

But in the end that theft of all that was best and progressive in the politics of the United Kingdom failed, because even Margaret Thatcher could not create a unified and civilized society by advocating a politics that sets individuals against each other in an unregulated struggle for survival. She could not do it in the UK and the Republicans have not been able to do it here either. There is a visible gap between the grand visions of their rhetoric and the realities within which we all live, a gap between promise and performance which cost the Republicans the White House in 2008. We once again enjoy the possibility of consolidating a *great moving left show*, of pulling the center of gravity of American politics back into the civilized center. But shows of that kind do not happen unless somebody puts them on: which is why it is now time for us to get the narratives back, time for us to sing our tunes again. To sing well and to sing together, we all have to learn the same words.[10] Here, in the chapters that follow, culled from the work of the finest think tanks of the democratic left, are some of those words. Let us hope that they help us to perform a little better under an Obama presidency than we managed to do under the Bush ones.

Notes

1. "In or Out of Favor," *New York Times*, March 7, 2009: according to Gallup Polls, on February 1, 2009 Rush Limbaugh's popularity rating was 28 percent while Barack Obama's was 66 percent.

2. President Obama is well aware of this, as he told his radio audience on February 28, 2009: "I know these steps won't sit well with the special interests and the lobbyists who are invested in the old way of doing business, and I know they're gearing up for a fight as we speak. My message to them is this: So am I."

3. R. H. Tawney, "The Choice before the Labour Party," *Political Quarterly*, vol. 3, 1932; reproduced in William A. Robson (editor), *The Political Quarterly in the 1930s*, London, Allen Lane, 1971, pp. 93–111.

4. Paul Starr, "The Realignment Opportunity," *American Prospect*, December 2008, p. 3.

5. On the persisting weakness of liberal think tanks – both in funding and in function – see Andy Rich, "War of Ideas," *Stanford Social Innovation Review*, Spring 2005, pp. 1–27.

6. The case has been laid out with great clarity and passion in Robert Reich's *Reason: Why Liberals Will Win the Battle for America*, Vintage Books, 2004.

7. To read more, and to see in detail the primary sources used as basic data here, see the sites linked to this volume: http://answeringbackdavidcoates.blogspot.com; http://liberaltoolkit.blogspot.com; and www.davidcoates.net.

8. Robert Reich, "The Lost Art of Democratic Narrative," *New Republic*, March 21, 2005.

9. Stuart Hall, "The Great Moving Right Show," in Stuart Hall and Martin Jacques (editors), *The Politics of Thatcherism*, London, Lawrence and Wishart, 1983, p. 39.

10. For a fascinating discussion of the importance of getting the words right, see Geoffrey Nunberg, *Talking Right*, New York PublicAffairs, 2006.

CHAPTER 2

Clearing the Decks

There are powerful conservative arguments out there which liberals need to think about with considerable care: arguments put forward with conviction by people of genuine integrity and by institutions of high academic repute. Debating with them is a serious and important endeavor. But there are other arguments out there too – arguments of less force and value – which need to be cleared away first. For these other arguments have a different purpose. They exist less to stimulate debate than to close it down, and are disseminated less by intellectuals within the conservative movement than by their more populist out-riders, who collectively make up a kind of right-wing "heavy brigade." We will have to compete with pedigree conservatives eventually, but first we need to deal with their rottweilers.

Republican rottweilers come in a number of forms. They come as private bloggers – in increasing numbers indeed. They come as right-wing shock jocks – now so plentiful as to have their own hierarchy of fame – and they come as journalists with their own weekly columns, newsletters, books and regular media appearances. As is to be expected in such a host, quality varies: but the best of them are very good indeed at what they do. Liberals may not care much for the Ann Coulter's, Sean Hannity's, Michael Savage's, Bill O'Reilly's and Rush Limbaugh's of this world; but these people are not to be ignored.

Indeed, and on the contrary, in the wake of the 2008 presidential election Rush Limbaugh in particular found himself vaulted into an unexpected unofficial leadership position within the broad Republican coalition. With a 60 percent approval rating among Republican voters, what Rush Limbaugh said to his 20 million listeners suddenly became national news. It also became party orthodoxy, such that any leading Republican disagreeing with Rush Limbaugh found himself quickly brought to heel.[1] What Rush Limbaugh said was that he wanted President Obama to fail: an assertion which he defended in this manner during an extensive lecture to the Conservative Political Action Conference (CPAC) in late February 2009.

> Do you know that President Obama, in six weeks of his administration, has proposed more spending than from the founding of the country to his Inauguration. Now this is not prosperity. It's not going to engender prosperity. It's not going to create prosperity and it's also not going to advance or promote freedom. It's going to be just the opposite. There are going to be more controls over what you can and can't do, how you can and can't do it, what you can and can't drive, what you can and can't say, where you can and can't say it. All of these things are coming down the pike, because it's not about revenue generation to them, it's about control. . . . and I'm supposed to say I don't want the President to fail. [Applause] We're in for a real battle. We are talking about the United States of America . . . we're talking about it remaining the country we were all born into and reared and grown into. And it's under assault. It's always under assault. But it's never been under assault like this from within before. And it's a serious, serious battle.[2]

For Rush Limbaugh, the greatest crime in that battle would be a surrender of principle, a breach from his core conservative beliefs and values, a false bipartisanship that would require "checking our core principles at the door." Facing a president who he believes "wants to destroy capitalism . . . wants to establish a very powerful socialist government,"[3] Limbaugh sees no space for false consensus. "Where is the compromise between good and evil," he asked his CPAC audience: "should Jesus have cut a different deal?"[4] Clearly not!

Rush Limbaugh and his equivalents on Fox News and across conservative talk radio see themselves as active warriors in a vital culture war, collectively orchestrating a powerful offensive against progressive positions and the individuals who articulate them.[5] It is an offensive that seeks not so much dialogue as closure. Its effect – and presumably also part of its purpose – is the construction in conservative ranks of a deep-rooted refusal even to listen to progressive arguments, let alone to be swayed by them: a refusal created in the main by the systematic denigration of all things liberal. There are even books out there telling you that liberals are not to be dealt with because they are seriously deficient, when compared to conservatives, on a long list of important personality and moral traits. Liberals are apparently less honest than conservatives. They are said to be also more selfish, more focused on money, less hardworking, less emotionally satisfied and – this is my favorite – *less* knowledgeable about economics and civic affairs.[6] Less knowledgeable! Wow, that really is quite a claim.

This jamming and blocking offensive has a set of standard components that we need to recognize and refute. Invariably, the first move in much of the blocking argument and literature is the creation of a "composite" liberal of extreme and unpalatable views, who is then used as a shorthand for liberals of all varieties. That composite and crazy progressive is labeled as profoundly un-American, and indeed anti-American, in impact and even in intention; and is often presented as in league with hostile foreigners, and as such a direct threat to the stability of core American values and institutions. The liberal message, we are told, is not to be argued with. It is to be defined out of court. Never go for the message. Go for the messenger. The message is not to be taken seriously. It is to be labeled and dismissed as the prime cause of the very social ills about which liberals so regularly complain: ills that would then quickly disappear if liberals would also do the same. We may have a liberal president now, but that is not a cause for celebration. It is a cause for shame.

Let's see how this works out in practice. Here's how to write like a conservative rottweiler.[7]

1. Straw men and Trojan horses

First you put together a composite liberal – a genuine straw person. You find one little-known radical, a Ward Churchill or the like, and you condemn him for believing something particularly outlandish. A few pages later, you find a different radical, and condemn him (or her) for believing something else equally bizarre.[8] Since the two named individuals are both labeled by you as liberals, you are quickly able to treat every liberal as though he and she believed both those things: even though in reality the views you have chosen are extreme ones, held as core opinions by very few liberals indeed. If anyone is then indelicate enough to point that out, you allow the lack of fit between the claim and the data to make no difference whatsoever. Instead you treat liberalism as a political tendency that is idea-prone to extreme radicalism, whether its adherents realize it or not; so enabling you to insist that even when your readers are only moderate liberals, they are still in bed with radicals and – like every Trojan horse – must stand condemned accordingly.

2. Patriots and traitors

The next key trick is to go "nativist," by wrapping your conservative views in the American flag. There are a number of ways of doing this: the more of them you use, the more effective the tactic becomes. Start by talking lovingly of an America of suburban peace and family values – a golden age of 1950s calm[9] – and then imply that one generation of liberal policies destroyed that calm and a second one now threatens the survival of the values on which it was based. Scan foreign experiences and cherry-pick some failures, and imply that liberal policies have foreign roots in exactly those same failures. Don't mention the positive European impact on the Founding Fathers. Talk only of America escaping the European yoke: and describe a unique city on a hill imperiled by liberal (foreign-inspired) policies that weaken security, run counter to American individualism, and erode the Protestant work ethic. And if in doubt, throw in a dash of anti-intellectualism too: comparing good American conservative common sense with the "soft Marxism" of Scandinavian social democracy or the arrogance of French statism.[10] That way, even when conservative administrations malfunction in Washington, the critique can be turned – not into one against conservatism (with its obvious liberal solution) – but into yet more antistatism. Not even conservative government works, you should imply, so let's keep the government out of things altogether!

3. Label the message, shoot the messenger

Make sure next that any policy or political position with which you disagree is labeled pejoratively, with as many "bad" tags as you can find. Do as much negative labeling as possible. Don't just disagree with a judicial ruling. Make sure that that ruling came from an "activist" judge.[11] Never miss the opportunity to characterize any federal initiative with which you disagree as, at best, "a challenge to states rights" and, at worst, as "socialistic." Keep before the American people a stark choice between "freedom" – understood as no public policy disturbance of the status quo – and "socialism": with the latter understood as any proposal likely to redress inequality, increase taxation, or restrict the rights of the rich.[12] And never simply disagree with your liberal opponent. Always denigrate that opponent, and talk of him or her in medical or animal terms: as an infection, a cancer or as vermin who need removing, cutting out, or putting down.[13] Always insist that "you don't have to compromise with depravity"[14]; and at the same time, always inflate the power and prestige that you attribute to those with whom you disagree. The less influential they are, the more you must label them as totally dominant in a set of institutions with which your readers are familiar but which they don't directly and intimately know: at the very least, in the media, higher education, the federal bureaucracy, the Democratic Party and the trade unions. Always present yourself, that is, as an oppressed and persecuted minority even when visibly you are not.

4. Blame the victim, demonize the do-gooder

If that does not work, then turn reality entirely on its head. Ignore the vast body of evidence now available to us on how inherited inequalities are denying to this generation of Americans the chance to begin their search for prosperity on a level playing field. Instead, build your arguments on a glorified and oversimplistic version of the American Dream, by insisting that rapid individual progress is still straightforwardly guaranteed to those who strive with sufficient individual zeal for its immediate attainment.[15] That approach will give you a series of huge advantages in the arguments stakes. It will enable you immediately to blame the victim, not the perpetrator, of any social ill that liberals bring up for policy debate.[16] You'll be able to blame poverty on the poor and unemployment on the jobless, pregnancy on the feckless young and divorce on the lack of faith. That will then free you of any moral obligation to do anything about any of those things. It will also enable you to put the entire blame for the social ills now besetting contemporary America on previous liberal attempts to set those ills to right. Current levels of income inequality can be blamed on Johnson's "War on Poverty." High levels of welfare dependency and the rise of single-parent families can be similarly explained away, though activist judges of a liberal persuasion can also be blamed for part of that: viz Roe v. Wade. Do not on any account give even an inch to any successful public welfare policy: not here, not in Europe, not even in the Third World; and if you find one, do not discuss the reason for its success at all. Instead, focus the discussion immediately on its necessarily greater adverse side effects on all sorts of important economic and social institutions – the more the merrier indeed – from economic growth and personal living standards to individual morality and the rise of the pornographic internet.

5. Outflank the Republican Party on its right

Make sure that you present the majority of the Republican leadership in Washington as closet liberals. Do not for a moment admit that the Bush administration was in any sense genuinely conservative.[17] To do that would be to throw away the two great advantages that playing the "outflanking card from the right" always gives you: namely a base from which continually to pull the Republican Party further and further away from government-imposed solutions of any kind; and iron-clad protection against liberal claims that conservative policies, when applied, invariably fail. For if you do consistently outflank George W. Bush on his right, every failure so listed can then be quickly redefined as a consequence, not of conservatism, but of its betrayal. Explaining inadequacies of Republican policy in that way – as the product of at best only a "flawed conservatism" – then leaves wonderfully intact the unchallengeable status of your basic premises: that societies work best when governed least, that private charity is always superior to any form of public welfare provision, and that government regulation is by definition some form of creeping socialism. The great thing about unchallengeable premises of that kind is that you can keep on recycling them for ever, in that way giving them the appearance of truth simply by the power of regular repetition. Also, do make certain that some of the things that you say about George W. Bush, or about liberals or Arabs . . . are so outlandish that not even a conservative media outlet like Fox News will disseminate them; because that will give you yet more evidence of how deeply entrenched within apparently rightwing institutions is the covert liberal monopoly of the entire American cultural network.[18] Do not talk to liberals. Do not concede for a second that it was conservatism that was rejected in November 2008.[19] Bush was rejected, but he was no conservative. Talk past liberals, and discount the election result as irrelevant, by talking past the conservative establishment too.

6. Paint the immediate future in truly apocalyptic terms

Finally this: treat the Obama administration as the embodiment of everything that is bad, blame it (and not George W. Bush) for our present economic difficulties, and talk of a conspiracy of evil that brought Obama to power by bringing America to the verge of ruin. Do more than criticize the new President's stimulus package for its largesse with your hard-earned and reluctantly surrendered tax dollar. Tell your listener/reader that such largesse is socialistic or communistic in intent and consequence.[20] Tell them it will take us toward a Soviet-style nightmare unless it is stopped. Explain the 2008 financial crash that scuppered the McCain-Palin ticket as Obama's creation,[21] the product of a carefully orchestrated plot between liberals in the Democratic Party and maverick financiers – George Soros is the normal favorite – deliberately to bring the markets down and manufacture a panic.[22] And cry wolf. Cry wolf big time. Say that the United States is on the brink of catastrophe.[23] Say it with genuine conviction and passion. Say it that way to, at the very least, regalvanize Republican energies for an electoral fight back in 2010 and 2012; and say it that way to, at worse, get awfully close to inviting a private violent intervention by some hothead that might yet save us from this disaster.[24]

A liberal response

We will deal with the individual claims made in the rottweiller literature about particular policy areas in the appropriate chapters. Here we need to establish some broad responses that apply across the literature as a whole: guidelines on how best to respond to the general attack being made.[25]

1. Get the target right

The first thing we have to insist upon is that the debate between conservatives and liberals be focused on actual arguments by actual people.

There can be no space in any intelligent debate on the future of the United States for the construction and chasing of "straw men." We must not do it ourselves; and we must not tolerate it in others. We must continually reassert the complexity of positions on both the left and the right. If conservative popularizers want to invent liberal monsters of their own imagination, the better to claim that they alone can slay them, they are free to do that; but they are not free then to claim that by so doing they have refuted real liberals with real policies. That political animal is far more difficult to kill: not least because it has more than one head. The liberal camp is a broad one, characterized by internal disagreements as well as by shared values; and though the center of gravity of liberal views is definitely to the left of conservative ones – that is not in dispute – there is also a considerable overlap between the ranges of opinion that cluster around those centers. Indeed, the most pressing responsibility on moderates in the face of this conservative onslaught, as Barack Obama repeatedly argues, is to seek out that common ground, and to pull political discussion back and away from the agenda-setting of the people who *are* the true radicals, the true outliers, in contemporary US politics: namely sections of the Republican Right itself.

2. Locate the real Trojan horse

For if there is a Trojan horse problem in US politics right now, it is one for the conservative coalition far more than for the liberal one; and not in the way that Michael Savage and Pat Buchanan would have it. George W. Bush may have been too liberal for their tastes on issues like immigration and foreign trade, or too fiscally irresponsible for the tax cutters in the coalition, but that is not the case we need to make. We need to ask instead just how many liberal Republicans voted for George Bush in 2000, expecting compassionate conservatism and global disengagement, only to get welfare retrenchment, tax breaks for the privileged and the erosion of environmental controls, not to mention the Bush family's private war? We need to ask just how many liberal conservatives took annual comfort in the carefully constructed moderation of George W. Bush's State of the Union Addresses – finding there a genuine desire to reach out across the aisle to the entirety of the American people – only to discover later that, in the pork barrel politics of Washington, well-placed Republican lobbyists effectively negated that outreach by slipping into law special privileges for the already overprivileged. We need constantly to remind moderate Republicans that a vote for George Bush in 2000 and 2004 was also a vote for the army of extreme conservatives who, between 2000 and 2006, slipped into positions of power and influence on the coattails of his claims about compassion, social justice and the protection of the weak. We need constantly to remind them that, in a very genuine sense, the inmates took over the asylum during the Bush years, and that we have only now captured it back.

3. Recapture the flag

"Nativism" is always the last refuge of the bankrupt, and we have to keep saying that. The flag is not just a Republican flag. There are many Americas and many Americans – some conservative, some liberal – all of them in their different ways passionate about this country and determined to see it prosperous and secure. The New Deal was not a foreign import, after all. On the contrary, it was just as home grown as the Pledge of Allegiance itself. In important and valuable ways the United States is a unique – and a uniquely free – society; but it is also one that shares many problems and processes with equivalent industrial democracies elsewhere. Given that commonality of situation and agenda, it is at the very least strange that a country so uniquely constructed by the migration to it of the brightest and the best should now choose to denigrate the contribution of foreign ideas – and even of foreign people – to its future internal development. National pride is an important virtue: but pride often comes before a fall. Some things the United States does well that others do not; and we should glory in that. But by the same token, there are economic and social dimensions of the United States that do not bear easy comparison with the best of the rest abroad. So it is always worth looking outward as well as inward, to see if there are things to be learned with profit from the way they are performed elsewhere; and we must keep insisting on that intellectual and political openness. It might suit the Republican Right on occasion to ridicule, for example, everything

French; but the Founding Fathers were not so indiscriminate in their reaction to the finest of European thought and practice. So who is our best guide in this – Jefferson or Limbaugh? You only have to put the question to see the answer.

4. Fight the adjectival war

Because a key element in the framing of political agendas is the language in which that frame is built, any successful rebuttal of a strident conservative voice must have as one of its first objectives the recapturing of the language itself.[26] We need a war on adjectives.[27] Judging is always an "active" exercise. Conservative judges are activist judges too. If they were not, the composition of the bench would not matter so much to conservatives and liberals alike! The choice is not between active and inactive judges. It is between progressive and conservative ones, and we should say so. By the same token, we should say too that a health care system to which everyone has access is not by that fact alone transformed into a socialist one. It would only be that if all the doctors inside it were also turned into state employees. A health care system to which everyone has access is merely a "universal" one. Calling it "socialistic," and implying it has old-style Russian overtones, makes it unappealing. Calling it a universal health care system, and implying it would be like Germany or the UK, changes the overtones entirely. That relabeling does not remove the need to ask whether a foreign model has any relevance here: but at least it allows the question to be put without the answer having been already predetermined. We should always insist on neutral terminology, and then ask of our conservative critics: what are you so afraid of, that you have to wrap your chosen solutions in loaded adjectival cling film? If your answers are so visibly superior, why do you need to build such a defensive linguistic wall around them?

5. Raise the standard of debate

Key too, to the reestablishment of the liberal voice as the dominant presence in American politics must be the insistence on a more measured and civilized form of debate between those who would participate in that debate. The intensity and speed of denigration of opponents now common on the American Right has happened before. It happened in very similar ways in Germany and Italy in the 1920s, as they headed to fascism rather than to FDR. If the contemporary debate is to be productive of long-term democratic outcomes, it has to be pulled to a higher and a calmer standard than that currently prevalent in many populist right-wing circles. Intellectual closure is always dangerous for democracy; and fundamentalism, in whatever form, always threatens the Enlightenment project in which the political freedoms of this country are embedded. Tolerance and dialogue, reason and reflection, the free exchange of ideas and information – these are the very lifeblood of an informed and democratic citizenry. One vital liberal task is to keep that tolerance, reason and untrammeled debate alive; and to do so both by setting high standards for ourselves (standards that privilege criticism over castigation) and by insisting on similar standards in our political opponents. There must be no replacement of civilized democratic discourse by the politics of the gutter.

6. Ridicule the nonsensical

Standards have also to be about more than tone of voice or mode of address. They have also to be about the quality of evidence, and the testing of assertion against data. Is it really the case, as Ann Coulter would have it, that "nationally renowned liberal female journalists have been known to offer oral sex to elected officials just for keeping abortion on demand legal"?[28] Are we really to believe, with Michael Savage, that many of America's leading universities "are often nothing more than houses of porn and scorn"?[29] Some of the propositions common in the popular writings of the Conservative Right – these included – are simply nonsensical, and have to be recognized as such. Try asking a Katrina victim if trickle down economics works when you're already up to your neck in water. See how many virgin "queens" you can find who decided to get pregnant because they wanted a welfare check. And see how many al-Qaeda terrorists you can name who supported a secular Baathist like Saddam Hussein before Dick Cheney decided that getting rid of him was the best way of blocking Osama bin Laden. Repetition of idiocy does not remove it. Self-deception is self-deception, no matter how many times it's practiced.

Just because conservative critics insist that their view of the world is more realistic than ours – that we, not they, are the hopeless romantics – it does not remove from them the obligation to study that reality rigorously; and we must say so.

7. Insist on the use of evidence

Lots of the disagreements between liberals and conservatives are open to resolution by the examination of appropriate evidence, so we must insist on the presence and use of carefully researched facts throughout the policy-debating process. Facts should not frighten us. If they frighten others, then that would suggest that much of what is now argued at us as axiomatic is in fact special pleading by the privileged. A free exchange of ideas and arguments should make that clear. Of course, in politics as in life, facts are not in the end determining. There will still be choices to be made. But in an informed democracy, those choices are made the better when the data in which they are set is secure. So what have we to lose? If we are wrong – if the data suggests things that we do not want to hear – then conservatives are entirely correct to insist that we surrender the field to them. But if we are not so in error – if the evidence, when examined, leaves holes in our opponents' proposals and underlying philosophies – then they too will need to respond in kind. This is not a matter of partisanship. It is a question of the quality of the research on which important political decisions are made. If the rush to war in Iraq in 2003 told us anything, it told us that bad data makes for bad policy. The systematic exploration of the facts can only improve the policy debate at home and abroad: so we should insist, on both sides of the aisle: *out* with cliché, *down* with half-truths, *in* with hard and systematic data, and *in* all the time, and not just when the evidence happens to fit our already entrenched preconceptions.

8. Slow the discussion down

Moreover, and for all its shrillness, the new conservative stridency seems extremely insecure. Indeed its stridency appears to be, as much as anything, a reaction to the dangerously thin foundations on which so much of the right-wing case now rests. A more firmly grounded and self-confident orthodoxy would not need to move with such speed to close down debate, fall back onto clichés, or denigrate the foreign and the different. Insisting that "French fries" be renamed as "freedom fries" tells us nothing about the quality of the fries; but it tells us a lot about the insecurities of those who would rename them. The penchant of so much of the right-wing media for rapid dialogue has two great advantages for them that we need to expose. It enables them to keep the discussion at the level of the superficial and the slick, privileging quick clichés over longer and more reflective forms of analysis. And it enables them quickly to circumvent data they dislike, arguments they cannot answer, and problems they wish not to discuss. We need to challenge these right-wing "scream-fests,"[30] insisting instead that major political issues receive the full historical and analytical treatment they deserve. Problems of the scale we now face will not succumb to the quick fix and the clichéd answer. They will succumb only to policy whose sophistication in design is a match for the complexity of the problems addressed. Prolonged thought, not easy strictures, needs to be the order of the day; and we must say so.

9. Expose the underlying hypocrisy

It was Anatole France who once pointed out that both the rich and the poor had the right to sleep under the bridges of Paris, but that oddly enough, the rich did not choose to do so. So often these days, the language of universal individual rights is used by conservative advocates to block off public policy that might strengthen collective rights, in the process reinforcing and protecting the positions of the privileged. Offering tax cuts to the rich as *the* one effective policy to help the poor really requires strong ideological balls; and we have to admit that the Republican Right are well endowed in that particular part of their political anatomy. Programmatic castration seems essential here. It is up to us to show, over and over again, the self-serving nature of many right-wing policies. If conservative opponents of the liberalization of immigration rules suddenly develop a deep concern for the impact of immigration on the wages of the working poor, then we need to ask them how they voted on the raising of the national minimum wage. And if conservative opponents of gay marriage argue that homosexuality offends the laws of God and undermines the sanctity of the family, we have to ask them why divorce rates are highest in the states of the Bible Belt? It is up to the liberals to raise time and time again the central question facing the whole compassionate conservatism project: compassion for exactly whom? Is it for the rich or for the poor, the privileged or the downtrodden? That is the issue. Too often on the Republican Right these days, the rhetoric is morally pretentious while the practice is sordidly self-serving; and we need to say so.

10. Clarify the value choice

For in the end, we cannot avoid issues of value. Nor should we try. Bill O'Reilly is right. There is a culture war going on in the United States right now, one rooted in different value-systems. The Republican Right might claim that its voice is less ideological than that of its progressive opponents, but that claim is ludicrous. If ideas were not important, Ann Coulter would not write her books. But she does, and no doubt she will go on writing, and she should. But what is good for the goose must also be good for the gander. It is our turn now to do exactly the same, and to do it with the weight of a progressive White House behind us. We have to ask our political opponents: what are your values? What offends you most? Are you more offended by the presence of widespread poverty amid affluence in the richest country on earth; or do you react with greater venom to the arrival of the Internal Revenue Service (IRS) to take from you some of your private wealth in order to apply it to the greater good? Is it more important to you that an employer can hire and fire at will than it is to see labor laws that give American citizens strong and dependable rights at work? Are you prepared to pay more for imported goods produced by overseas workers paid decent wages, or do you not care about the conditions of the foreign poor if any easing of their conditions would corrode your capacity to consume? How wide does your commitment to individual rights stretch – out from you through your family to whom? Does it extend from the basic political right to vote to the wider social right of children to grow up in houses free of poverty and with access to adequate health care? Are you selfless just on a Sunday, or does your Christian morality – your concern for your fellow man/woman – last all week? We have to ask, and we need to know.

The need for healthy democratic dialogue

Given what has happened to the intensity of political debate in the United States since November 4, 2008, the fifth of those ten guidelines is worth reemphasizing as we go forward. For with conservative radio hosts currently playing so visible a role in the orchestration of the conservative push-back against liberal policies, an alarming stridency has crept into the dialogue of American politics. Rush Limbaugh, Ann Coulter and their conservative colleagues offer themselves as defenders of basic American freedoms: but their mode of argumentation – their tone, their vitriol, their denigration of alternatives, their underlying fundamentalism – all jeopardize the very freedoms that they claim to defend. At the very least, we have to say back to them that respect for opponents, and tolerance for the give and take of points of view, is the very basis of a democratic culture, a basis that would currently appear to be safer in our hands than in theirs.

Maybe this is the real legacy of the Bush years – or more accurately, of the Rove years – a willingness to win votes by any means necessary; a willingness to move quickly to the politics of smear and fear if the politics of give and take are not immediately enough to win the day; and a willingness to treat opponents as worthy of denigration as well as of disagreement. After all, it was the politics of fear that conservative talk radio deployed big time in 2007, to prevent Republican legislators facing looming primaries from supporting bipartisan proposals for comprehensive immigration reform.[31] It was the politics of smear that, a year later, left a significant minority of the US electorate convinced that Barack Obama was Muslim rather than Christian, and a Kenyan rather than an American. Misinformation spread by e-mail was a particularly disturbing feature of the 2008 presidential campaign.[32] Barack Obama won in spite of a series of dirty tricks of the kind that had swift-boated the less charismatic John Kerry four years earlier. He won too in spite of the only thinly veiled racism of certain of his Republican opponents.

So we are at a critical time for the *quality* of democracy in this country, as well as for the direction of its politics. A culture of intolerance is building in the far reaches of the American Right, and a hectoring style of argumentation is fast becoming the norm in conservative media circles.[33] If, day after day, you live wholly immersed in the world of conservative talk radio and *Fox News*, your vision of the world is not only likely to be seriously impaired. It is also likely to be seriously overdramatized and underpopulated.

- *Impaired* because liberals are not poised to demand "a Marxist revolution against the rich," no matter how often Ann Coulter tells you that they are;[34]
- *overdramatized* because you will be convinced that evil liberal elites are conspiring to destroy the basic fabric of democratic America, even though they are not; and
- *underpopulated* because your vision of the world will be occupied only by evil liberals and valiant conservatives, instead of by the rich tapestry of nuanced political disagreement actually in play.

Such an impoverished world vision does not invite mutual tolerance and the celebration of diversity. It does not invite careful research and calm reflection. It does not invite an understanding of complexity and balance. Yet it is precisely in times of great economic difficulty and foreign entanglement that world visions of that paucity are at their most dangerous. The Great Depression of the 1930s sparked authoritarianism on both wings of the political spectrum – fascism on the Right, communism on the Left – and we must not go down that route again. And we will not if we sustain and deepen a democratic debate in the United States that privileges mutual respect for competing positions, honest attention to evidence and detail, and a clear specification of values and preferences. The chapters that follow have been written in the manner that they have precisely to make their own small contribution to the sustenance of just such a dialogue: a dialogue in the sane center of politics where, fortunately, the aspirations and understandings of most Americans continue to reside.

Notes

1. The new chairman of the Republican National Committee, Michael Steele, was quick to apologize to Limbaugh after calling his program "incendiary" and "ugly." Steele, Limbaugh and the Louisiana Governor Bobby Jindal (who gave the Party's official response to the President's Address to a Joint Session of Congress in February 2009) were famously dismissed by Charles Blow as "the axis of drivel" (*New York Times,* March 7, 2009). Clearly there is no love lost between the two camps.
2. Address to the Conservative Political Action Conference, February 28, 2009.
3. Rush Limbaugh, *Barack Obama's Cruel Socialism*, transcript of radio program, February 27, 2009.
4. Address to the Conservative Political Action Conference, February 28, 2009.
5. Bill O'Reilly, *Culture Warrior*, New York, Broadway Books, 2006, pp. 26–7. His target is people he labels "secular progressives." I guess that would include me.
6. Peter Schweizer, *Makers and Takers: Why Conservatives Work Harder, Feel Happier, Have Closer Families, Take Fewer Drugs, Give More Generously, Value Honesty More, Are Less Materialistic and Envious, Whine Less . . . and Even Hug Their Children More than Liberals*, New York, Bantam Books, 2008.
7. The construction of this section draws heavily on books, newsletters and Websites created by, among others, Rush Limbaugh, Bill O'Reilly, Ann Coulter, Sean Hannity, Mark Levine, Tammy Bruce and Michael Savage.
8. So, for example, this from Michael Savage: "at many of our colleges – which are often nothing more than houses of porn and scorn – proterrorist professors like Ward Churchill at the University of Colorado at Boulder spew speeches that transcend the treacherous. For example, ensconced in his twisted Lilliputian world, Churchill told Fox News that 'Bush, at least in symbolic terms, is the world's leading terrorist'. . . . Listen to this lunatic, a spokeschick for the Fish Empathy Project, a new . . . initiative to harass business. She explained, 'Fish are so misunderstood, because they're so far removed from our daily lives. They're such interesting, fascinating individuals, but they're so incredibly abused'." Michael Savage, *Liberalism is a Mental Disorder* (New York, Nelson Current, 2003, pp. xxiii–iv, 94–5).
9. "I remember an America that was beautiful, free and safe. Sure, some of the politicians may have been just as corrupt as now. But somehow you could tell they still loved America. That's the difference I've discovered

over time. There has always been a tension between Democrats and Republicans, but there were no traitors like there are today: it was unheard of." Michael Savage, *The Enemy Within: Saving America from the Liberal Assault on Our Schools, Faith and Military* (Nashville, WND Books, 2003, p. 21).

10. "The emergence of an international social liberalism, which is at its core soft-communism, is a very real threat to the sovereignty of our nation. Forces from within and without our country continue to try to tell us that we are out of step with the rest of the world. The 'sophisticated' Europeans laugh at us for our naïveté and our clinging to religion and family values. . . . Our children are being inculcated with the international-socialist credos from crib to college. They are being taught that European socialist leaders are men of superior brains who must triumph over the ignorance, the stupidity, and the short-sighted selfishness of the American masses . . . in other words, under the soft Marxism of Bill Clinton, America was weakened – morally, militarily and spiritually" (Michael Savage, *Liberalism is a Mental Disorder*, pp. xiii, xiv, 200).

11. Mark Levine, *Men in Black: How the Supreme Court is Destroying America* (Washington, DC, Regnery Publishing Inc., 2005, p. 10).

12. "Granted, true Democrats, the so-called blue-America, probably consider themselves just as patriotic (if not more so) than the residents of so-called red-America (the Republicans). But in their zeal to help the unfortunate, they are now largely espousing the tenets of socialism, not democracy" (Michael Savage, *Liberalism is a Mental Disorder*, pp. xix–xx).

13. "Extreme liberalism is a mental disease. It's a destructive contagion more deadly than any force this country has ever faced . . . Modern distorted liberalism is the Enemy Within" (Michael Savage, *The Enemy Within*, p. 14).

14. Rush Limbaugh, to the Heritage Foundation, November 2004. Available at www.heritage.org/support/presidentsclub_110804.cfm.

15. "So when people call up and tell me you can't make it in America – or that it takes welfare or a bunch of government handouts – I tell them they're crazy. *Of course* you can make it. If I'm doing it, you can. You don't have to make it big – that often takes breaks beyond one's total control. But you can make it and do quite well, if you're willing to invest the effort" (Sean Hannity, *Let Freedom Ring*, New York, Harper-Collins, 2004, p. 282).

16. Anne Coulter recently had an interesting list of groups she called "fake victims": "illegal immigrants, the Muslims, the gays, [her] favorite victim group, wealthy white women living in Scarsdale who were bored

being housewives – that's Betty Friedan victim . . ." (in conversation with Rush Limbaugh, radio transcript, January 16, 2009).

17. "The conservative moment is dead. I take no pleasure in making that observation. Let's face facts. . . . When I first voted for George W. Bush, I didn't think I was getting Bill Clinton-Lite" (Michael Savage, *Liberalism is a Mental Disorder*, pp. xi, 89). The case is argued far more carefully and fully in Bruce Bartlett, *Impostor, How George W. Bush Bankrupted America and Betrayed the Reagan Legacy*, New York, Doubleday, 2006; and in Pat Buchanan, *Where the Right Went Wrong*, New York, Thomas Dunne Books, 2004.

18. "In the major media, if you're a lib, you're protected. If you're a conservative, you're crucified. Case in point . . . I was fired from MSNBC" (Michael Savage, *The Enemy Within*, pp. 217, 218, 219).

19. "Moderates in our party, and liberal elements outside it, have tried to steer this debate towards the suggestion that we need to change our core views, desert our convictions and give up our conservative philosophy. This is nonsense. The country did not become liberal on November 4th. In fact, just the reverse is true" (Michael Steele, RNC Chairman, cited by Ed Kilgore on the *Huffington Post*, January 6, 2009).

20. My Friday, March 6 e-mail from the conservative book club *Human Events* was headed *Obama's Socialist Agenda is Crippling America*, and told me that Obama, Pelosi and the liberals in Congress were "using our economic down-turn as a pathetic excuse to transform the United States into a socialist country." It also told me to get "plumb mad-dog mean" (a quotation from *The Outlaw Josie Wales*!).

21. Rush Limbaugh regularly refers to the recession as "Obama's recession." He also refers to Obama as "The Messiah" and "The One." Ann Coulter prefers "B. Hussein Obama"!

22. My March 8, 2009 *Human Events* e-mail was headed *Obama-Soros Plot to Ruin Economy?* The question mark was rhetorical. The e-mail was a pitch for *Obama Unmasked*, containing all the appropriate evidence.

23. On Day One of what Limbaugh referred to as "Obamalot" ("yesterday doesn't count because he had to share that day with Bush"), Rush Limbaugh said this to a caller about health care reform: "one thing we gotta stop is health care. I'm serious now. If they get that, then that's the tipping point. Democracy as we know it is finished."

24. This is not Limbaugh's position, of course. His energies are directed to persuading the Republican Party to pick a genuine and powerful conservative leader. As he told CPAC, the Party has to get back to its Reaganite roots. For him, it was a "no brainer." But some of the

intemperate remarks made by other conservative shock jocks do worry me on this score. Their rhetoric against Obama is so venomous!

25. For balance, we should note here that Ann Coulter has an equivalent set of what she calls "pointers," for conservatives to use against liberals. They are: don't surrender out of the gate; you don't need to be defensive; you must outrage the enemy; never apologize; never compliment a Democrat; never show graciousness toward a Democrat; never flatter a Democrat; do not succumb to liberal bribery; prepare for your darkest secrets to become liberal talking points; and always be open to liberals in transition (Ann Coulter, *How to Talk to a Liberal (if You Must)*, New York, Three Rivers Press, 2004, pp. 11–19).

26. The case for the importance of a reframing of the debate is at its clearest in George Lakoff's, *Don't Think of an Elephant: Know Your Values and Frame the Debate*, River Junction Vermont, Chelsea Green Publishing, 2004. For a more light-hearted demonstration of the same truth, see Katrina vanden Heuvel, *Dictionary of Republicanism,* New York, Nation Books, 2005.

27. In the interest of balance, it should be noted that Ann Coulter makes a similar criticism of liberals, accusing them of "hate speech," not least in their regular habit of attaching the adjective "stupid" to the proper noun "George W. Bush" (Ann Coulter, *Slander*, New York, Three Rivers Press, 2002, p. 43).

28. Ann Coulter, *How to Talk to a Liberal (if You Must)*, p. 16.

29. Michael Savage, *Liberalism is a Mental Disorder*, p. xxiii.

30. The term is Kevin Mattson's, in his "The Book of Liberal Values," *Prospect*, February 2006, p. 32.

31. Mike Allen, "Talk Radio Helped Sink Immigration Reform," *Politico*, August 20, 2007.

32. Christopher Hayes, "The New Right-Wing Smear Machine," *Nation*, November 12, 2007, pp. 11–17.

33. Those media outlets are now extensive. Ever since the late 1980s, when the Federal Communications Commission repealed the Fairness Doctrine which obliged broadcasters to provide balance content, especially on political issues, conservative talk radio has exploded in volume and range. Data from the Spring of 2007 suggested that 91 percent of the political talk radio programming on the stations owned by the top five commercial station owners was conservative – 91 percent! NPR, of course, is a great exception: it still subscribes to the Fairness Doctrine: but commercial radio stations – and television channels like Fox – do not. In the top 10 radio markets in the country, three-quarters of

all news/talk programming is conservative. In four of the top 10 – Philadelphia, Dallas, Houston and Atlanta, the figure is 96 percent. The center-left is developing its own shock–jock response – primarily on *Air America* and *MSNBC* – but that response is significantly less strident, more nuanced and less generally available than its conservative equivalent.

34. This in Ann Coulter's "Are 'Hope' and 'Change' Still Tax–Deductible?" posted March 11, 2009.

CHAPTER 3

The Wonders of "Trickle-Down" Economics

A decade that has contained two recessions and two presidents constitutes an almost perfect test case for the evaluation of competing economic philosophies. Faced with a major recession in 2009, Barack Obama's first budget cut taxes for 95 percent of America's working families while modestly increasing them for the 5 percent earning the most. Eight years earlier, faced with a less severe but still substantial downturn in the wake of 9/11, George W. Bush cut taxes modestly for the bottom 90 percent of US taxpayers but cut them more generously for the top 10 percent. One president went for trickle-up economics, one for trickle-down. Since even in this economy money can't move in two different directions at the same time, we do need a clear position on which is best: cutting taxes on the wealthy or cutting taxes on the poor.

The Obama tax strategy was made clear in his first budget, issued in February 2009. "Over the past two or three decades, the top 1% of Americans have experienced a dramatic increase from 10 percent to more than 20% in the share of national income that is accruing to them," the president's director of the Office of Management and Budget told the press corps, "so we're asking them to pitch in a bit more."[1]

The Bush tax cuts would be allowed to lapse for those earning more than $250,000 a year; and from 2011 those same people would only receive a tax break of 28 cents on the dollar for the charitable contributions that they make, rather than the 35 cents allowed hitherto. That, in the context of a budget proposing to maintain the Bush tax cuts for everyone earning less than $250,000, and in the wake of a stimulus package that gave those same lower and middle-class earners a tax rebate that the president now hoped to make permanent.

The Bush strategy had been different because it was based on an entirely different philosophy. In 2001, the Bush administration launched a $1.35 trillion package of tax cuts – the largest since 1981 and one designed to last until 2010 – a package phasing in reductions in individual tax rates and estate taxes, and increases in child tax credit, while reserving the largest tax cuts for those on the highest incomes rather than on the lowest. In 2003 the President signed into law a further round of legislation that lowered until 2008 tax rates on capital gains, dividends and business investment, and brought into immediate effect the reductions in individual income tax rates legislated in 2001. In 2006 the President then brought forward a further $70 billion worth of tax cuts, extending the main elements of the 2003 package until 2010. In his final days in office, George W. Bush defended his trademark tax strategy by saying this:[2]

> [T]he benefits of the tax cuts have been obscured by the recent economic crisis, no question about it. But when they finally take a look back at whether or not tax cuts were effective or not, it's hard to argue against 52 uninterrupted months of job growth as a result of tax policy. And so my hope is, that after this crisis passes – and it will – that people continue to write about and articulate a public policy of low taxes.

Though the Bush administration is no longer with us, the differences in taxation philosophy still are. The initial Obama stimulus package met an unprecedented level and intensity of Republican opposition – total opposition in the House, and all but total in the Senate – because its balance of taxation and spending was not to Republican tastes. Their alternative "American Option" plan was entirely tax-focused: cutting business taxes from 35 percent to 25 percent, cutting estate tax to 15 percent, keeping tax rates on dividends and capital gains at 15 percent, and making the 2001 and 2003 tax cuts permanent for everyone regardless of income. "No American family," the Plan's chief architect wrote, "should be forced to pay the federal government more than 25% of the fruits of their hard labor."[3] Supporters of the 2009 Obama budget might deny it was excessively redistributive – all that "President Obama is doing is rebalancing from Wall Street to Main Street," the head of America's fastest growing trade union told the *Financial Times* – but opponents were less sanguine. Describing the Obama proposals as the "most distributionist in modern American history," the chief economist at the US Chamber of Commerce declined to tell the paper "the views of our members" because "they contain too many expletives for a family newspaper. We were happy to be invited to the dinner," he said, "we just didn't realize we were going to be the main course"![4]

Clearly the clash of philosophies is still firmly in play. Conservative forces in the United States continue to rally around a taxation agenda built on broadly the following foundations.

1. Taxation in the United States is at historically high levels, and needs to be brought down as a matter of urgency

Western Europeans often recognize the existence of two kinds of wage – the private wage and the social wage – and then treat taxation as a legitimate payment for important forms of social provision.[5] But that is not the way taxes are understood and presented by the Republican Party and its conservative allies here in the United States. Here, it is the private wage which is uniquely privileged. It is your money. It is hard earned. Taxation is a burden on it, something from which any sane person automatically seeks maximum "relief." Over time that tax burden has grown: "in 1913 the highest American federal individual income tax rate was 7 percent on $500,000. Today, the equivalent tax rate is 35% on $357,000."[6] Americans currently work 120 days each year just to pay their taxes, "with April 30th being the nationally estimated date of completion. . . . longer to pay for government than they will for food, clothing and housing combined."[7] Nearly four dollars in every ten – "an all-time high,"[8] conservative commentators regularly tell us – is now "taken" in taxes by various levels of government: taken in direct and in hidden ways.

That tax "take" hurts us all. It hurts American businesses, burdening them with the administrative costs of complex tax codes that distort investment;

and it hurts American families, whose wages are squeezed by ever-rising taxes. The entire tax code is said to be riddled with anomalies and lack of fairness. Dividends are taxed twice; and through the estate tax, even death itself is taxed: so imposing "an undue, unfair and frankly, un-American burden on families, farmers and entrepreneurs."[9] "Our current tax system," Neal Boortz has written,[10]

> *... is one that punishes the behaviors Americans value and rewards the behaviors we abhor. Those in our society who work hard and achieve are punished with taxes that approach confiscatory levels. Eschew hard work, follow the path of least resistance, and your tax burden all but disappears while the tax-payer funded government largesse pours in.*

The tax code in the United States is said to already be far too redistributive downwards,[11] and to have grown into such a monster that no one can now operate legally within it without the help of a growing army of tax specialists, and without surrendering to the government ever larger quantities of private information that no public agency should possess. "Working families are paying four times more in taxes today than they did in the 1950s," Sean Hannity has written, and "many are struggling just to make ends meet";[12] which is why good news in the world of taxation – according to former President Bush at least – occurs only when "Americans keep more of their hard-earned dollars because of tax cuts."[13]

2. Tax cuts are the quickest and most effective way of generating economic growth and rising employment

"Our economy prospers," George W. Bush told us in April 2006, "when Americans like you make the decisions on how best to spend, save and invest."[14] The most effective way to generate output and employment is simultaneously to ease the tax burden on consumers and companies. The goal of tax policy should be "to minimize the impediments to the behaviors – work, saving, investment and entrepreneurship – that generate production and income. Fundamental tax reform is capable of generating growth."[15] Particularly in a recession marked by a slump in business investment, it makes sense to go for an "aggressive tax-cutting policy . . . to get the capital investment engine running again."[16] Lowering corporate taxation frees companies to invest, so strengthening their competitive position. It frees them to add workers to their

payroll, thus boosting demand; and "when Americans have money to spend, everyone wins, because jobs are created by that spending."[17] Increasing marginal tax rates, by contrast,

> *greatly harms the economy – when more of the money goes to the government, there's less incentive for "the rich" to work, save, invest, and create and expand business. This affects people trying to start businesses with investment money from wealthy folks. Not to mention people looking for jobs, which usually come from businesspeople with money.[18]*

The lower the tax burden on the employment of labor, the more jobs can be created. The less taxation discourages investment and innovation, the greater will be the rate of economic growth. In fact, tax cuts enhance the flows of revenue within the economy, on which taxation itself can then be levied. Cutting taxes, therefore, is paradoxically the best way of generating a virtuous cycle of company growth, private affluence and taxation revenue. It contrasts favorably with the "tax rates/tax revenue downward spiral"[19] associated with liberal-inspired tax increases, which only suppress consumer demand, discourage investment and employment, and erode the tax base. "The message is clear. Republicans giveth, Democrats taketh away."[20]

3. Big Government needs to be rolled back, to stop it crowding out the private enterprise on which long-term economic prosperity depends

That rising flow of taxable revenue is the part of the antitax argument that then troubles many within the Republican coalition: the observable paradox that "starving the beast"[21] of tax revenues will not itself curb the growth of government. For fiscal conservatives, "deficits are a symptom" but "spending is the disease," because "government spending diverts resources from the productive sector of the economy."[22] Government borrowing pushes up interest rates, squeezing out marginal investment initiatives in the private sector. Heavy taxation discourages foreign investment; and government regulations pull the allocation of domestic resources away from what, in a perfectly competitive environment, would be optimally efficient. So if government has to be in the economy at all – and only pure libertarians within the Republican coalition deny the existence of a limited list of vital public functions that have to be financed by taxation of some kind[23] – then conservative forces in the United States tend to favor as flat a tax as possible.[24] An ideal tax system, for the Republican Right, would tax all economic activity equally at one rate, would have that rate set at the lowest possible level, would eliminate all forms of double taxation, would levy taxes on purchases rather than on incomes, and would be so simple as to remove the need for the existing plethora of accountants and tax-return software.[25] As Bill O'Reilly puts it in a press release to Edward Kennedy: "hard work and self-reliance leads to success on the job, Senator. Wise up and spread the word, and get your hand out of my pocket."[26]

4. Taxes need to be minimized because market solutions are always preferable to government ones

It is not simply that Republicans do not like paying taxes. In a very real sense, they do not like government either. There is a deeper premise at work inside this argument about lowering taxation: the belief that money spent by government is necessarily inferior – in the quality of what is provided and in the freedoms that it brings – to money spent privately by citizens. Republicans habitually treat markets as Adam Smith did: as the one place in which – as if by an invisible hand – people are led to serve the general interest by single-mindedly pursuing their own. Anything disturbing such market exchanges is then treated as, at best, an interference with freedom and at worst, as a challenge to liberty itself. It is simply no use trying to buck the market. If you want the wages of the poor to rise, for example, the last thing you must do is increase the minimum wage. That will only stop small firms creating the jobs that pay the wage, and inflate labor costs across the entire economy, creating unemployment in sectors that have to compete with cheap labor-based companies abroad. And never of course give trade unions an inch. Labor market regulation actually makes worse the job loss and poverty that it pretends to make better. For there is no "invisible hand" at work in the world of politics, pulling everything into good order. That only occurs in unregulated markets. In a political world free of market discipline, office-holders are always high on promise and low on performance: so it's better not to give them any more dollars than is absolutely necessary. Keeping your dollars, and using them yourself, will always produce a better outcome, and not just for you, but for everyone else as well.[27]

5. Cut the red tape, scrap the regulations

On this argument, it is not simply a matter of shrinking the public sector down to the size that will enable Grover Norquist to drown it in the bath.[28] *It is also essential to remove, as quickly and extensively as possible, the dead weight of government regulation on the freedom of action of American business. Low corporate and personal taxation, and low business regulation, go together. The principle that governments govern best which govern least applies to all spheres of private life, including the economic. If prosperity is to be sustained, markets need to be expanded and the players inside them allowed to work. When once asked by a conservative radio host why American prosperity and Republican economic leadership so regularly go together, George Bush's original Treasury secretary, John Snow, said they go together because, unlike Democrats, Republicans "have adopted, on a scale beyond that of any other country, a reliance on market forces." "Markets work. We let markets work. The market is a marvelous mechanism for high GDP growth, high job creation and high wages."*[29] *Because long-term economic growth depends on American ingenuity and enterprise, removing regulations and red tape that blocks ingenuity and enterprise becomes an essential part of well-designed economic policy. Low taxes and the deregulation of economic activity − tax cuts and a regular bonfire of politically imposed constraints on American enterprise and initiative − thus becomes the only guarantor of rising wealth for all.*

6. Rising tides raise all ships, so cutting the taxes of the rich is the most effective way of helping the poor

The surest route out of poverty is through paid employment, and the only route to paid employment is through job creation by the private sector. Liberal taxation policies, dictated by outmoded class ideology − policies that take money from the rich and give it to the poor − are exactly the kind of thing that hurts the poor most. As Abraham Lincoln said, "you can't raise the wage earner by holding down the wage giver." The only truly reliable route to a general rise in living standards is through a taxation system that rewards effort and enterprise. Since it's successful entrepreneurs who pay by far the largest slice of federal income tax, cutting the taxes of the successful makes most sense in the pursuit of economic growth. As Rush Limbaugh put it: "how in the world can anyone with a brain come forth and say 'I am against tax cuts for the rich. I'm only going to have a tax cut for the middle class.' If you give a tax cut to people in the bottom 20%, you're not going to stimulate anything."[30] The fastest way to reduce the number of the American poor is to let the companies who can generate employment get on with the business of doing so. Republicans understand that "government does not create prosperity, and nobody in Washington can wave a wand and create jobs."[31] They know that government works best by getting out of the way: by cutting unnecessary regulation, removing barriers to investment and job creation; and allowing those who can make money to actually make it: and then keep it, and so invest it in their (and their country's) future. There's a powerful faith in trickle-down economics at the core of the Republican Party's current conviction that "to keep our economy strong and growing . . . tax relief needs to be made permanent."[32] Money made by the rich, so the argument goes, will pull the poor up behind it.

A liberal response

So what could possibly be wrong with that? These things at least.

1. Don't be so sure that it was the tax cuts that triggered economic growth

The impression that is often given by advocates of sweeping tax cuts in the United States – of an economy so overburdened by taxation that it will immediately leap into life once that burden is removed – is an entirely false one. Until the financial meltdown of 2008 prompted a temporary and unusual level of government involvement in the economy, the share of GDP passing through the hands of the US state had been no larger than that passing through the hands of governments in most industrial democracies,[33] and under Republican leadership after 2001 was not significantly different to the share passing through the hands of the Clinton administration after 1993 when the US economy boomed. In fact in 2004, at 27.8 percent of national income, the tax take was actually the lowest in 37 years.

Taxation levels and economic growth rates rarely move inversely together. In the 1990s, the "burden of taxation" carried by companies and consumers in the United States was significantly lower than that carried by their Swedish equivalents, and yet Sweden was the other major industrial economy that grew rapidly, alongside the American, in that decade. There have even been times in postwar US economic history when the relationship between taxation levels and economic growth rates has been exactly the *reverse* of that canvassed by the Republicans: times when rates of economic growth have been higher with capital gains taxes at 45 percent than at 20 percent.[34] Certainly the tax cuts of the Bush years did *not* coincide with a spectacular leap in growth performance. On the contrary, the US economic cycle that began in March 2001 and ended in December 2007 registered the weakest jobs and incomes growth of any business cycle in the postwar period.[35] And that should not surprise us, because no matter what the Republicans now claim, there is no simple one-to-one relationship between tax levels and growth spurts in modern economic systems. The factors triggering economic growth are way more complex than that. Politicians like to lay claim to economic success when it happens, and to blame others for economic downturns when they come. But the truth is that they are always riding the tiger; and they are not in full control of the animal in any of the phases of its existence, no matter how often they tell us that they are.

2. The kind of tax cuts that might have triggered growth were precisely the kind of tax cuts that George Bush did not introduce

The more sophisticated advocates of tax cuts normally differentiate between types of taxes to be done away with in the interest of economic growth: differentiating between tax cuts designed to placate the Republicans' political base and taxes cut to trigger economic performance. Increasing the child tax credit in 2001 was an example of the first. Lowering the taxation rates on dividends in 2003 was an example of the second. The claim normally made is that, over time, the Bush administration did refocus its taxation reforms properly, away from social engineering and toward the encouragement of saving and investment.[36] Yet ironically, just as it did so, in 2003 – reducing taxes on capital to their lowest level since the 1930s – "personal savings as a percentage of after-tax income fell . . . for the first time since the Depression. Americans not only spent their incomes, they dipped into savings to borrow to pay for their purchases."[37] And of course we did: because the tax changes made in 2001 and 2003 hardly touched the bulk of us at all.

The 2001 change in income tax rates gave the majority of taxpayers a rebate of just $300. The top 10 percent of American taxpayers, by contrast, saw their annual tax bill fall by more than $50,000. The 2003 capital gains and dividend tax cuts were similarly skewed in impact: "57% of the tax cuts accrued to the top 1 percent of income earners and 40 percent to millionaires alone."[38] They – not the average American taxpayer – were the great beneficiaries of the Bush tax changes launched to lift America out of recession:[39] the very people indeed whose saving and consumption patterns were already so well-fixed – because of their excessive affluence – that they were almost entirely immune to the Bush administration's determined attempt to trigger economic growth by making them more affluent still. If the Bush administration had really wanted to kick-start economic growth in 2001 by boosting consumer demand, it would have directed its tax cuts *downwards* – away from the rich, into the hands of Middle America and the working poor – by cutting payroll taxes (which make up 60 percent of the taxes paid by the bottom 80 percent of income earners) rather than income tax (which makes up 60 percent of the taxes paid by the richest 20 percent).[40] But strangely enough, it was only in 2008 that, very belatedly, the Bush administration quietly adopted a bottom-up approach, launching a nearly $150 billion stimulus package, two-thirds of which went as tax rebates to low income earners: $600 to individuals earning less than $75,000 a year, or $1200 to couples earning less than $150,000.[41] The Bush administration only learned slowly that trickle-down economics was not enough – slow-learning that cost the rest of us dear.

3. Republicans are not as keen on deregulation as they like to claim

The Republicans like to present the strongest sections of the US economy as tax free because "government free," with themselves as the great defenders of both those freedoms; but in reality those sectors are often strongest precisely because they are *not* government-free, and the Republicans know it. Large numbers of American engineering firms rely on demand from the Pentagon for their profits; and you cannot get closer to government than that. Large agribusinesses, and a swathe of small independent farmers, rely on extensive farm subsidies; and a significant number of legislators from both parties pride themselves on the amount of "pork" they bring back to their particular constituencies. The Bush administration did not retreat from the economy, no matter what its spokespeople claimed. Rather it practiced big government *military Keynesianism* – deficit spending that was primarily of benefit to the military-industrial complex. The American corporate sector spends billions of dollars a year on lobby activity, and puts huge amounts of money into party-coffers whenever an election looms;[42] and it does that, not simply to keep government regulation at bay, but to generate regulations that suit American companies and orders that keep them in business. Whatever else the US economy may be, free of government it is not: and no Republican Party will make it so – or even wants to – no matter what the Republican leadership says at the top of each election cycle.

When Republicans talk about deregulation, they normally mean one of two things. They mean removing blockages on the ability of corporate America to make quick and easy profits, or they mean removing regulations that are protective of the American worker. The Bush administration systematically extended deregulation on both fronts: putting Bush loyalists in charge of regulatory agencies, whittling away existing Occupational Health and Safety standards, blocking new regulations and cutting funding for the inspection of existing ones.[43] Under the euphemism of "reforming OSHA," the Republicans in Congress used their monopoly of power in Washington between 2004 and 2006 to replace compulsory regulations with voluntary codes of practice that eroded labor standards and made litigation in defense of them progressively more difficult to win.[44] Yet even to use the same term "deregulation" to cover the removal of responsibilities from companies and rights from workers helps to obscure the asymmetries of power at play here. Companies need regulating, whether they like it or nor, to ensure that the externalities they generate (the social consequences of what they do) are figured into their calculations of costs. Such corporate regulation is essential to protect the long-term public interest. But for workers, regulation has a more immediate and direct function. Labor market regulation is necessary, short-term as well as long-term, to protect individual workers from excessive exploitation and danger as they labor. An individual worker facing a large employer has little power of his/her own. Regulations bring the government in on the worker's side, ensuring adequate minimum standards of pay, working conditions and human rights. Republicans talk the language of deregulation, but they are normally very reluctant to withdraw subsidies and special favors from the corporations that fund them. They are characteristically less restrained, however, when stripping away protective regulations from the people those companies employ. "One rule for capital but another for labor" is very much the Republican way.[45] Such selective deregulation is a class project. It is reactionary and unnecessary, and we should say so.

4. If this is "trickle-down", the money's going in the wrong direction

For all the claims about rising tides raising all ships, we did not see any significant "trickle-down" effect on the distribution of wealth, and on the fate of general living standards, in the America presided over by George W. Bush. On the contrary, all the data suggests that inequalities in wealth in the United States were still rising on his watch, and are now of an unprecedented scale (both comparatively and over time).[46] The data also suggests that the bulk of American workers have experienced at best only a limited increase in their living standards in the last quarter century, in spite of the remarkable growth and productivity performance of the US economy, particularly in the 1990s. Well might Paul Krugman ask "where's my trickle?"[47] Krugman's trickle, like everyone else's had gone, because "in a global economy, investments don't trickle down; they trickle out to wherever on the planet the rich can get the highest returns."[48]

The research data on the distribution of wealth is clear and disturbing. Reversing a long-term trend to greater wealth equality that began in 1929 and persisted through the 1970s, the last two decades have seen a sharp increase in inequality. "The share of the top 1% of wealth holders rose by 5 percent" between 1983 and 1998, Edward Wolff has reported, while "that of the bottom 40 percent showed an absolute decline. Almost all the absolute gains in real wealth accrued to the top 20 percent of wealth holders."[49] And that at a time, between 1973 and 1995, when income inequality also surged and real wages effectively stagnated for at least the bottom 40 percent of US wage earners.[50] There was modest wage growth between 1995 and 2000, but it was not sustained. Indeed, the weekly earnings of median workers – those in the middle of the income range – actually fell by 3.2 percent in real terms between October 2001 and late 2005.[51] Even the modest progress in real incomes made in 2007 still left median household incomes 2.6 percent *lower* in 2007 than in 2000.[52] Hourly compensation for median workers did not grow at all between 2001 and 2007 in spite of historically high productivity growth.[53] What increase in consumption Middle America has experienced of late has come, not via any trickle down of wealth and income from above – except for that modest increase in real wages between 1995 and 2000 – but from a steady increase in the *hours* worked, and the personal *debt* levels carried, by the average American household.

No one would deny that there was significant growth in the total stock of wealth and income inside the US economy in the 1990s: but what is remarkable is how little of that growth actually trickled down into higher living standards for Middle America. It should have done, but it did not. Instead, the fruits of the 1990s' boom were largely monopolized by the top 10 percent of US income earners, often taken in the form of outrageously generous payments that CEOs made to themselves. Between 1997 and 2001, the top 1 percent of US earners took an amazing 24 percent of all the growth in aggregate wages and salaries. The top 10 percent took just a fraction under a half of that growth. The bottom 50 percent held on to only 13 cents in every extra dollar.[54] The result was a change in the ratio of CEO salary packages to average earnings from 27:1 in 1973 to a staggering 300:1 by the end of the century.[55] The EPI calculated the ratio for 2007 as 275:1. "In other words, in 2007 a CEO earned more in one workday (there are 260 in a year) than the typical worker earned all year."[56] If that was "trickle-down economics" at work, then Newton's laws of gravity are clearly wrong: under present arrangements in the

US, money trickles upwards, it would appear, not downwards, and in some volume!

5. If rising tides raise all ships, why is there still so much poverty in the United States?

The United States is not only the richest country on earth, it is also the one that is most scarred by the persistence of poverty among affluence. Poverty is a notoriously difficult thing to measure, and different countries do it in different ways. The US, in fact, has one of the more restricted definitions of poverty – defining it in absolute terms, with different levels depending on family size – rather than as a percentage of average income, as is the norm elsewhere; but even so it remains unique in the scale of its child poverty and second only to the United Kingdom among Western nations in the severity of the poverty that its adult poor experience.[57] As we will see in more detail in Chapter 4, 12.5 percent of all Americans lived in officially defined poverty in 2007 – some 37.3 million Americans in total – down almost ten percentage points from 1959 (the first year that an official measure was taken) but higher in percentage and absolute terms, year on year, for each twelve-months of the Bush administration. The real wealth of the US economy (measured in terms of output and productivity) rose between 1992 and 2007 as never before – the tide genuinely went up – but not all the boats rose with it. Prosperity certainly did *not* rise for one African-American in four, or for one Hispanic-American in five, or for 21.9 percent of all American children. We all saw the images: when the waters rose in New Orleans, it was the poor who were left to sink.

Nor, within these tidal flows, have small boats found it easy to grow on their own. Within any one generation, individual mobility within the wage structure has proved extraordinarily difficult to achieve. Indeed, the rate of mobility has actually slowed slightly of late. As many as 77 percent of all low wage earners in the late 1980s (those in the bottom 40 percent of the wage distribution) were still there a decade later – and that decade was, after all, one of unprecedented prosperity and growth.[58] And between generations, cycles of deprivation, like cycles of privilege, still conspire to lock the children of the poor into poverty as they age. Run-down housing, inadequate schooling, depressed neighborhoods, the predominance of low-paid work, and the absence of adequate skill and training programs: all conspire to deny – to large sections of the young American poor – the full reality of the American dream. And that should come as no surprise. There is plenty of well-established research data to show –in relation both to whole economies, and to groups and individuals within them – that unregulated markets *reproduce inequalities* rather than reduce them in scale.

We need always to remember, and always to stress, who exactly is going to benefit, and who is going to be hurt, if taxes are cut the Republican way. A successful campaign for a flat tax – a 17 percent sales tax has recently being canvassed by the Heritage Foundation[59] and a 23 percent one by Neal Boortz.[60] By relocating taxes from income to goods, a flat tax would shift the burden of taxation in a dramatic fashion *downwards* – away from the rich on to Middle America and on to the working poor. If that shift is not then to be too excessive, government programs would also have to be cut on a very large scale – and that would be a second hit on the poorest and the least privileged in the United States. In a Washington dominated by the kind of political forces capable of introducing a flat tax, defense spending – and the flow of tax dollars to the firms wallowing in the corporate welfare of the arms industry – would not take the bulk of the reformers' knife. It would be welfare programs of the poor that would feel the blade most. Tax cutting may sound populist, progressive and liberating; but in Republican hands it has invariably been exactly the reverse.

6. Let's try "trickle-up" economics for a change

Since all the Bush administration's trickle-down largesse to the American rich did not help the American poor – or indeed even Middle America in the main – it is good to have a new administration in power in Washington, one that is prepared to use public policy (a higher minimum wage, more generous earned income tax credits and the like) to put a floor under low wages and to help ratchet up wage levels in total. It is good, but it is also likely to be contested;

because for all the talk about the desirability of bipartisanship in contemporary American politics there remain powerful think tanks within the Republican coalition prepared to spend a vast amount of time preaching the dangers, to the American poor, of such interference in the "natural" workings of labor markets.[61]

But if those dangers – of pricing people out of work by the creation of an "artificial" wage floor – are so obvious, why is such a vast effort of persuasion necessary? It is necessary, of course, because the dangers are overstated. It is necessary because raising the national minimum wage, as study after study has demonstrated, would have at most only the most marginal effect on levels of employment.[62] And that should not surprise us, given that the vast majority of low-paid workers in contemporary America are employed in service sectors that are free of international competition. Raising their minimum wage will not affect the competitiveness of one service firm relative to another. It simply inflates prices across the service sector as a whole. People end up paying slightly more for their burgers – a modest cost, one would have thought, for a genuine erosion of poverty – particularly if at the same time, raising the minimum wage helps to discourage sub-contracting and boosts the purchasing power of the working poor.

If there are then sectors – and there are, not many, but some – in which wage rises can weaken the competitiveness of those US-based companies which are obliged to compete with cheap labor-based producers abroad, that is an issue to be addressed, not through wage policy but through policy on trade and exchange rates. Industrious and low-paid American workers should not carry that cross alone. There is simply no justification for allowing unfair competition with underpaid workers abroad to add to the plight of the American working poor. What is desperately needed instead is a set of policies capable of creating a dynamic of rising wages here *and* abroad. Far from being a bad thing, a consistent raising of minimum wages in the United States – embedded in a new and more sophisticated trade policy – could be a key element in the generation of that dynamic, and we need to say so: because the alternative – of a perpetual race to the bottom – will have social and political consequences too tragic to contemplate. Are American conservatives really in favor of perennially low wages for one family in five? Do they really think the minimum wage should remain frozen year after year, with a current real value lower now than in 1955? If they are, let them tell us: and let us see the electoral consequences of such honesty; and if they are not, then let them step aside, and allow the national minimum wage to rise incrementally as it should.

7. Not all government spending is bad, and Republicans know it

Finally, this more complicated issue – one that might need to be tackled if the argument for tax cuts persists – the legitimacy of the claim, common in Republican circles, that by their very natures "big government" is bad and unregulated private enterprise is good. The polarity is a false one, and needs to be challenged at both of its ends.

On the "big government" end, the conservative claim, as we saw, is that too much government spending crowds out the private investment vital to long-term economic growth. But this "crowding out thesis" is way too overplayed.[63] There is a case to be made for big government that fiscal conservatives regularly fail to concede. In economies operating at less than full employment – like the US economy in 2008 and 2009 – government spending actually stimulates economic growth and private sector job creation, "crowding in" private investment rather than crowding it out. The public orchestration of private R&D can also often be a huge stimulus to growth. It certainly has been in the United States. The Pentagon has long been the US equivalent of the much-vaunted Japanese industry ministry, MITI. Nor is the taxation that the IRS gathers into Washington somehow then "lost" to the private sector. On the contrary, it is immediately recycled back into the economy through the government programs it sustains, in the process funding institutions (like schools) that are absolutely vital to the long-term health of both the private economy and the wider society. There are forms of public expenditure that progressives ought to question and contain – much of it "pork" added to spending bills to keep local interests placated and votes in place.[64] But it is quite wrong to imply that a private economy, low taxed and little governed, would easily sustain the vast range of public goods defining of a civilized democracy. The test of spending by governments and private companies alike should be the outcome, not the actor: not who is doing the spending, but on what the resources are being spent. A private sector replete with industries of pornography and prostitution is not to be preferred to a public sector supporting art galleries and museums. Any society worth its salt needs a lot of public spending on lots of socially desirable things – and we need to say so.

8. Labor markets must be regulated, whether Republicans like it or not

Nor should we easily swallow the assumption that unregulated markets, particularly labor markets, generate patterns of reward that reflect genuine differences of skill and effort. How often do we hear, from the Republican Right, that the present tax code distorts the proper allocation of labor, by altering the prices and rewards of effort and initiative? But does it? Does a salary ratio of 300:1 between CEOs and the average worker mean that CEOs are three hundred times more skilled, industrious, vital . . . than the people they employ? No, it simply means that CEOs are in a better position – through their ownership and management of capital – to lay claim as their private salary to more and more of the collectively generated revenues of the companies they head. The strange thing about unregulated labor markets is that they often generate an *inverse* relationship between reward and effort, and between reward and competence. Think of all the incompetent CEOs still paid huge salaries, or discretely ditched with generous severance packages. And think of all the really terrible jobs on which we depend: the collection of trash, the digging of ditches, the nursing of the infirm, the defense of the country at war. Are those the jobs to which an unregulated labor market gives the greatest rewards? No. An unregulated labor market gives most of what it has to give to those who monopolize a sellable skill, a piece of property or a position of power. Of course, pay should reflect the years of study and sacrifice that people put into their training. There has to be some reward for skill, some differentiation of salary level. But how much? What is the right ratio of top salaries to bottom ones? Is it 50:1, 25:1, 6:1? There is genuine scope for disagreement here, but presumably most of us would agree that there has to be some limit to the kind of ratio that is acceptable. Henry Paulson reportedly earned $38 million in 2005 alone, as chairman and CEO of Goldman Sachs.[65] $38 million! If that is the kind of outcome that unregulated markets produce, then they are generating, not freedom, but excess – and must be managed back, in the manner of the initial 2009 AIG bonuses, into some proper proportion.

Sadly, it is not a form of management that we can expect from Republican tax cutters, is it? Just the reverse, really: fat cats rarely slim voluntarily. Their diet has usually to be imposed. If, in these times of large budget deficits, someone or something has to be slimmed down, this is the key question to ask. Why start on programs for the poor, who are already thin, when in richer circles there is so much obesity waiting for the knife?

Notes

1. Peter Orszag, quoted in the *New York Times*, February 27, 2009.
2. Speaking to the American Enterprise Institute, December 8, 2008.
3. Jim DeMint, *The American Option: A Job Plan That Works*, The Heritage Foundation, Web memo 1108, January 29, 2009.
4. Andy Stern and Martin Regalia, quoted in the *Financial Times*, February 28/March 1, 2009, p. 3.
5. See, for example, Polly Toynbee, "Taxes are a moral good, and avoiding your fair share is a moral disgrace," *Guardian*, September 15, 2006.
6. Samuel Gregg, "What's 'Just' about Taxes?" *Acton Institute Commentary*, March 5, 2008.
7. National Center for Policy Analysis, *Taxing Times*, April 27, 2007. "High taxes force families to work harder each year to fuel a growing government. Overall, Americans now work over four months of the year to fund government at all levels." The White House, *The President's Agenda for Tax Relief: Executive Summary*, February 2006.
8. Dean Stansel, *The Hidden Burden of Taxation*, The Cato Institute, Policy Analysis No 302, April 15, 1998.
9. Senator Rick Santorum, "It's time to kill the Death Tax," *townhall.com*, June 8, 2006.
10. Neal Boortz, *The Fair Tax Book*, Harper, 2005, p. xv.
11. Kevin A. Hassett, *Re: Distribution*, American Enterprise Institute Website, posted November 21, 2008.

12. Sean Hannity, *Let Freedom Ring*, New York, Harper Collins, 2004, p. 206.
13. George W. Bush's radio address, April 15, 2006.
14. Ibid.
15. Daniel Mitchell, "A Benchmark for Assessing the Recommendations of the President's Tax Reform Panel," *The Heritage Foundation*, Web memo 890, October 24, 2005.
16. Chris Edwards, *Business Tax Cuts Crucial in a Slowdown*, Cato Institute Website, October 5, 2001.
17. Bill O'Reilly, *Working for a Living*, BillOReilly.com, August 11, 2005.
18. Peter Ferrara, *Obama's New Tax Welfare*, DividedWeFall.org, October 21, 2008.
19. Daniel Mitchell, *The President's Tax Agenda*, Heritage Foundation, Web memo #992, February 7, 2006.
20. Jim Gilmore, chair of the Republican National Committee, quoted in Hannity, *Let Freedom Ring*, p. 211.
21. The term was invented by David Stockman, Ronald Reagan's budget director, the theory being that tax cuts would create budget deficits and so induce cuts in programs, ultimately pulling government back to a 1920s level of activity.
22. Daniel Mitchell, *The President's Tax Agenda*.
23. This list is normally pure Adam Smith; Book V, Chapter XI, *The Wealth of Nations*, New York, Bantam Books, 2003.
24. See Steve Forbes, *Flat Tax Revolution*, Washington, DC, Regnery Publishing Inc., 2005.
25. Such a flat tax would avoid the standard four "costs" normally attributed by conservatives to the complexity of the tax code: the army of tax consultants it sustains; the barriers to efficient corporate and personal decision-making it creates; the invasion of privacy with which it is associated; and the extent of noncompliance it induces. On these, see Chris Edwards, *The Simple Tax Life*, Cato Institute Website, April 17, 2006.
26. Bill O'Reilly, *Working for a Living*.
27. The *Cato Handbook on Policy* put the case against high taxation this way.

> "The most obvious cost is that Americans are left with less money to meet their needs for food, clothing, housing and other items, and businesses are left with fewer funds to invest and build the economy. In addition the tax system imposes large compliance burdens and 'deadweight losses' on the economy. *Compliance burdens* are the time and administrative costs of dealing with the tax system's rules and paperwork. *Deadweight losses* are created by taxes distorting the market economy by changing relative prices and altering the behavior of workers, investors, businesses and entrepreneurs." (2004, p. 118)

28. For details, see Chapter 5, note 18.

29. Radio interview, November 4, 2005.

30. Rush Limbaugh, *Top 20% Pay 80% of Taxes*, Welcome to Rush 24/7, August 13, 2004.

31. Dick Cheney, speaking at the Harley-Davidson plant in Kansas City, January 6, 2006.

32. George W. Bush, quoted in the *Washington Post*, May 3, 2006.

33. Actually less (if by total public spending you mean spending on social programs) – at 14.6 percent of GDP – than all but Ireland in the top 18 OECD economies in 2001; and by some margin. The Italian figure was 23.9 percent of GDP, the Swedish 27.5 percent, the UK 21.5 percent, even the Japanese 16.6 percent (Jonas Pontusson, *Inequality and Prosperity*, Century Foundation, 2005, p. 145).

34. The two periods in question being 1974–78 and 1979–83. This from the Century Foundation's *Why It's Good to be Rich – and Getting Better All the Time* (2004).

35. See Joshua Picker, *Before the Bush Recession*, Center for American Progress, February 2009; and the earlier Josh Bivens and John Irons, *A Feeble Recovery*, Economic Policy Institute Briefing Paper 214, May 1, 2008.

36. For this argument, see Daniel Mitchell, *State of the Union 2006: A Mixed Message on Tax Policy*, The Heritage Foundation, Web memo #981, February 1, 2006.

37. Jill Barshay, "The Labor versus Capital Debate," *CQ Weekly*, February 6, 2006, p. 4.

38. Gene Sperling and Christian Weller, *Five Economic Challenges that Need More Policy Attention*, Canter for American Progress, January 22, 2007, p. 5 of 7.

39. "Much has recently been made of the fact that the share of taxes paid by the rich has gone up over the past twenty years. But this is not because *tax rates* have gone up substantially for the rich, but because *incomes* have gone up much for the rich than for the average family in the 1980s and 1990s. In fact . . . there was relatively little variation in the percentage of income paid at constant income levels between 1979 and 997" (Bernard Wasow, *Why the Rich Have Been Paying More Taxes*, Century Foundation, January 14, 2003).

40. For these percentages, see Bernard Wasow, "Myth 1: The rich deserve most of the tax cuts because they pay most of the taxes," *Class Warfare Fact and Fiction* (New York, The Century Foundation, 2004).

41. There was even a moment in March 2009 when as many as 85 House Republicans supported a 90 percent tax rate on unwarranted executive

bonuses, particularly from AIG. This conversion to a progressive tax code was very short-lived!

42. Lobbyists in Washington are currently spending about $25 million a year per politician (source: *Guardian*, January 6, 2006). There are now more than 34,000 registered lobbyists in Washington, a number that has *doubled* since 2000 (*Washington Post*, June 25, 2005).

43. The details are in V. Mogensen (editor), *Worker Safety under Siege*, New York, M. E. Sharpe, 2006.

44. For more examples, see Steven Greenhouse, "Labor Agency is Failing Workers, Report Says," *New York Times*, March 25, 2009.

45. In 2009 Republican lawmakers demanded that the UAW tear up its contracts with the big three auto companies before federal assistance was given, but made no such demand on the contracts signed by AIG executives.

46. Hutton estimates the rate of inequality in the US as *twice* that in Japan, Germany and France (Will Hutton, *A Declaration of Independence*, New York, W. W. Norton, 2003, p. 130).

47. Writing in the *New York Times*, September 10, 2007.

48. Robert Reich, "Paying for It," *The American Prospect*, December 2007, p. 44.

49. Edward N. Wolff, *Top Heavy: The increasing Inequality of Wealth in America and What Can Be Done about It*, New York, The New Press, 2002, pp. 8–9.

50. Paul Ryscavage, *Income Inequality in America: An Analysis of Trends*, New York, M. E. Sharpe, 1999; and Lawrence Mishel, Jared Bernstein and Sylvia Allegretto, *The State of Working America*, Ithaca, ILR Press, 2005, pp. 39–105.

51. Data in the *Financial Times*, July 25, 2006.

52. Data published by the Center for American Progress, August 26, 2008.

53. *The State of Working America 2008/9*, Washington, DC, Economic Policy Institute, 2009, p. 6.

54. This, after a similar pattern through the 1983–1998 period when, "to put it succinctly, the top quintile received a little less than 90 percent of the total increase in income and over 90 percent of the increase in wealth" (Edward N. Wolff, *Top Heavy*, pp. 37–8).

55. It fell back to a mere 237:1 in 2001 as stock values fell, and stood at 262:1 in 2005. (See Ian Dew-Becker and Robert Gordon, *Where Did the Productivity Growth Go?* National Bureau of Economic Research working paper 11842, December 2005.)

56. *State of Working America 2008/9*, p. 220.

57. This calculation is based on data from the Luxemburg Income study, reported in *The New American Economy: A Rising Tide that Lifts Only Yachts* (New York, Century Foundation, 2004, pp. 7–9).
58. Lawrence Mishel, Jared Bernstein and Sylvia Allegretto, *The State of Working America*, p. 3.
59. Edwin Feulner, *Flat-Out Smart*, The Heritage Foundation Web memo, October 25, 2005.
60. Neal Boortz, *The Fair Tax Book*, passim.
61. The Employment Policy Institute springs most readily to mind. See, for example, their press release, *Labor Day 2005: Five Reasons Not to Increase the Minimum Wage*.
62. For a recent survey of the debate and the evidence, see CQ Researcher, *Minimum Wage*, December 16, 2005: also Liana Fox, *Minimum Wage Trends*, Economic Policy Institute Briefing Paper 178, October 24, 2006.
63. The more sophisticated of the conservative theorists often quietly concede that. This from Daniel Mitchell: "contrary to what both political parties argue, there does not seem to be a strong relationship between the budget deficit and interest rates. Nor is there much reason to believe that lower interest rates, by themselves, will have a pronounced effect on investment" (*Taxes, Deficits and Economic Growth*, The Heritage Foundation Website, May 14, 1996).
64. For the remarkable scale of this "pork" in the Republican-controlled 109th Congress, see Robert Reich, "An Economy Raised on Pork," *New York Times*, September 3, 2005; and Ryan Sager, *The Elephant in the Room* (Hoboken, John Wiley, 2006), p. 102.
65. *Time*, June 12, 2006, p. 21.

CHAPTER 4

Cutting "Welfare" to Help the Poor

Welfare states in the modern world are not very old – 60, 70 years at most. Some parts are older – the German social insurance system started with Bismarck – but in general the provision of government help to the poor, the sick, the disabled and the elderly is a very recent phenomenon. Not all governments make that provision even now: but most do. Certainly in recent times, all governments in the advanced democracies have taken on a major welfare role; and that includes federal and state authorities here in the United States.

Yet in this, as in so much else, the US has proved to be unique. Unique in coverage: no universal system of health care, free at the point of use, emerged here in the late 1940s as it did in much of Western Europe. Unique in delivery system: from the early 1950s pensions and health care were tied directly to wage settlements here, in wages-and-benefits packages with few foreign parallels. Unique in timing: the US set the pace in the 1930s with the New Deal, and again in the late 1960s with its own War on Poverty. Unique in vocabulary: here the state pension system is known as "social security" and the term "welfare" is restricted to payments to the poor, giving it a stigma it lacks in much of Western Europe.[1] And unique in fragility: the

United States is the only major industrial democracy formally committed to the "ending of welfare as we know it": through the 1996 Personal Responsibility and Work Opportunity Reconciliation Act.

The result has been the consolidation in the United States of a publicly financed welfare system which, in comparative terms, is now both residual and modest. It is residual, in that it leaves the bulk of provision for the sick and the old to the private sector. It is modest, in that the public provision made available is – pensions apart – less generous than that now commonplace in Western Europe and Japan.[2] For many American liberals, there is something profoundly embarrassing about the richest country on earth getting by with the most limited welfare system in the advanced industrial world. But that is not how the Conservative Right sees it. On the contrary, having a residual and modest welfare state is, for them, one of the key reasons why the USA *is* the richest country on earth. Protecting that economic success then requires welfare provision here to be made ever more residual and modest over time. In a manner and scale without precedence elsewhere, *cutting welfare* – either to the bone, or away completely – is regularly and seriously canvassed by conservative forces in the United States as the best way of helping the poor. Their argument goes like this.

1. There is not as much poverty in America as liberals like to claim

The liberal media is way too quick to exaggerate and at times misreport the data on poverty in the United States. We have to be very careful here. "For most Americans, the word 'poverty' suggests destitution"; but in truth only a tiny portion of the 37 million people reported as living in poverty by the Census Bureau are poor in any meaningful sense of that term. "Overall, the living standards of most poor Americans are far higher than is generally appreciated."[3] Most of them have a fridge, a stove, a television – normally two, both color – a microwave, air-conditioning and a car. The bulk of the American poor has basic but decent housing, and access to food and health care. In fact, "the average poor American has more living space than the average individual living in Paris . . . and other cities throughout Europe."[4] This is not poverty by world standards. It is in Asia and Africa that poverty stunts the growth of children. Not the United States. What poverty there is here is often short-lived.

"More than half of all poverty 'spells' (time spent in poverty) last less than four months, and about 80 percent last less than a year."[5] There is a lot of upward and downward social mobility in the United States. One household in three escapes poverty within three years; and one rich family in three slips down into a lower income bracket during that same period. "In fact, very few people – only about 2 percent of the total population – are chronically poor in America, as defined by living in poverty for four years or more";[6] and all societies have a stratum of folk like that. Poverty, after all, is natural. The poor are always with us; so it is ridiculous to criticize the United States for simply being like all the rest. We are not denying that there is real hardship for roughly one poor household in three. We are simply saying that "even those households would be judged to have high living standards compared to most people in the world."[7] So we need to keep a sense of proportion when discussing poverty – a sense of proportion that, on this as on so much else, liberals normally lack.

2. What poverty there is in the United States is almost entirely self-induced

America is still a society where, by hard work and personal effort, all things are possible. You do not have to be poor. Poverty is, in that sense, a question of choice. "It has a behavior-based component. Women who cannot afford to care for children should not have them. People who can work should do so. Young children should remain in school."[8] If you want to stay out of poverty, make sure that you stay first at school and then in work; and make sure too that you don't have children until you have established a stable and well-funded relationship. School, work and marriage are the great barriers to poverty here, and all three are readily available if you look for them.

So if you don't, that tells us something, not about the society in which you are poor, but about you as someone who remains poor when you do not need to. Why are you still there, trapped in your own poverty? Perhaps it is because you do not have the right skills, or the willingness to acquire them. Or perhaps it is because you blew school, and now are paying the price. There might even be an IQ issue here.[9] Or perhaps it is simply that you moved too quickly into casual and careless sex, and are now looking for support from people less feckless than yourself. Not that everyone is guilty here, of course. There are innocents caught up in poverty too – widows, the genetically infirm and overwhelmingly the children you so casually bred — innocents who, if not helped, will find themselves trapped in a culture of poverty from which it is very hard to escape. We know that "nearly two-thirds of poor children reside in single-parent families," Robert Rector has written, but we also know that "if poor mothers married the fathers of their children, nearly 75 percent would immediately be lifted out of poverty."[10]

So there are things that can be done, and there is a role for public policy. But it has to be policy anchored in a clear recognition of at least three things. That, in the main, people put themselves into poverty, rather than being put there. Policy has therefore to be designed primarily to stop them doing that. That it is not the rich who cause poverty, but the poor themselves. Tax the rich into oblivion — play class politics — and you will end up with even more poverty. And that public policy can only do so much, and can easily overreach itself. "The government can force your parents to send you to school, but it can't force you to learn." There's a matter of personal responsibility here. "If you do not educate yourself or develop a marketable skill, the chances are you will be poor and powerless";[11] and that will be nobody's fault but your own.

3. The big thing that's wrong with liberal welfare programs is that they create more poverty than they remove

The liberal welfare programs of the 1960s were designed on the premise that what the poor lacked, more than anything else, was money and skills. Liberal-minded politicians threw trillions of tax dollars into the urban ghettos, offering what they termed "a hand but not a handout." In the main, this largesse was well-intentioned: though some of it did also reflect a Democratic Party desire to build up a dependent client base. But even when welfare policy was well-intentioned, it was entirely counterproductive. It got nowhere near the real causes of poverty, rooted as those are in illegitimacy and idleness. It simply transferred hard-earned resources from the working-poor to the nonworking-poor: in the process sending out entirely the wrong message about effort and personal responsibility, and squeezing the very people whose industry and personal morality were and remain the backbone of the American success story.

In designing their welfare programs, liberals ignored the warning, given long ago by FDR, that "continued dependence on relief induces a spiritual and moral disintegration fundamentally destructive to the national fiber."[12]

They chose instead to dole out ever larger quantities of that relief — to administer what he had called in 1935 "a narcotic, a subtle destroyer of the human spirit" — tolerating as they did so the existence of far too many "welfare queens."[13] *The relief they doled out so indiscriminately to both the deserving and the undeserving poor then literally cost a fortune — $8.3 trillion since 1973 alone*[14] *— but failed entirely to remove the poverty it was designed to end. Even Jimmy Carter admitted as much: that the liberal welfare system was "anti-work, anti-family, inequitable in its treatment of the poor and wasteful of the taxpayers' dollars."*[15] *But like all Democrats, he never tackled its inadequacies. He had far too many dependent constituencies to service to be able to match his understanding of the system's defects with policy adequate to its reform.*

4. Many of today's social ills can and must be laid at the door of welfare itself

The War on Poverty was a disaster; and because it was, the liberal establishment in Washington still bears a huge responsibility for the level and scale of deprivation in America's inner cities. As Ronald Reagan said in his last State of the Union address, "Some years ago the federal government declared war on poverty, and poverty won." Like all welfare states, the War on Poverty, by making it "profitable to be poor,"[16] *"degrade[d] the tradition of work, thrift and neighborliness that enabled a society to work at the outset," and then spawned "social and economic problems that it [was] powerless to solve."*[17] *What had started as a "safety net" quickly became nothing less than a "hammock."*[18]

The incentive structures in its programs locked people into the very poverty on which the war was being waged. Welfare programs developed in the late 1960s and early 1970s made it far too easy for young men to shirk their parental responsibilities and for young women to have children without being able to afford them. "One out-of-wedlock birth every 35 seconds," Robert Rector told Congress in February 2005. Those same programs built in powerful disincentives to work: reducing the potential US labor supply by nearly 5 percent and lowering the work effort of welfare recipients by as much as 30 percent.[19] *They also helped to consolidate a culture of instant gratification and moral fecklessness among welfare recipients that ran counter to the work ethic that had lifted previous generations of the poor into their contemporary affluence. Far from raising living standards in America's urban heartlands, the*

War on Poverty created an underclass of people excluded by their welfare dependency from full participation in the values and practices of mainstream American life; and at the core of that underclass, this well-meaning but ill-informed expansion of welfare programs then marooned in poverty a whole generation of ghetto kids.

5. Suffer the little children . . .

It was, and still is, these children of the poor who are welfare's greatest casualties. These are the kids who lack the guidance of an ever-present and hardworking father. They are the ones who, in consequence, are disproportionately exposed to "emotional and behavioral problems, school failure, drug and alcohol abuse, crime and incarceration."[20] It is they who face the bleakest future: since "the longer a child remains on [welfare] in childhood the lower will be his earnings as an adult"[21] and the greater will be the likelihood of him dropping out of school and ending up back on welfare when older. The driver here is not poverty. It is welfare itself. It is welfare, not poverty, that produces dependency; and it is dependency that lowers a child's IQ. Hold everything else constant – income, race, parental IQ . . . everything you want – and then test for cognitive capacity in kids on welfare and kids who are not. You will find a 20 percent drop in cognitive capacity among kids who have spent at least a sixth of their life on welfare.[22] "The traditional welfare state's core dilemma," Robert Rector has written, "is that profligate spending intended to alleviate material poverty" actually "led to a dramatic increase in behavioral poverty . . . dependency and an eroded work ethic, lack of educational aspirations and achievement, inability or unwillingness to control one's children, increased single parenthood and illegitimacy, criminal activity, and drug and alcohol abuse."[23] The liberals' welfare programs did more than simply fail to solve poverty. They also damaged those to whom they were given.

6. Fortunately, there is a better way out of poverty than welfare

Once the true answers to poverty – school, work and marriage – were recognized by the Republicans who swept to power in Congress in 1994, the solution was to hand. Instead of handouts and entitlements, the Gingrich Contract with America ushered in an era of personal responsibility, workfare and the promotion of responsible parenthood. The 1996 Act took away entitlements to permanent welfare support: replacing the New Deal's Aid to Families with Dependent Children with a new Temporary Assistance to Needy Families program linking welfare to a commitment to work/seek work. The Act set a firm time limit – five years – on the receipt of welfare, and established targets for the percentage of recipients in work or job training schemes by 2001 and 2002; triggering a move from welfare to work. It also began systematically to reinforce the institution of marriage, by encouraging states to establish pater-nity and collect child support, and by obliging teenage mothers to remain in school and to live with an adult. According to its advocates, the 1996 Act worked. Contrary to the fears of increased poverty expressed by liberals at the time,[24] there were 2.3 million fewer children in poverty in 2001 than in 1996, the rates of poverty among African-American children and among families headed by single mothers were at all-time lows, welfare caseloads were significantly down, the growth rate of illegitimate births had slowed, and employ-ment among single mothers was up by anything between 50 and 100 percent.[25] With Earned Income Tax Credit and noncash benefits from the remaining 69 federal welfare programs added in, the number of people in poverty in the United States actually fell between 1996 and 2001 by more than 4 million – a rate of poverty down in just 5 years from 10.2 percent to 8.8.[26]

One section of the Republican coalition – that anchored in the Heritage Foundation and in sections of the Christian Right – now wants a second round of welfare reform, focusing on a stricter and wider application of the work-rules established in 1996,[27] and on a more powerful advocacy of marriage. They want work rules added to the other main welfare programs – public housing and food stamps. They supported George W. Bush's "healthy marriage initiative," and now want that augmented by a wider advocacy of sexual absti-nence before marriage. Their argument is that the 1996 Act was a step in the right direction. It began a welfare revolution that must now be carried forward – on the certain conviction that "by increasing work and marriage, our nation can virtually eliminate remaining child poverty"[28] within our lifetime.

The more libertarian elements within the Republican coalition, however – those closer to the Cato Institute – are less comfortable with state orchestration of marriage vows than are the Heritage people. They remain convinced that even the 1996 reform failed to reduce out-of-wedlock births on any significant scale, or to enable welfare recipients to become self-sustaining. They do not believe that even Republican-inspired welfare reforms can ever adequately do either of those things. So they favor a different tack: initially the complete

removal of welfare benefits from "young women who continue to make unten-
able life decisions";[29] the return of all welfare funds from the federal govern-
ment to the states; and eventually the replacement of all welfare payments with
a negative income tax[30] and the complete privatization of welfare. Charities
are so much better than governments, they insist, in dealing with poverty. They
are more responsive to their donors and to their clients, more flexible, more
efficient and more effective. The federal government should therefore return
"responsibility for the poor first to the states, then to the private sector."[31]
Cato-based libertarians see the 1996 Act as a mixed blessing – as a necessary
first step, but one freezing the policy debate in the wrong place: by implying
that, if properly designed, welfare can be made to work. No it can't, they say.
Welfare will only work by being totally abolished. "When it comes to welfare,"
as Michael Tanner has written, "we should end it, not mend it."[32]

A liberal response

Oh that it was that simple. But it is not: for the following reasons
at least.

1. There's more poverty out there than you might think

It takes strong political nerves to get up in the morning, put on the
expensive suit, and go tell Congress that being poor in the United
States isn't really being poor at all. Perhaps those who feel this way
should try it for themselves. After all, the United States possesses one
of the more idiosyncratic and limited definitions of poverty in the
advanced industrial world, one designed as late as 1963 by a minor civil
servant in the Department of Agriculture.[33] What Mollie Orshansky
came up with was not a relative measure of poverty but an absolute
one – an income figure sensitive to family size and to rates of inflation – one that by 2007 defined the poverty threshold for a single
individual as $10,787, and for a family of four as $21,027. Those are
very low figures, especially if you live in an expensive urban area –
just try living on welfare and even paying the rent in a place like
Chicago[34] – and yet even so, as we saw in Chapter 3, in 2007 12.5 percent of all Americans were living on incomes that fell at/below the

official poverty lines. What was even worse: of the 37 million people living in officially defined poverty in 2007, 13 million were children. That is equivalent to the entire populations of Sweden and Norway. The poverty rate for very young children in the United States in the first half-decade of the twenty-first century was slightly under 20 percent: nearly one preschool child in every five! Around them are what the EPI calls the *twice-poor*. Americans living on or below incomes that are only twice the officially defined level for their family size.[35] Amazingly, over 89 million Americans fell into that broader category in 2003 – all close to poverty and all accordingly obliged to watch every penny. (The EPI calculated that on average nationwide, a family of four currently requires a yearly income of $48,778 to meet its basic needs, and that nearly a third of all American family earns less than that.[36]) Collectively the poor and the twice-poor now constitute 31 percent of the population: nearly three Americans in every ten.[37] That's a huge number of people living in or near the margin of poverty, no matter what Congress is or is not being told by the people in suits.

What those three Americans in ten experience is real poverty, in both the absolute and relative senses of the term. The percentage of American families currently classified as "food insecure" is 11.1, and not just the unemployed – 40 percent of all those using food banks live in families in which at least one adult is working.[38] People in poverty here know, and know on a daily basis, that they don't have what most Americans have; and that they lack those things in a culture which repeatedly defines success in consumption and income terms. The poor in America are not only poor. They are continually reminded of their economic condition by every billboard they pass. So it does not help them – or indeed us – to be told that most of them have cars. Of course they have cars: given the absence of adequate systems of public transport in vast swathes of the United States, how else are they meant to get to the shops, or to the food bank. A car in the United States is not a luxury. It is a necessity; an extra financial burden that cannot be avoided if doing the ordinary things of life is not to become nearly impossible. The Western European poor do not need cars to anything like the same degree, because the scale of public provision – the size of the social wage that everyone enjoys regardless of income – is so much higher there.

That is one reason why it is simply untrue to claim that the American poor are better off than most ordinary Europeans and better off than the entirety of the Western European poor. Sadly, they are not. On the contrary, the child poverty rate in the United States is currently *four* times that of northern Europe.[39] There are *only three* Western European countries whose poor children have a lower living standard than do poor children in the United States.[40] UNICEF found the US ranking three from bottom in 2007 on its measure of child material well-being in the 20 most advanced industrial economies.[41] There are at least *nine* OECD countries in which the cash and noncash benefits flowing to families in poverty exceed the flows reaching their American equivalents.[42] As early as 1990, there were at least *ten* OECD countries in which, after tax and transfers, the rate of poverty (measured in American terms) was lower than in the US itself.[43] And at the start of the new millennium, life expectancy among African-Americans was actually running *lower* than that of low-income Indians in the impoverished state of Kerala.[44]

2. If all this poverty is self-inflicted, then masochism in the United States is amazingly rife

If poverty is genuinely something that people choose, then it is remarkable how many people in America seem keen to make that choice. It is even more remarkable that the children of the poor consistently make that choice again and again as they get older; that women (especially single mothers) make that choice more than men; and that African-Americans and Hispanic-Americans consistently make that choice in greater numbers than do their white equivalents. There seem to be patterns here, patterns reproduced by a myriad of isolated individual decisions, but patterns that hold regardless of the individuals whose decisions call them into existence. And when patterns build up like that, it seems sensible to treat them like patterns. After all, if it looks like a duck and quacks like a duck, perhaps it is a duck.

Which is why there is something particularly offensive about the speed and ease with which so many commentators on the American Right, instead of probing beneath the surface for the underlying causes of the "pathologies" of poverty they so dislike, move instead to demonize the poor, endlessly blaming them for making "bad choices" as though good ones were plentiful and immediately at hand. Telling young black women to marry the fathers of their children, for example, carries with it the premise that the men are there to be married. Yet one in nine African-American men between the ages of 20 and 34 is currently in jail,[45] a bigger proportion of "men away" than the US as a whole experienced during the entirety of the Second World War; and unemployment rates among young black men are double those among their white contemporaries. "The problem is not that the nation's poorest women have systematically passed up good jobs and good marriage partners. The problem is that there are significant economic and cultural inadequacies in the choices available to them."[46] They, like the rest of America, value children; but unlike the rest of America, they cannot easily support them.

Conservative commentators roll into the ghetto, see individuals acting quite rationally within the parameters of what is possible there, and then condemn those individuals for not doing what they could have done had the parameters been wider. They see the last act in the drama but never the prologue. Margaret Thatcher's great ally, Norman Tebbit, used to tell the UK poor to "get on their bikes and go find work," as his father had before him. But when jobs are scarce, you have to peddle further. If you are already trapped in urban poverty, the incline up which you have to cycle is steeper than in the suburban flatlands. If the world around you is racist, cycling alone can be dangerous if you are black. If it is sexist, women cyclists beware! The level playing field on which all of us are supposed to act with responsibility is just not there in a world scarred by inequalities of class, race and gender that have built up over the generations. So advocate peddling by all means. Personal responsibility *is* the necessary last moment. We can all agree on that. But if the Republican audience genuinely wants the American social play to have the happy ending they desire, they will have to do something too about the inequalities and inadequacies that currently characterize the stage set on which it is being performed. If they do not work on the *positions* that create poverty, and focus instead only on the individuals currently occupying them, all that can happen is that some of those individuals will escape to affluence, but the positions of the poor will still be there, to be filled by the next generation of the under-resourced. People will rotate in and out of poverty, but poverty itself will remain.

3. The true lessons of Katrina

For what else are we to make of the images released on the world by the impact of Katrina on New Orleans in 2005: images of Americans too poor to escape their own drowning, and of Americans without bank accounts or even the money to buy a ride? We can go the right-wing route, of course. We can deny or downplay those images. We can even tell Congress that the American poor are not like the Sudanese poor. Or we can indirectly blame the Louisiana poor for their own drowning, by using their plight as a warning to other Americans to stay in school or to go to work, however menial that work may be. Or – and this would be the more honest, liberal thing to do – we can face the reality of poverty and racism in the United States, and recognize the strength of the cycles of deprivation that lock themselves around the poor. We can even go the extra mile and concede that, although there are many poor whites – that poverty is not a monopoly of black and Latino communities[47] – even so, exposure to poverty is still overwhelmingly organized by the color of your skin. If you are born black and poor, your chances of remaining poor remain significantly higher than if you are born white and poor.[48] That is not because, being black, you are lazier or less intelligent than your white counterpart. It is because your color – for all the years of civil rights legislation and affirmative action since the 1960s – still acts as a barrier to equal access to the opportunities of American life.

Conservative forces will no doubt then tell us that affirmative action breeds a white racist counterreaction. It undoubtedly does. That is one of the dilemmas of liberal politics. The libertarian wing of the Conservative coalition will no doubt even go so far as to demand the repeal of all civil rights legislation, in order to set everyone on a level playing field. But such demands are either disingenuous or naive. For there is racism out there – racism that does not create poverty, the system does that, but racism that determines which parts of American society will be most vulnerable to any poverty that happens to be around. Take away affirmative action and racism will not disappear.

There can be no genuine equality of rights when the individuals exercising them are endowed with such unequal amounts of social power and personal capital. Telling the black poor to pull themselves up by their bootstraps is one thing. Telling the white middle class to pull hard on the pink ribbons of their daughters' ballet shoes is quite another. To stop a repetition of the tragedy of New Orleans, we need more than stronger levees and lectures on self-help. We need policy addressed to the structural causes of poverty, and an honest debate on how best to eradicate the long shadow of slavery.

4. Given a chance, welfare works better than is claimed

The payment of welfare stands accused by many on the American Right of creating poverty and of damaging those to whom it is given; but with one important caveat – about welfare traps – to which we will come later, the claim is literally ludicrous. Welfare did not create poverty in America. There was poverty here long before the New Deal, and long before Johnson's "War." Neither set of welfare initiatives created their clienteles. They simply responded to their prior existence. The poverty of the 1930s was of a mass kind, the product of a general economic collapse that was rectified not by welfare programs but by the United States' mobilization for war. Within it, however, were categories of the poor that had existed before 1929 and that continued to do so after 1941: the temporarily unemployed, the genetically infirm, widows and the elderly. By the 1960s those categories of the poor had been joined by another, one explicitly excluded from the coverage of the original New Deal. To get any sort of legislative package through a Congress whose committees were dominated by southern Democrats, FDR had excluded black workers in the south. Servants and agricultural workers gained no benefits from the core programs of the New Deal. They survived instead in invisible southern poverty, poverty which – as prosperity returned with the war – then drew them out of the south into the cities and industries of the north-east and the mid-west. In the first half of the postwar period, African-Americans increasingly exchanged *invisible* southern rural poverty for its *visible* urban northern equivalent. It was an exchange to which the welfare programs of the 1960s were a belated response.

So it was a case of poverty first, and welfare second; not the other way around. It was also a case of a welfare response that, when properly funded, took the rate of poverty *down*, not up: a response which over time definitely improved the lives of many categories of the American poor. The official poverty rate in 1959 – the first year in the United States that it was taken – was 22.4 percent. By 1973, with the war on poverty at its height, that rate had halved. Then, as programs were cut back in the 1970s and 1980s, the rate grew again. It was back to 14.5 percent by 1992, although it is slightly lower now, as we have seen. Behind the numbers there always was, and is, movement. Over 7 million Americans moved out of poverty in the 1990s, and 4 million moved back between 2001 and 2004. Behind the numbers too, there was and is more than welfare. The growth rate of the economy has also to be factored in; but so too do the programs – three in particular. *Social Security* has had a huge impact on the plight of a key category of the American poor, providing an index-linked floor under the income of retirees. The poverty rate among the American old was 35.2 percent in 1959. By 1995 it was only 10.5 percent. *Food stamps* have played a vital role in maintaining at least a moderate flow of adequate food to families on low incomes: in 2000 helping some 17 million people.[49] In its last full year of operation (1995), Aid to Families with Dependent Children was providing money to about 14 million adults and children. None of these programs lifted any of their recipients into average-income lifestyles.[50] "None achieved spectacular results ... spectacular results are, of course, difficult to achieve."[51] But collectively they put a safety net under the American poor which, if absent, could only have intensified their poverty. There is thus an important if negative defense of welfare in the United States: that without it, the condition of the poor would have been significantly worse.

5. The charity illusion

Unless, of course, as the Cato people would have it, private charity would have stepped into the breach, and done a better job. But there is just no evidence for that. There is certainly no evidence that private charity could, or did, scratch more than the surface of the poverty experienced by the old, the infirm and the widowed prior to the New Deal. And of the nature of things, there can be no evidence to sustain the claim that if welfare was entirely removed (and tax levels cut accordingly), those benefiting from the tax cuts would then redirect all/most of their extra income into charitable endeavors. American altruism – though impressive by international standards – is not without limit, and because it is not, the private sector cannot be treated as a reliable and problem-free alternative to existing welfare programs. Charity-based welfare contains no mechanisms to guard against unevenness of provision, or against moralizing in the terms set for aid given, or simply against the onset of "gift exhaustion" over time. The gathering of funds by private charities is in any case always time-consuming, intrusive and administratively inefficient; and the distribution of funds as private handouts only serves to reinforce – in those who receive them – the very sense of dependency and impotence which conservatives are apparently so keen to avoid.

The libertarian Right talk the language of "rights" for the affluent and of "entitlements" for the poor, and prefer charities to governments because only government programs are entitlement-based. They imply that only the poor have an entitlement culture in contemporary America. They advocate dependency on wages but not dependency on welfare. They favor dependency on the stock market but not on the welfare check. Some of them support the private dependency of married women on their husbands but not the public dependency of the poor on the state. That is, they rank different kinds of dependency without ever adequately explaining why just one of those kinds is inferior to the rest, or without factoring in the entitlement culture of the corporate rich. But they are correct in this much at least. In a welfare regime based on charities the poor do indeed lose all their entitlements. They get only what they are given. They literally have *no* rights. But is that what we really want – states-based or charity-based welfare systems that produce unevenness, particularism and parsimony? Do we really want the poor in Alabama less protected than the poor in Massachusetts, or the Catholic poor less protected than Baptist poor in the south? I do hope not. We need to remember that the best sort of charity starts at home, in a middle-class willingness to contribute through taxation to the provision of an adequate social wage that alone can guarantee basic quality-of-life rights to all

Americans. It is not the sort of charity that the intellectuals at the Cato Institute favor, but it is the only kind of charity for which American liberals ought regularly to campaign.

6. The fallacy of the incompetent state

In any event, in making the pitch for the full privatization of welfare, the Charles Murray's and Michael Tanner's of this world are not comparing like with like. They are also generalizing from an extraordinarily parochial base. They advocate the replacement of the American welfare system by an idealized and untested network of private charities, using as their evidence inadequacies in American public welfare policy since the 1970s. With few exceptions, they do not appear to have looked in any systematic way at Western Europe, where states have run welfare systems successfully for years. Nor have they engaged with – indeed have they even read – the fabulous and extensive scholarly literature on comparative welfare systems. If they had, they would quickly have come to see that the great tragedy of Lyndon Johnson's war on poverty was not that poverty won here, but that the war itself was not pursued with sufficient consistency and zeal.

All governments – European and American alike – distribute income and dispense welfare. They are all, in James Galbraith's telling term, "transfer states," and inequality always shows what he called "the fingerprints of state policy." [52] The war on poverty required those fingerprints to distribute income downwards, and initially it did. General poverty levels fell. But command of the war then shifted. Under Reagan and the Bushes, the fingerprints were deployed differently. Income was consciously moved upwards. Welfare systems can always be made to fail, if inadequately financed and incompetently led. A FEMA will always fail if led by cronies and managed by fools. But by the same token, welfare systems can always be made to work well if supplied with sufficient funds and commitment. Indeed, take a welfare system up to about 40 percent of GDP – when it is servicing the entire community and not just the poor – and popular support for it will rise, not fall. That has been the universal Western European experience. [53]

Charles Murray is wrong: the limitations of welfare states are not structural and endemic. They're political and contingent. You get the welfare state you fight for. It is income inequality in the US that makes welfare seem burdensome and unfair to those many Middle Americans who are so financially hard pressed by those above them that they are reluctant to fund those who stand below them on the social food chain. You solve that pressure on Middle America not by cutting welfare but by cutting inequality: by shortening the chain. Welfare provision works in Western Europe because income inequality there is less, and because European Conservative/Christian Democratic parties are genuinely compassionate in their conservatism. They have to be. To be elected, they have to say – as even Margaret Thatcher was obliged to do – that the "national health service is safe in our hands." But not here; here the Democratic Left is much weaker than in Western Europe, and the political and electoral center of gravity is accordingly much further to the right. Saving welfare does not require its privatization. It requires the Democratic Party to get its act together, and to pull that center of gravity leftwards in a more civilized direction. Thank goodness that at long last that is beginning to happen again.

7. The limits of welfare-to-work in a world of low pay

The 1996 Act was the Republicans' ace card in their attempt to roll back the American welfare state, and they have one huge piece of evidence going in their favor: the dramatic fall in the number of people – especially young single mothers – in receipt of welfare since its passing. But the figures on caseload reduction, though real, are also deceptive, and we need to say so. They are deceptive in a *causal* sense: in that the full implementation of the Act coincided with a significant period of job growth in the American economy. When that growth stalled, so too did the rate of job take-up by single mothers.[54] The figures on caseload reduction are deceptive too in a *social* sense. People came off welfare, but then ran into a whole series of new problems which the figures don't catch. Women fleeing domestic violence lost a vital source of autonomy from the men who had violated them.[55]

Young women with small children lost a significant percentage of their new wages on child care and transport costs; and the children themselves – whose enhanced well-being was, after all, a key aim of the new legislation – often found themselves in inadequate child care, looked after by under-trained and underpaid female staff. Women did not stop doing child care. They simply stopped doing their own. And overwhelmingly, the figures on caseload reduction are deceptive in an *economic* sense. Going off welfare, though it reduced the numbers, did not reduce the scale and rate of poverty among those who previously had been in receipt of aid. The Cato Institute's Michael Tanner has conceded as much, noting that "self-sufficiency appears to be eluding the grasp of many, if not most, former recipients."[56] And of course it is, because (quite predictably) the vast majority of the jobs into which former welfare recipients were moved turned out to be *low-paid* ones. Welfare-to-work moved people from government-sponsored poverty to private sector-based poverty, adding to their transport and child care costs as it did so. Workfare changed the source of poverty, but not the poverty itself.

All of which underscores the key issue that the Right will *not* adequately address: how to restructure the American economy in ways that will reduce the number of low-paid jobs it sustains. Cato's Michael Tanner wants welfare reduction to go hand in hand with the encouragement of enterprise and job creation. Fine, but where is the evidence that enterprise alone – without trade union pressure – will automatically create a high-wage growth strategy. There is none. If there were, China would currently have the highest wages on earth. Yet without that high-wage dynamic – put into play by government policy or by the strength of the labor movement – moving people from welfare to work will not bring down the rate of poverty. It will simply add to the pool of workers seeking low-paid jobs, reducing already low levels of pay as it does so, and forcing even more Americans into that most intolerable of situations: full-time work which fails to provide an adequate living wage. Oh that the Republican coalition in the United States would put half the effort it does into welfare reform into the design of a labor market policy protective of adequate wages. That would be an effective antipoverty policy indeed – but don't hold your breath. That kind of sanity is definitely not coming, not from this generation of Republicans anyway!

8. The "welfare-poor" and the "working-poor" are on the same side

Republicans like to present themselves as champions of the working-poor against the welfare-poor, implying that the interests of the two groups are in tension, and painting the Democratic Party into a "tax and spend" corner as they do so. But the argument is false in both of its premises: the interests of the two are not in tension, and the Republicans are not the defenders of the real interests of the working-poor.

The existence of a large group of full-time workers paid so little that they themselves are on the margin of poverty actually traps the welfare-poor a second time. If you are on welfare, you are poor. If you get out of welfare and into work, you will still be poor; because the move will only take you into the bottom tier of the poorly paid. If the people in that low-pay group are then financially pressed – and they definitely are – it is not because of the weight of any welfare taxation which they carry. It is because their wages are low. It is not taxes that make them poor, but lack of income growth. What really hurts the low paid is not the poverty of the people below them but the greed of the people above.[57] As we saw in Chapter 3, the truly unique feature of the recent American income story is the proportion of total income growth taken by the ultra-rich. You remember, 24 percent of all income growth in the US economy between 1997 and 2001 taken by just 1 percent of the population, at the end of a quarter-century in which wages remained flat for the majority of working Americans. What the working-poor need is not welfare retrenchment but higher wages. They *and* the welfare-poor need the creation of a high-wage, high-growth economy to ease the burden of poverty on them both. They both need full employment and rising wages in an economy in which there is a fair distribution of rewards. That's the kind of economy that the Republicans always promise in the run-up to elections; but it is also the kind that after elections, for 90 million Americans at least, they regularly fail to deliver.

The promise, however, does indicate one thing: even Republicans agree that public policy can make a difference here. The existence of the working-poor is not an act of God, as "natural" as poverty itself. It's the direct product of an unregulated market system in which the rights of workers are regularly eroded and taxation policy is repeatedly redesigned to favor the already privileged. Relative wages are always "much more a matter of politics, and much less a matter of markets, than is generally believed."[58] Even before the 1996 Act and the later Bush tax cuts, the US came in last – and by a huge margin – in the number of low-income families raised to half-median income by government programs: only 38 percent of families here, as against 87 percent in Sweden and 78 percent in Germany.[59] The problems of the working-poor are "directly traceable to actions of the government, the most prominent" being "the redistribution of tax burdens, government hostility to trade unions, and an indifference to preserving the real value of the minimum wage."[60] It is not the welfare-poor who live off the hard work of ordinary Americans. It is the super-rich. It is time to straighten out the twisted logic of an argument that blames the poverty of the nearly poor on the existence of those even poorer than themselves, while the rich get away blame-free. If poverty, and the fear of poverty, is genuinely to be lifted off the shoulders of those at the bottom of this society, those in its upper layers will need to do the lifting: not by cutting welfare to the poor but by cutting welfare to themselves.[61]

9. Welfare doesn't trap the poor in an underclass. We do

Welfare critics are right on at least this: there is a "welfare-trap/work-disincentive" issue in any welfare system. As people come off welfare, and lose benefits, the effective tax rate on their own earnings can be extraordinarily high. Depending on the rules, in the move from welfare-to-work you might lose 60 cents of welfare provision for every dollar you earn, and effectively be only 40 cents better off: a rate of taxation against which the rich regularly howl when experiencing it themselves. So there is a problem of "disincentives to work" associated with welfare, one on which conservatives regularly latch. But it is not the only, or indeed the main, problem currently facing young mothers in search of good jobs in America's inner cities. Good jobs are scarce there because the middle class have left, taking the jobs with them. Available child care is poor because the programs have been cut. Young men are scarce because incarceration rates have been systematically ratcheted up. Suburban flight, welfare retrenchment, drugs and the rise of a prison-economy are the real villains here. As Barack Obama said, "the people of New Orleans just weren't abandoned during the Hurricane. They were abandoned long ago – to murder and mayhem in the streets, to substandard schools, to dilapidated housing, to inadequate health care, to a pervasive sense of hopelessness."[62] Underclasses do not create themselves. They are created. You cannot be trapped unless somebody does the trapping.

The great thing about traps, however, is that they can be sprung. The solution to the disincentive effect of welfare payments is to phase-in benefit reductions slowly – allowing people to earn and receive benefits in parallel until their incomes reach a tolerable level. Middle-class college kids paying back student loans experience a similar kind of phasing. They are allowed to link the repayment of their loans to the growth of their salaries, and to pay lower than market rates of interest as they do so. So if it works for one class, it should for another. It costs money, of course, and goes to the poor: so it is not a solution that appeals to many Republicans. Their preference is the more penal one: cutting off the flow of aid, to force people to make "right choices" and get themselves out of the ghetto. But that is easier said than done. Cut the money away from teenage mothers, and you leave their babies even more disadvantaged than before.[63] Deny those mothers adequate training programs and child support and to what then can they turn? It is as likely to be to vice as to virtue[64]: particularly if, at the same time, three-strike incarceration policies are taking away the men who might support them – and taking them away in ever greater numbers for ever longer periods of time. There is a problem of illegitimacy rates among young African-American women. It is one rooted in a longer standing crisis of the African-American family that stretches back to the Civil War and beyond.[65] But welfare did not cause that problem. At most, it amplifies it at the margin; and so cutting welfare alone will not solve it. Cycles of deprivation are not broken by denying help to those locked within them. Breaking entrenched patterns of social exclusion requires the deployment of *more*, not fewer, resources; and the careful orchestration of policies from the full range of government agencies seeking to deal with them.[66] Faced with entrenched social exclusion, you do not pull welfare out. You put it in. Liberal solutions are not easy. They are not cheap; and they are not quick. But at least they are solutions.

Cutting welfare is not. Cutting welfare can only make the social exclusion of the poor worse.

10. Poverty is a matter of choice – it's just not a choice made by the poor

The ultimate irony here is that poverty, as the Republican Right regularly claims, is indeed a matter of choice. It is just not a choice that the poor themselves are called upon to make. It is a choice made by the rest of us. In the main, for most of us, by how we vote; and for those who govern us, by how they legislate. They and us, not the poor, have the power to choose. We can chose, as an economy and a society, to meet the arrival of intensified global competition by outsourcing production, lowering American wages and increasing income inequality. Or we can chose to reset the way we organize the economy and regulate trade, in order to pull jobs back here, and to improve the quality of work and levels of remuneration attached to them. There is a choice to be made. If we take the first route, we will create new sources of poverty for those low-skilled American workers currently in employment, and extra barriers to those trying to move into work from welfare dependency. If we take the second, we will have to dismantle much of the hidden welfare state now going to the rich: and perhaps not just to them. A proper system of rent subsidy for people on low incomes, for example, may have to be financed by phasing out the enormous tax subsidy currently provided to those of us fortunate enough to be buying rather than renting our houses. But at least the more affluent among us have a choice. The poor do not. Or perhaps more accurately, the affluent have the choice of making a big difference by a small sacrifice. The poor, by contrast, have to labor mightily just to change their individual circumstances by merely an inch.

"Poor people and investment bankers have one thing in common. They both spend considerable energy thinking about money."[67] Which is why, on this topic at least, the Republicans are both right and wrong. They are right: when discussing poverty, policy is ultimately a matter of making right choices. But they are also wrong. Over and over again, the choices they make are the wrong ones – and we need to say so.

Notes

1. Welfare policies in the US are means-tested policies, unlike social insurance policies of the Social Security kind. To qualify for the former, you have to demonstrate *need*. For the latter, you only have to demonstrate *contributions*. In 2005, the US welfare system had more than 70 means-tested aid programs providing cash, food, housing, medical care and social services to low-income persons.
2. For a scholarly if idiosyncratic challenge to this assertion, see chapter 1 of Christopher Howard, *The Welfare State Nobody Knows*, Princeton, Princeton University Press, 2007. Yet even he ultimately concludes (p. 209) that his (larger) welfare state "does not do much to lift the poor out of poverty, or to close the gap between rich and poor."
3. There is a parallel argument among conservative academics and commentators about real wages – that they have *not* stagnated over the last 30 years, as is conventionally believed. See, for example, Christian Broda and David E. Weistein, *Prices, Poverty and Inequality*, Washington, DC, AEI Press, 2008.
4. Robert Rector and Kirk Johnson, *Understanding Poverty in America*, Research, Welfare, The Heritage Foundation, January 5, 2004.
5. Kirk Johnson, *The Data on Poverty and Health Insurance You're Not Reading*, Research, Welfare, The Heritage Foundation, August 27, 2004.
6. Ibid.
7. Robert Rector and Kirk Johnson, *Understanding Poverty in America*.
8. Michael Tanner, *Leviathan on the Right*, Cato Institute, 2007, p. 82.
9. For the claim that "low IQ continues to be a much stronger precursor of poverty than the socioeconomic circumstances in which people grow up," see Richard Herrnstein and Charles Murray, *The Bell Curve: Intelligence and Class Structure in American Life*, New York, The Free Press, 1994, p. 127.
10. Robert Rector, "Poverty and Inequality," *Issues 2006: The Candidate's Briefing Book*, Heritage Foundation, 2006, p. 110.
11. Bill O'Reilly, "Katrina and the Poor," BillOReilly.com, September 8, 2005.
12. In his 1935 State of the Union Address.
13. Like the one made famous by Ronald Reagan in 1980: "ripping off $150,000 from the government, using 80 aliases, 30 addresses, a dozen social security cards, and four fictional dead husbands." This, in the 1980 presidential campaign: the woman referred to was actually convicted for using two different aliases to collect $8,000; but the story continued to be told even after the true facts were made known.

14. Michael Tanner, *The Poverty of Welfare*, Cato Institute, 2003, p. 158.

15. Quoted in Robert Rector, *The Good News about Welfare Reform*, Research Welfare, The Heritage Foundation, September 20, 2001, p. 9 of 12.

16. Charles Murray, *Losing Ground*, p. 9.

17. Charles Murray, *In Our Hands*, Washington, DC, AEI Press, 2006, pp. 3–4.

18. The imagery is that of Monica Charen, on page 96 of her *Do-Gooders*, New York, Sentinel, 2006.

19. Michael Tanner, *The End of Welfare*, Cato Institute, 1996, p. 88.

20. Robert Rector, before the Sub-Committee on Human Resources of the Committee on Ways and Means, House of Representatives, February 10, 2005.

21. Robert Rector, *The Effects of Welfare Reform*, Research Welfare, The Heritage Foundation, March 15, 2001, p. 1 of 12.

22. This, in Robert Rector, *The Effects of Welfare Reform*, p. 4 of 12.

23. Robert Rector, "Poverty and Inequality," p. 109: italics added.

24. Senator Daniel Patrick Moynihan called it "the most brutal act of social policy since Reconstruction."

25. Robert Rector, *Welfare Reform*, p. 114; Robert Rector and Patrick Fagan, *The Continuing Good News about Welfare Reform*, The Heritage Foundation Backgrounder, Executive Summary, No. 1620, February 6, 2003.

26. Robert Rector, *The Good News about Welfare Reform*, p. 3 of 12.

27. Such rules were implemented by the Bush administration in June 2006.

28. Robert Rector and Kirk Johnson, *Understanding Poverty in America*, p. 14 of 18.

29. Michael Tanner, *Welfare Reform Less than Meets the Eye*, Policy Analysis No 473, Cato Institute, April 1, 2003, p. 23.

30. The idea is Charles Murray's, initially a $10,000 a year basic income, and *no* other federal or state program benefiting some citizens but not others. See his *In Our Hands*, pp. 8–14.

31. Cato Handbook for 105th Congress, *Welfare Reform*, Cato Institute, p. 4 of 4.

32. Michael Tanner, *Welfare Reform Less than Meets the Eye*, p. 1. He really doesn't like welfare! See, for example, this from his *Leviathan on the Right* (p. 77): "We know that welfare is a failure. It has neither reduced poverty nor made the poor self-sufficient. It has torn at the social fabric of the country and been a significant factor in increasing out-of-wedlock births with all of their attendant problems. It has weakened the work ethic and contributed to rising crime rates. Most tragically of all,

the pathologies it engenders have been passed on from parent to child, from generation to generation."

33. Her story is told in John Cassidy's "Relatively Deprived: How Poor is Poor?" *The New Yorker*, April 3, 2006. There is now a widespread view, across the political spectrum, that the US needs a new way of measuring poverty. See for example, Nicholas Eberstadt, *The Poverty of the Official Poverty Rate* (AEI, November 2008); The Hamilton Project, *Improving the Measurement of Poverty* (The Brookings Institution, December 2008); and Jared Bernstein, *Economic Opportunity and Poverty in America* (Economic Policy Institute, February 2007).

34. On rent as a problem for the poor, see Barbara Ehrenreich, "Earth to Wal-Mars," in James Lardner and David A Smith (editors), *Inequality Matters*, New York, The Free Press, 2005, p. 53; and Jason DeParle, *American Dream*, New York, Penguin, 2004, p. 11.

35. The EPI credibly defend this "twice the poverty threshold" as corresponding "closely to more rigorously defined measures of a family's ability to meet its basic needs" (Lawrence Mishel, Jared Bernstein and Sylvia Allegretto, *The State of Working America 2004/2005*, Ithaca, ILR Press, 2005, p. 310).

36. EPI Briefing Paper No. 224, October 29, 2008.

37. Ibid., p. 313.

38. This, from USDA figures on food security, and from Howard Berkes, "A rural struggle to keep the family fed," *National Public Radio*, November 21, 2005.

39. Lee Rainwater and Timothy Smeeding, *Poor Kids in a Rich Country* New York, Russell Sage Foundation, 2003, p. 22.

40. UK, Spain and Italy (ibid., p. 45).

41. UNICEF, *Child Poverty in Perspective*, Florence, Italy, 2007, p. 7.

42. Lawrence Mishel, Jared Bernstein and Sylvia Allegretto, *The State of Working America 2004/2005*, p. 411.

43. Jonas Pontusson, *Inequality and Prosperity: Social Europe versus Liberal America*, Ithaca, Cornell University Press, 2005, p. 171.

44. Amartya Sen's 1999 data, cited in Cassidy, "Relatively Deprived: How Poor is Poor?"

45. *One in Hundred Behind Bars*, Public Performance Safety Project, 2008, p. 6.

46. Sharon Hays, *Flat Broke with Children*, New York, Oxford University Press, 2003, p. 231.

47. The predominant images of New Orleans were of African-American poverty; but the images of the other smaller towns on the Gulf shore hit by Katrina were often images of white poverty – in one-industry towns

without unions, high wages or decent benefits. There was a class story as well as a race story in Katrina: and ultimately a story of a tragedy, of an American working class seriously weakened by divisions of ethnicity and race. James Cobb wrote a very powerful essay on this, "Southern Exposure," in the *New York Times*, November 19, 2005.

48. In 2002, 47.8 percent of all African-Americans were living on/below the "twice-poverty threshold," as were 52 percent of all Hispanics. The equivalent figure for white Americans was 27.7% (Lawrence Mishel, Jared Bernstein and Sylvia Allegretto, *The State of Working America 2004/2005*, p. 318). More generally, see the National Urban League's annual *State of Black America* report.

49. In 2004, the WIC program run by the Department of Agriculture helped feed 7.9 million more – 6 million of them children in poor families.

50. It was only briefly in the early 1970s, for example, that the rate of benefit increase outstripped that of wages. The value of the typical welfare check fell by 40 percent over the next two decades.

51. Gary Burtless, "Public Spending on the Poor: Historical Trends and economic Limits," in Sheldon Danziger, Gary D. Sandefur and Daniel H. Weinberg (editors), *Confronting Poverty*, Cambridge, Harvard University press, 1994, p. 51.

52. James K. Galbraith, *Created Unequal*, New York, The Free Press, 1998, p. 20.

53. Ibid., p. 16.

54. Christopher Jencks et al., "Welfare Redux," *The American Prospect*, March 2006, p. 37. It was noticeable too that, as the caseloads fell, the proportion of those still on them who were long-term welfare recipients increased. Even the Cato Institute people have commented on that: "those remaining on the rolls are a hard-core of long-term unemployed and difficult-to-place recipients" (Michael Tanner, *The Poverty of Welfare*, p. 61). As the recession deepened in 2008/9, welfare rolls continued to fall (See Jason DeParle, "Welfare Aid not Growing as Economy Drops Off," *New York Times*, February 2, 2009).

55. Domestic violence is a huge hidden issue here. "Over 50 percent of homeless women and children cite domestic violence as the reason they are homeless. Many depend on welfare to provide an escape from the abuse … a significant proportion of the welfare caseload – consistently between 15 percent and 25 percent – consists of current victims of serious domestic violence" (Sarah Glazer, "Welfare Reform", *CQ Researcher*, vol. 11, number 27, August 3, 2001, p. 20 of 26). For details, see Demie

Kurz, "Women, Welfare, and Domestic Violence," in Gwendolyn Mink, *Whose Welfare*, Ithaca, Cornell University Press, 1999, pp. 132–51.

56. Michael Tanner, *The Poverty of Welfare*, p. 80. Hence his overall conclusion: "if welfare reform has not been the disaster claimed by critics, neither has it been quite the success claimed by supporters" (p. 56).

57. The existence of the welfare-poor beneath them only hurts them to the extent that welfare-to-work programs create an even bigger supply of people in pursuit of their low paid jobs. As the 1996 Act was first being implemented Nobel Laureate Robert Solow estimated that to get even a 1 percent increase in demand for labor to increase to absorb them, wages would have to fall by 2 or 3 percent in real terms, with most of that fall hitting already employed low wage workers (Robert Solow, *Work and Welfare*, Princeton, Princeton University Press, 1998).

58. James K. Galbraith, *Created Unequal*, p. 10.

59. These figures in J. Schwarz and Thomas Volgy, *The Forgotten Americans; Thirty Million Working Poor in the Land of Opportunity*, New York, W. W. Norton, 1993, p. 14.

60. James K. Galbraith, *Created Unequal*, p. 20.

61. If a notion of the "welfare state for the rich" shocks, consider this: "we have in place today not one but two competing welfare systems. One is the private one disproportionately for the rich, based on the ownership of financial assets. The other is a public one, mainly for the retired population, with dribs and drabs for the younger poor. Both are financed mainly by working Americans, who pay taxes to the state and interest to their creditors, and then try to live on the remainder" (James, K. Galbraith, *Created Unequal*, pp. 13–14).

62. Cited in Jonathan Alter, "The Other America: an Enduring Shame," *Newsweek*, September 19, 2005, p. 42.

63. To give credit where it is due, Charles Murray for one does recognize that: that work and welfare will have to go together unless we're willing to let a lot of children starve. On this, see his 'Can We replace Welfare With Work?' in Michael Darby (editor), *Reducing Poverty in America*, Thousand Oaks, Sage, 1996, p. 81.

64. Sharon Hays, *Flat Broke with Children*, p. 278.

65. Thomas Sowell, among others, denies that, claiming that "the black family, which had survived centuries of slavery and discrimination, began rapidly disintegrating in the liberal welfare state that subsidized unwed pregnancy and changed welfare from an emergency rescue to a way of life" (Thomas Sowell, *A Painful Anniversary*, townhall.com, August 17, 2004). But the sources of fragility here are deeper and older

than that. If they were not, welfare could not have been so caustic. Discussing them used to be taboo on the Left – remember the reaction to the leaked report in the 1960s by the young Daniel Patrick Moynihan. But no longer. The interplay of racism and its legacies on the one side, and urban decay and welfare support on the other, has produced a new form of social exclusion with its own *internal* motor of reproduction: especially hostility to learning among young African-American males in families on low income. But it is not just internal. There is not space here to discuss all the external forces in detail, but a full analysis would need to factor in such things as commercial sport as a new form of athletic share-cropping, and the commercialization of rap music.

66. That's certainly been the experience of the New Labour Government in the UK since 1997, when it created a separate Social Exclusion Unit to coordinate antipoverty policy in inner cities. See, for example, the SEU Report, *Tackling Social Exclusion: Taking Stock and Looking to the Future*, March 2004. David Shipler came to a similar conclusion from his study of the American working poor. "All of the problems," he said, "have to be attacked at once" (*The Working Poor: Invisible in America*, Alfred A. Knopf, 2004, p. 285). I am sure that he is right.

67. David Shipler, *The Working Poor*, p. 27.

CHAPTER 5

Reforming Social Security

George W. Bush made "reform" of the Social Security[1] system the centerpiece of his 2005 State of the Union address. He warned us then – as on many other occasions later – that for young workers in particular, the system had "serious problems that will grow worse with time": so serious, in fact, that by 2042 "the entire system would be exhausted and bankrupt." He presented an image of a system, based on payroll taxes, that was running out of payroll; and he argued for its replacement, little by little, by a system based on voluntary personal retirement accounts. He was very careful that night to reassure older workers that none of these changes would touch them. He also hedged his proposals about with a series of limitations on how and where young workers would be allowed to invest, in order to minimize the risks involved in the new responsibilities he was planning to lay on them. But he was clear. The Social Security system needed to be reset – made "permanently sound," as he put it – and that resetting had to involve at least its partial privatization.

Though that particular presidential initiative failed to gather traction, the issue of Social Security reform did not go away. On the contrary, both major political parties addressed it in their 2008 platforms, and at least one presidential candidate that year (Fred Thompson) made Social Security reform the centerpiece of his bid for the Republican Party nomination. Barack Obama entered office in 2009 committed to asking "those making over $250,000 to contribute a bit more to Social Security to keep it sound"; and within a month of entering the White House had held a "fiscal responsibility summit" to discuss ways of reducing the federal deficit. Expenditures on Social Security were high on the agenda at that summit; and although there was no formal State of the Union Address in 2009 that did not prevent the new president from calling on Congress to "begin a conversation" on how best to strengthen Social Security "while creating tax-free universal savings accounts for all Americans."[2]

Both the specification of the problem made by his predecessor, and George Bush's preferred solution, were fully in line with mainstream Republican thinking on the issue of pension reform. Five major themes currently run through conservative analyses and prescriptions for Social Security, each visible in what George Bush chose to say in 2005. The general conservative argument goes something like this.

1. The demographic base for a viable system of Social Security has changed qualitatively since the system was first created

In the 1930s there were 16 people available for work for every retiree eligible for the new system of Social Security; and with an average life expectancy of only 61, very few of those 16 could legitimately anticipate any kind of pension at all. But that's no longer the case. Now the ratio of workers to retirees is about 3:1, and falling. It will be 2:1 soon, when the baby boomers start retiring; and government actuaries project that the ratio will be lower still by century's end. As a population, we are aging: as recently as 1960 only one American in ten was over 65; by 2025 that figure will be one in four. We are not breeding or dying in the same proportions and at the same rate as earlier generations did. We are having fewer babies and we are living longer; and because we are, a Social Security system designed to meet the needs of the 1930s will have to be changed. Five million Americans received Social Security in 1945. Forty-seven million do today. Young workers in particular have lost faith in the system. There was even a poll showing that twice as many of them "believe in flying saucers as believe they will receive a Social Security check when they retire."[3] Something has to go.

2. Those demographic changes mean that the financing of Social Security – 1930s style – will not work in the long term, and needs fixing

Right now, there is no immediate financial crunch. The payroll taxes levied on the salaries of the baby boomers are still much larger than the monies being handed out to current retirees from the Trust Fund: not least because the relevant tax levels have been raised at least 30 times since Social Security was first legislated. But this excess of revenues over expenditures will not last. Sometime around 2015 the Fund will begin to pay out more than it takes in. Even then, for two or three decades at least, it will be able to survive by drawing on the surpluses built up in the years when workers did outnumber pensioners. But eventually – around the year 2041 – the money will all be gone; then to balance the books pension benefits will have to be cut, or the age of retirement raised, or levels of taxation significantly increased. Accordingly, the country faces "a looming fiscal crisis as the baby boom generation moves into retirement"[4]: a crisis that, according to the Trust Fund's critics, will be ever more expensive to resolve, the longer it is allowed to fester. "We have a huge fiscal gap, a huge generational imbalance, and we can't let one generation's social insurance be paid for by bankrupting" the next.[5] "Estimates suggest," the Cato Institute's Michael Tanner has said, "that each year we wait to reform Social Security costs between $150 billion and $600 billion more. That sure looks like a crisis to me."[6]

3. The existing system has deeply disturbing consequences for the wider economy, which will only intensify if allowed to continue unreformed

Even now Social Security has some pretty unpleasant indirect consequences that we would do well to avoid. True, it provides some security for 95 percent of all Americans in their old age: but that very security discourages private savings: and America's uniquely low savings rate is one of the key things undermining the economy's long-term competitiveness. "Social Security," Cato's Ferrara and Tanner have argued, "likely reduces US GDP by 10 percent or more each year."[7] Americans are not saving and investing enough. Instead they are getting big government on the cheap, because politicians are able to raid the Trust Fund surplus to finance programs they would otherwise have to cover with new taxation. In that way, Social Security is currently making a double contribution to the creation of an undesirable culture of welfare dependency: entrenching dependency on state handouts in old age, and dependency when younger on other welfare programs that its payroll tax helps indirectly to finance.[8] Right now, there is no Trust Fund. It has been raided to oblivion by welfare-minded politicians, replaced by a set of worthless government IOUs that a later generation will have to pick up and pay. Even the liberals' claim that Social Security is mildly redistributive of income from rich to poor is not right. Social Security is not redistributive downwards but upwards – disadvantaging African-American men worst of all – because most of them (and the low paid in general) do not live long enough after retirement to recoup all the monies they have paid in. Those monies end up by default in the pockets of the more affluent longer-lasting old. Which is why it is so much better, the conservative argument runs, to let the low-paid build up their own investment accounts while they are working, enabling them by their own savings to break out of cycles of poverty that otherwise so debilitate them.

4. A more market-based funding system would give future generations of pensioners a better and a more secure pension

Ultimately Social Security is just a big pyramid scheme, and a very poor one at that: the pension it generates is appallingly low. If the private sector had designed it, people would have been jailed for fraud! If Social Security is all you have to live on in old age, you will be very poor indeed. So rather than compound its defects by ignoring them, leaving future generations to cope with huge tax rises or substantial benefit cuts, the system should be progressively privatized as quickly as possible. The rights of existing workers must be protected, of course; but the financing of pensions by younger workers needs to change. If workers entering the labor force now are encouraged or obliged to build up their own individual savings accounts, four benefits will follow over time. (1) Young workers will avoid overpaying into the Social Security Fund, in effect no longer transferring so much of their earnings into the pensions of the baby boomer generation. (2) The rate of return that they will earn on their private savings will be much greater than that guaranteed now by federally provided Social Security: their pensions, when they eventually arrive, will be bigger. (3) Those pensions will be entirely theirs. No set of politicians will be able to take them away from the workers who've saved for them. A market-based solution, that is, will make pensions not only larger but also more secure. (4) It will also set workers free from the existing curbs, imposed by the Social Security system, on their liberty to buy what insurance they want from whoever they want. "The larger crisis," Michael Tanner has written, "is not about the system's finances. . . . It is about a system where workers have no real ownership of their benefits, and where low- and middle-income workers cannot accumulate wealth that they can use in retirement and pass along to their heirs."[9] As late as August 31, 2008, just two weeks before the financial meltdown, Michael Tanner was still telling readers of the Indianapolis Star *that "a much better approach would be to take advantage of the higher rates of return from private investment by allowing young workers the option of saving some of their Social Security taxes through personal accounts."[10]*

5. The route to a secure and prosperous retirement for all lies through the creation of a system of personal investment accounts

These are now being canvassed by the Cato Institute and others as the way forward, and as the one most widely adopted outside the US – famously in Chile – to overcome the lack of viability, unfairness and low rates of return that are endemic to government-run pay-as-you-go pension schemes of the Social Security type. Advocates of such a transition argue that the introduction of such personal savings accounts, if properly organized, can avoid the central criticism often made of such a radical move – namely that the first generation building them will be double-burdened by the need simultaneously to pay existing pensions and to save for their own. Those transition costs will be cushioned, advocates of privatization claim, by the enhanced economic growth triggered by the savings and investments of young workers, by the temporary continuation of a reduced payroll tax, by the taxation of the returns on these rapidly expanding ISA nest-eggs and by much-needed cutbacks in other government programs. The great strength of individual savings accounts, Cato President Edward Crane has written, lies in their capacity "to take advantage of the higher returns available from private investment, what Einstein called 'the most powerful force in the universe' – compound interest."[11] Individual Savings Accounts, not Social Security, are the way forward: because by "investing through the private system and earning modest returns, the average two-earner couple would retire with a trust fund of about $1 million in today's *dollars,"*[12] *enough to pay them more than Social Security off the interest alone.*

The Cato claim for individual accounts remains considerable. *In their briefing to the 2008 Congress the Institute said again that allowing younger workers to invest their Social Security taxes through individual accounts would:*[13]

- *help restore Social Security to long-term solvency, without massive tax increases;*
- *provide workers with higher benefits than Social Security would otherwise be able to pay;*
- *create a system that treats women, minorities and young people more fairly;*
- *increase national savings and economic growth;*
- *allow low-income workers to accumulate real, inheritable wealth . . . and*
- *give workers ownership of and control over their retirement funds.*

A liberal response

So if Peter Ferrara and Michael Tanner are right, and average couples could end up controlling their own million-dollar trust funds if Social Security was privatized, why should liberals object? The following reasons spring to mind.

1. Don't take the jewel from the crown

The first is this. We need to say to right-wing doom merchants in the debate on Social Security that the scheme they're critiquing is actually one of the New Deal's finest legacies. The Social Security system initiated under FDR's leadership in 1935 has developed into one of the strongest state-provided pension systems in the industrial world. So before we knock it, we should praise it. It is, as George McGovern said, "a true success story."[14] Under the New Deal, the United States equipped itself with a near universal publicly provided pension system, and did so well before most other industrial democracies.[15] Then, with genuine bipartisan support, later administrations developed that near universal system from its original character as a limited safety net for the aged poor into a pension scheme giving the vast majority of US citizens a unique and unprecedented peace of mind: a guarantee that for the first time in American history, their living standards would not cataclysmically fall with retirement, and that if disabled at work, they would not be left to starve. There is still poverty in old age for many Americans, of course, because many Americans are poor; but with the Social Security system fully developed, even the poorest Americans are now guaranteed that retirement will not make that poverty worse. The key developments here occurred under Republican rather than Democratic leadership – under Richard Nixon in 1971 and under Ronald Reagan in 1983 – *1971*, when the level of Social Security payment was not simply raised but also index-linked; and *1983*, when the payroll tax rate supporting Social Security was significantly increased. Both these dates were bipartisan milestones in the steady expansion of Social Security's coverage and benefits from the 15 percent of the US workforce originally covered to the 95 percent now within its umbrella – currently over 130 million workers and their dependents. In December 2007 Social Security provided monthly payments to nearly 50 million beneficiaries (34 million retirees, 6 million survivors of deceased workers and 9 million disabled workers and their dependents): collectively, one American in six.[16]

The critics are right in this – the "expense" of Social Security has in consequence grown: grown, indeed, to the point at which the United States, when compared to other industrial democracies, now has one of the more generous of state-provided pension schemes. It also has one of the more financially sound: the Social Security Trust Fund took in $200 billion dollars more than it dispensed in 2007, and had an accumulated surplus of $2.2 trillion.[17] That is presumably one reason why Conservatives – keen as Grover Norquist once so famously said, to reduce government "to the size where I can drag it into the bathroom and drown it in the bathtub"[18] – have set their sights on Social Security privatization with such determination. The Cato Institute has had privatization as a major policy goal since 1980. The Heritage Foundation has been equally active; as has Norquist's "Americans for Tax Reform" organization. No wonder, because in the sphere of pension provision, with all its actuarial uncertainties, state provision really works!

2. If it ain't broke, don't fix it

We should say too that much of the scaremongering about the viability of the Social Security Trust Fund is just that – scaremongering. The dire scenarios that are regularly painted, by those who see the Fund drained of all monies by 2040, rest on a set of problematic premises that are rarely aired, let alone contested. The main one is the yield from the payroll tax: but that undershoots only if two other things undershoot as well: the growth rate of the US economy and the total wage fund that it sustains. The Conservatives' worse case scenarios are normally built on the Trustees' growth rate projection for the economy of only 1.5 percent per annum over a 75-year period (and a productivity growth rate of only 1.3 percent): growth and productivity rates that the US economy has regularly exceeded, and by some margin. In fact, there's an important and serious paradox here: that those who would have us believe the Trust Fund to be doomed (because of low growth rates in the economy as a whole) would also have us believe that individual savings (withdrawn from the Fund and invested on Wall Street) would simultaneously soar in value. But it's not obvious how, unless we are to project a bubble economy in which the real economy stagnates but paper assets inflate – hardly a basis for long-term pension stability – or unless we buy into the argument that payroll taxes alone depress economic growth. A much more realistic projection would have the economy expanding on average at 3 percent per year between now and 2040, and productivity at 2.5 percent, with wages rising at least in line with growth.[19] If that happens – and all that is being projected is that the US economy function as well in the next half century as it has in the last – then there will be more than enough money in the Trust Fund, secured by US Treasury bonds, to continue paying full benefits well past 2040 and on.

3. If you're genuinely worried, try tinkering instead

That may be to bend the stick too far the other way.[20] It may be that a payment shortfall will eventually open up – though it is hard to see why it should come as early as 2040 – but if it does, all the policy-makers would then have to do, to put matters right, would be one or more of three very modest things. They would have to (a) make small adjustments in the payroll tax rate;[21] (b) alter slightly the investment strategy adopted by the Fund[22]; and/or (c) raise (or indeed entirely remove) the $107,000 cap on payroll taxation currently in place.[23] The image we are being given by the Trust Fund's critics is of an America burdened by the old: and yet in truth the rate of aging of the population is far lower – and will continue to be far lower – than the rate of growth of the economy as a whole.[24] Compound interest works on economic growth, productivity improvements and wage levels as well as on individual savings accounts; which is why running the economy at full employment, and triggering labor-saving capital investment and associated productivity and wage growth, would be a much more effective guarantee of Trust Fund solvency in 2040 than any privatization proposal currently on the table. In fact, the creation of individual savings accounts, by redirecting away part of the payroll tax, can only intensify the problems of balancing the Trust Fund's books. We need to say – loud and long – that if the Conservative Right is really concerned about the Fund's long-run viability, a modest set of tax and benefit changes is easily available to it. The fact that such a set is not being canvassed by them must at least put on the table the question of the real motives involved in their call for rapid privatization: is it pensioner security or market ideology?

4. If you want to mend something, focus your efforts on the bits that are really broken

One of the great paradoxes of this whole debate about Social Security insolvency is that there *is* a part of the US pension system that is genuinely in crisis – it just doesn't happen to be the government-provided section of it.[25] The other great leg of retirement support in the postwar United States has been a system of company-financed pensions negotiated into existence by trade unions in bargaining processes with major corporations. In 1994 these pensions were in place for at least 45 percent of all Americans between the ages of 21 and 65. But that employer-based pension system is now in internal free-fall. Major US corporations claim that they can no longer afford its continued provision, citing intensified competition in domestic and global markets as the cause. Accordingly, three things at least are now underway. Many companies are resetting their pension schemes for their younger workers from "defined benefit" to "defined contribution" ones: no longer, that is, guaranteeing a pension of a certain value, but only a flow of funds into some 401(k) or its equivalent. Verizon, Lockheed Martin, Motorola, even IBM, have all gone down this route, shifting pension investment risks from the company to the worker. A number of major corporations have also reneged on the pensions they promised – General Motors for one, United Airlines for another. And firms going bankrupt, like Enron, have often raided their pension funds as a first line of defense: taking away pension rights in order to pay off debtors, ease the burden on shareholders, or provide golden parachutes for a chosen few.

Time and again, we are told in this debate that taking pension provision away from the government, and placing it in the private sector, increases pension security. But nothing could be further from the truth. "Social Security is now the only secure source of retirement income that retirees can count on."[26] No serious politician is willing – if present practice is any guide – to risk the wrath of the gray vote by reducing current pension rights by so much as a dollar; but in the private sector, CEOs in trouble regularly completely restructure or do away with the pensions that, in easier times, had been traded for moderate wage settlements. And the irony is that, when they do, it is the much derided government funding system that then rides to the rescue, in the form of the Pension Benefit Guaranty Corporation.[27] It is big corporations, not the government, which have the worse record for robbing pensioners: robbing them as workers by holding their wages back in return for pension-funding, and robbing them as pensioners by defaulting on some or all of the pension provision they had previously promised. Nor are even solvent companies free from the danger of pension default. The collapse of stock market values in the last quarter of 2008 left corporate pension plans severely underfinanced – to the tune of $409 billion if Mercer, an international consulting firm, is to be believed.[28] We need to remember that every time we are told something different!

5. Remember that privatization can damage your health

As the advocates of privatization do occasionally concede, playing the market produces losers as well as winners. It takes skill, capacity and time to play the market well; and as we now know only too well after the 2008 financial crisis, markets – and particularly money markets – have a disturbing way of going down as well as going up. The value of people's 401(k)s has plummeted recently – by 14 percent on average according to Hewitt Associates, or in Fidelity's case, 27 percent[29] – making retirements based on their earnings either precarious or impossible for many. Private retirement portfolios have proved to be high on promise but low on performance. Social Security, by contrast, continues to provide just what its name implies – security. As a defined benefit rather than defined contribution form of pension, people know exactly what flow of funds they can rely upon as they age, and because of Richard Nixon they also know that those funds will be continually indexed to inflation. The critics say that that flow is too small, but even they recognize that (political intervention apart) it is secure. Indeed, the more they recognize the risks involved, the more they follow George W. Bush's example, and hedge individual savings accounts around with politically imposed constraints. In his 2005 State of the Union Address, the former president promised "careful guidelines for personal accounts . . . a conservative mix of bonds and stock funds" plus protection from "hidden Wall Street fees" and "sudden market swings on the eve of your retirement." But if such a scale of constraints is necessary by pensioners taking money out of Social Security, why do it in the first place? Why go to a casino to gamble, when by staying away from one your pension will remain secure? And why make that move now, when the other leg of the pension system – company-based private pension provision – is itself looking less and less secure. Why trade one secure and one insecure leg for two insecure ones? It makes no sense.

Except perhaps for this: the only people who make money longterm in casinos are the people who run them, which is presumably why – in the Bush years – the privatization of Social Security was so attractive to sections of Wall Street. One hundred and thirty million new individual savings accounts would be literally, for them, a license to print money. The administrative costs of private brokerage will act as an extra tax (albeit a private one) on the money held back from the payroll taxes going into the Social Security Trust Fund. It is almost certain that those private fees will take out of any privatized system far more monies than are currently absorbed by administrative overheads in the Social Security system. Estimates vary, but normally the gap between the two is projected to be at least several percentage points.[30] And since the Social Security system is one that provides benefits to both the disabled and the widowed, as well as to the old, where are we to find private insurers prepared to pick up their cover, at rates that are in any way comparable to the rate of payroll tax? Presumably the gap in charges between the two systems will be higher again for anyone unfortunate enough to lose a limb, a husband or a father before their pension kicks in.

6. The dangers of speculation

Those extra charges might be worth absorbing, of course, if individual savings accounts were indeed a guaranteed route to the accumulation of million dollar trust funds by the average American earner. But are they? The answer is almost certainly that they are not. The numbers put together to sustain this part of the privatization argument are, to put it mildly, extremely optimistic. The 7 percent annual rate of return available to well-managed individual savings accounts often cited by the advocates of privatization would indeed double an investor's money every decade; but that rate was achieved in the US in the postwar period only by widening the gap between stock prices and the earnings of their underlying assets to a dangerously large 33:1. You have to factor in the 1990s Stock Market bubble before projecting forward. Projecting the same 7 percent forward for another half-century would give us a gap between stock prices and underlying earnings of something in excess of 200:1 by 2055. A speculative bubble of that scale would be unsustainable; and because of that, and if we take the economic growth assumptions used by the Social Security trustees as our guide, a rate of stock price growth of probably 3.5 percent seems far more likely.[31]

So not quite so many millionaires as promised, apparently: particularly because of the two linked pieces of evidence on which the advocates of privatization tend not to dwell: the volatility of stock values over time; and the way in which significant numbers of American workers, no doubt for very pressing and immediate financial reasons, raid/empty their savings accounts long before those savings mature.[32] Even before the 2008 financial meltdown reduced the ability of companies to fund 401(k)s and drove many 401(k)-holders to raid them for current living, 47 percent of American workers worked for companies that did not even offer 401(k) plans, and less than half of all private sector workers took advantage of them even when they did. Social Security's coverage was and remains near universal. Privatization's coverage is not and will not be. We therefore need to ask: where is the security in all of this? And where is the gain, to the society at large, in the reproduction, within the pension system, of the unevenness of coverage that so bedevils American health care?

7. Take the direct route to income equality, if equality is actually what you want

The capacity of savers to enjoy Edward Crane's compound interest bonanza will critically turn on how much they are able to put into their personal savings accounts. Any privatization of Social Security will only compound income and wealth inequality in the United States, not level it as the Conservative Right now claims. True, a rising tide raises all ships, but as we saw in Chapter 3, compound interest makes big ships bigger on a grander scale than small ones. Whatever else the privatization of Social Security will or will not deliver, an egalitarian society is certainly not going to be one of its outcomes. In data collected since 2001, "the Social Security Administration found that Social Security provided more than half of the total income for almost two-thirds of households comprised exclusively of those aged 65 and over, and provided at least 90 percent of income for a third of this group."[33] We also know that Social Security makes up 55 percent of the income of older women, and that for many elderly unmarried women, it is often their *only* source of money.[34] It is hard to see any kind of private savings account that can give similar proportions of the working poor, and particularly the elderly female poor, the indexing protection of the current system, or the cushioning of their pension rights against low earning years as is the case now.

Indeed, there is something particularly unseemly in the libertarian insistence that Social Security should be privatized because it is failing the poor, when Social Security currently provides so great a proportion of the income of those who need income most. As Henry Aaron has rightly said, Social Security is by "far and away the most important US antipoverty program"[35] – and the Cato people want to do away with it! If they really want to improve the lot of America's working and elderly poor, there are at least two far more direct routes that they could take. Instead of campaigning to run down government-provided pensions, the Cato Institute could campaign for, say, a doubling by the government of the pensions provided to the lowest paid, with means testing of Social Security benefits for the rest. And it could support a significant increase in the minimum wage, attacking poverty directly at its source. After all, poverty in work is due to low wages, not to payroll taxes; and African-Americans die on average earlier than white Americans, not because they lack individual savings accounts but because they are disproportionately poor. Alas, as far as I'm aware, no such Cato campaigns have been forthcoming.

8. It pays to place this issue in a wider, more comparative context

As its critics often point out, the United States' Social Security system is built on a confidence trick. Young workers are told that they are paying into a fund that will be waiting for them when they retire. But in reality they are paying into a fund that then pays the pensions of the existing old; so that when the time comes for them to retire they will need a new generation of workers committed to the same illusion. Like pension schemes in many other industrial societies, Social Security is a pay-as-you-go scheme; with all the strengths and weaknesses that schemes of that kind necessarily have.

The strengths come early. When the scheme is young and the ratio of workers to retirees is a high one, the money that flows into the Fund is way in excess of the money being paid out; and that is particularly true if – as was indeed the case for most of the postwar period – the productivity and wages of those workers were rising rapidly. Then generous schemes could be, and were, consolidated: delaying until now any day of reckoning when the growth rates of productivity and wages slowed, and the demographics changed. At that moment, altering the system becomes particularly difficult, because any attempt to replace it with a actuarially sound one – where workers genuinely save for their own retirement – then creates, for the generation caught up in the transition, the "cost" of simultaneously saving for their pension and funding the pensions of others. The change is also difficult because the regular repetition of the illusion helps to build up in the minds of those paying the payroll tax a quasi-property attitude to the pensions promised: a belief that they have in some meaningful sense already "bought" their pension, which the government is therefore obliged to give them. Many governments in other countries have lately also faced these endemic elements of pay-as-you-go pension schemes, and have quite properly ducked them.[36] Once in such a system, reform at the margin, not a fundamental resetting, seems the appropriate order of the day. The system works so long as the illusion holds, and breaking it brings transition costs of too great a scale to make the resetting worthwhile.

The big canvassed exception has been Chile, but the Chilean experiment is now widely recognized – outside ideologically blinkered circles at least – to have been a disturbing failure.[37] Many of the Chileans who opted for the private accounts, particularly those on low incomes, found the yield too low to sustain their retirement, and lower in many cases than the pensions provided to their equivalents by the state system. Heavy administrative fees also eroded their benefits, in a private system that is still heavily underwritten by the Chilean taxpayer: to the point indeed that pension reform was a key issue in the election campaign that brought the center-left's Michelle Bachelet to power in 2006. Even the parties of the center-right campaigned during that election for public subsidization of contributions to private accounts – hardly what former president Bush can have had in mind when suggesting in 2004 that the US could learn some "lessons from Chile, especially when it comes to how to run our pension plans."[38] If there were lessons, George W. Bush did not seem to realize that they were entirely negative ones!

9. Don't let the flows of money fool you

Those who would privatize Social Security treat it as a dead weight on the economy in at least two different senses: as a barrier to saving (and hence investment and economic growth) by this generation of workers and as a debt burden (and hence a barrier to consumption and economic growth) on generations of workers to come. But neither is true. The payroll tax is itself a major form of saving – taking money from the consumption of workers now and depositing it in the Trust Fund. That money is not then lost to the economy. It finances public expenditures on other programs and it finances the spending of the old. It only slows economic growth if you subscribe to the theory that savings trigger investment, rather than – as Keynesian economics would have it – that investment triggers savings, or if you believe that the balance of bondholding and equities in the contemporary US economy is too bond-heavy. If it is, that balance can be altered in many ways without touching Social Security at all. And debts do not flow between generations, but *within* them. If, at some point in the future, governments have to borrow money to finance pensions, they will borrow that money from institutions actually functioning and people actually alive at the time![39] Each generation has to decide on the appropriate balance between the consumption of the young and that of the old, and between the holders of government debt and the recipients of government spending. Decisions in one generation do not predetermine those choices for the next, because beneath the circuits of money that lubricate consumption and welfare in any one generation, real resources move. A generation can only consume what it makes. Social Security does not increase or decrease that total stock of goods and services. It just gives the old a secure claim on a small part of it; and what, we must ask, is in any way wrong with it doing that?

10. Ultimately it's a question of values

In the end, as always, this discussion comes down – as all important ones do – to a question of values. How important is it to you to give your parents, as they age, a secure and prosperous retirement? If it is important, then two things should follow.

The first is this. If the prosperity of the old matters to you, then far from curtailing Social Security, you should be pushing to raise its minimum levels; for current levels of provision are – as its critics say – still too low to lift out of poverty elderly Americans dependent on Social Security alone. Not privatization but expansion should be the order of the day. Not less Social Security but more!

Then, if the security of that prosperity also matters to you, then so too should the defense of the existing system, because Social Security provides benefits that "no government Thrift Savings Plan or 401(k) can match: an inflation-indexed annuity, life insurance and disability insurance

> . . . Social Security's guaranteed benefit does not depend upon the outcome of the stock market and is not tied to the decisions of individual investors. Rather, Social Security automatically adjusts the benefit to reflect a worker's earning history, which insures a worker against underestimating her earning ability. Social Security also follows workers from job to job, and, unlike a private fund, is not affected by breaks in payment in times when workers are unemployed. Private accounts lack the important social insurance properties of Social Security. Social Security adjusts for inflation; is guaranteed to last an entire lifetime, no matter how long; is shielded from stock market losses; and, when young workers become disabled or die, provides substantial income replacement to multiple beneficiaries across generations (e.g. to surviving family members for their lifetime). Private accounts and 401(k)s have none of these protections. . . . In essence private accounts would fundamentally shift the risk from the government to the individual, changing the Social Security program into an "Individual Insecurity" program.[40]

This is not to deny that the present rules and trustee policies need review. Undoubtedly they do: change *within* the system is visibly needed, both to generate a better rate of return for the Fund as a whole, and to strengthen the benefits flowing to groups currently disadvantaged under existing regulations – most notably African-Americans and elderly women among the poor.[41] The roots of inequality in this society do not lie in its pension scheme, but that inequality is definitely reproduced there. So any serious attempt to eradicate poverty in this – the richest society on earth – must have, as one of its dimensions – pension reform.

Markets, however, are the great creators of inequality: so they are the least suitable device for its elimination. Those who advocate market-based pension systems in preference to government-funded universal provision would be much more convincing if they were also advocating programs of income equalization – so that everyone within the market could operate on a level playing field. But no such advocacy is forthcoming from the members of what Jacob Hacker has so aptly labeled as "the personal responsibility crusade":[42] which is why the ostensible concern of the Social Security privatizers for the poor and underprivileged ultimately sounds so bogus. We need to say back to them, over and over again, that *they are simply wrong*. There may indeed be many incremental changes to be made to the Social Security system, now and in the future, in order to maintain its capacity to meet its important social function. But of one thing we can be absolutely certain. The privatization of the system – either in part or in whole – is not going to be one of those necessary changes. Any privatization that is done will simply be right-wing Republican ideology run amok!

Notes

1. Social Security's formal name is Old Age, Survivors and Disability Insurance: a scheme providing pensions and insurance to workers and their families in the event of disability and death.
2. Address to Joint Session of Congress, February 24, 2009.
3. Peter J. Ferrara and Michael Tanner, *A New Deal for Social Security*, Washington, DC, Cato Institute, 1998, p. 1. For doubts on the authenticity of that claim, see Teresa Ghilarducci, *When I'm Sixty-Four*, Princeton, Princeton University Press, 2008, p. 151.
4. The chairman of the Trustee's Panel, quoted in the *Winston-Salem Journal*, May 2, 2006, p. A7.
5. Laurence Kotlikoff, quoted in Mary H. Cooper, "Social Security Reform," *CQ Researcher*, vol. 14, number 33, September 24, 2004, p. 4.
6. Michael Tanner, "Signs of Crisis are Clear," *USA Today*, February 1, 2005 (reproduced on the Cato Institute Website). See also Laurence Kotlikoff and Scott Burns, *The Coming Generational Storm*, Cambridge, MIT Press, 2004.
7. Ferrara, Peter J. and Tanner, Michael. *A New Deal for Social Security*, Washington, DC, Cato Institute, 1998, p. 111.
8. Some of the claims here are very serious indeed: that, for example, "socialized old-age pensions intentionally displace private economic bonds of families, and so contribute to the progressive destruction of society by the state" (this from Allan Carlson, cited in Ferrara and Tanner, *A New Deal for Social Security*, p. 106).

9. Ibid.

10. Michael Tanner, "Taking Advantage of Private Accounts' High return Rate," *Indianapolis Star*, August 31, 2008 (added to *cato.org* on September 4, 2008).

11. Edward H. Crane, "Simple Rules for Social Security Reform," The Cato Institute Website, September 21, 2004.

12. Ferrara and Tanner, *A New Deal for Social Security*, p. 82.

13. *Cato Handbook for Policymakers*, 2008, p. 181.

14. George McGovern, *Social Security and the Golden Age*, Golden, Colorado, Fulcrum Publishing, 2005, p. 2.

15. Not to mention the even earlier Civil War pension scheme, with half a million men on its rolls by 1910, almost one in three of all men then over 65 in the US. That pension scheme paid about 30 percent of average wages, at a time when the fledgling German pension scheme – Bismarck's – was paying about 17 percent (E. Amenta and T. Skocpol, "Taking exception: explaining the distinctiveness of American public policies in the last century," in F. Castles (editor), *The Comparative History of Public Policy*, Cheltenham UK, Edward Elgar, 1999, p. 297).

16. *Annual Report of the Trustees of the Federal Old Age and Survivors Insurance and Federal Disability Insurance Trust Funds*, April 10, 2008 (US Government Printing office 41–188, Washington, DC, 2008, p. 2).

17. Ibid.

18. Interview with Mara Liasson, "Morning Edition," *NPR*, May 25, 2001.

19. The figures are Dean Baker and Mark Weisbrot's, in their *Social Security: The Phony Crisis*, Chicago, University of Chicago Press, 1999.

20. It all depends on which projection you take. The Social Security Trustees' "intermediate" scenario in their 2008 report had the fund in surplus right through to 2041. Their more optimistic "low cost" scenario had the surplus still intact in 2080.

21. Given that wages by 2040 will be at least 30 percent higher than now, even if payroll taxes then have to be slightly increased, "it will take a great deal of imagination to perceive this as some sort of highway robbery by tomorrow's senior citizens against the youth of today" (Baker and Weisbrot, *Social Security*, p. 2).

22. If the Fund earns less on its investments than is normal among private pension fund managers, then the solution seems obvious. Do what they do. The Brookings Institute's Barry P. Bosworth and Gary Burtless regularly canvas this as a more effective and immediate to any "problem" deemed to be looming by the Fund's conservative critics. (See for example, Gary Burtless's evidence to the Senate Committee on the Budget, January 19, 1999.) For a similar argument, see Nancy Altman, *The Battle for Social Security*, Hoboken, NJ, Wiley, 2005, p. 305.

23. Taking away the cap ought to be the one to go for first; since its removal would, at a stroke, improve Social Security's capacity slightly to redistribute income from the rich to the poor. It would also release into the Trust Fund much needed tax revenues to offset any shortfall thought to be looming. The percentage of total payroll now escaping taxation – because it's over the $107,000 cap – has risen from 10 percent to 15 percent since 1983, in line with the growing inequality of income and wealth in the US. Raising the cap would therefore be entirely in line with the original goals of the Social Security program.

24. "... the proportion of people over 65 is 12.7 percent today and will grow to 20% by 2030. At the same time, the economy is projected to grow by 59 percent. Can an economy that is 59 percent bigger support an increase of this size in its retired population? There is little reason to doubt that it can ... with little adverse impact on the rising living standards of the rest of the nation" (Baker and Weisbrot, *Social Security*, p. 32).

25. Or if it is, it is not the Social Security bit. Pension schemes funded by state governments for state employees are in crisis, and were even before the financial meltdown that began in September 2008. Data that month showed losses by state pension funds for the first three-quarters of the year as averaging 14.8 percent, leaving maybe 40 percent of all such funds seriously underfunded (*Financial Times*, October 27, 2008, p. 1).

26. Mary H. Cooper, "Social Security Reform," *CQ Researcher*, vol. 14, number 33, September 24, 2004, p. 4.

27. Which accordingly has itself been pushed unto deficit: reportedly some $11 billion by 2009 (*Associated Press*, February 19, 2009).

28. Ibid.

29. *US News and World Report*, February 25, 2009 (data first posted, February 12).

30. Baker and Weisbrot put it as wide as 11–13 percent (*Social Security*, p. 13). The administration of the current Social Security system takes only 0.8 percent of total revenues.

31. I am dependent here on Baker and Weisbrot's calculations: *Social Security*, pp. 8–9. But there are many others, equally sanguine about future stock price growth.

32. "A safe retirement based on a 401(k) account requires decades of discipline, something many people don't have. A recent study by Hewitt Associates, the employee benefits research firm, found that 45 percent of workers cashed out their 401(k)s when leaving a company, instead of leaving the money in the plan or rolling it over into a new one. And some workers cannot or do not participate in the retirement plans

available to them." (*New York Times*, editorial, "The Pensions Deep Freeze", January14, 2006).

33. Economic Policy Institute, *Social Security: Facts at a Glance*, Washington, DC, EPI, 2005.

34. National Organization of Women, *Talking Points about Women, Social Security and Privatization*, Washington, DC, March 4, 2005.

35. Henry J. Aaron, "Privatizing Social Security: A Bad Idea Whose Time Will Never Come," *The Brookings Review*, vol. 21, 2003, pp. 16–23.

36. On this, see John Myles and Paul Pierson, "The comparative political economy of pension reform," in Paul Pierson (editor), *The New Politics of the Welfare State*, Oxford, Oxford University Press, 2001, pp. 305–15.

37. See, for example, The Century Foundation Report, *Chile's Experience with Social Security Privatization: a Model for the United States* (on its Website 3/10/1999); or Manuel Riesco, *Private Pensions in Chile, a Quarter Century On* (CENDA, Santiago, Chile: Website www.cep.cl). It is significant that the Chilean reform, introduced under the Pinochet dictatorship, did not extend to either the military or the police. They remained in their state-financed scheme!

38. Cited in the *Financial Times*, November 28, 2005, p. 11. Details of the proposed reforms can be found in the *New York Times*, December 20, 2006, p. A18.

39. "Any debt owed *by* future generations will also be owed *to* future generations, because each generation that pays interest on the national debt pays that money to members of the same generation who own the Treasury bonds" (Baker and Weisbrot, *Social Security*, pp. 17–18).

40. Economic Policy Institute, *Social Security, Frequently Asked Questions*, Washington, DC, EPI, 2005.

41. On this, see Robert Eisner, *Social Security: More Not Less* (Century Foundation/Twentieth Century Fund Report), New York, Century Foundation Press, 1998, pp. 4, 41–2; and Heidi Hartmann and Catherine Hill, *Strengthening Social Security for Women*, Washington, DC, National Council of Women's Organizations, 1999.

42. Jacob Hacker, *The Great Risk Shift*, Oxford, Oxford University Press, 2006, p. 38.

CHAPTER 6

Bringing Health to the Health Care System

Like people abroad, people here tend to believe that we possess "the finest health care system in the world."[1] That claim is the common currency of the health debate in many countries these days. But what is less common elsewhere is the scale of anxiety evident across the entirety of the United States about the cost and availability of the health care of which we are so proud. And that is not surprising because, for all its huge strengths, American medicine also has huge problems, problems that are understood in a broadly similar fashion on both sides of the aisle.

- The American medical system has a problem of *size*. In 2008 US spending on heath care, at $2.4 trillion, took up 17 percent of GDP, nearly twice the percentage common in other industrial democracies and twice the OECD's median per capita spending.[2] We are currently headed toward $1 of every $5 going towards health care.[3]

- It has a problem of *costs*. "Since 1999, employment-based health insurance premiums have increased 120 percent, compared to cumulative inflation of 44 percent and cumulative wage growth of 29 percent during the same period."[4] Per person health care expenditure has risen 6.5 percent per year since 2000. Inflation has averaged just 2.6 percent.[5]

- It has a problem of *access*. In 2007, 45.7 million Americans lacked any health insurance, maybe twice that number spent some months without health insurance, and in total 75 million adults (42 percent of all adults aged 19–64) were either uninsured or underinsured.[6]

- It has a problem of *public fundability*. The two great federally funded systems of health cover (Medicare for the elderly and Medicaid for the poor) take up between a quarter and a fifth of the entire federal budget, and without major tax hikes face insolvency within our lifetime.[7]

- It also has a problem of *private fundability*. Increasingly, employer-sponsored insurance coverage is being reset, with higher co-payments and deductibles levied on employees, and with more limited access to medical services per dollar of cover provided. That private coverage is also shrinking: the proportion of firms offering insurance coverage dropped from 69 to 60 percent between 2000 and 2007, and the number of working Americans covered by such insurance fell accordingly: from 67.8 percent to 63 percent.[8]

- It has a problem of *international under-performance*. In 2008, the Commonwealth Fund's National Scorecard, ranking countries against 37 leading international performance benchmarks, found the US scoring only out 65 out of a possible 100; and that included coming last out of 19 leading countries on avoiding preventable deaths. According to the Fund, "up to 101,000 fewer people would die prematurely if the US could achieve leading, benchmark country rates."[9]

- It has a problem of *quality control*. As many as 195,000 people may well be dying in American hospitals each year because of avoidable medical errors, and as many as 1.5 million may well be being misdiagnosed.[10] More serious still, the trend data suggests that "performance compared with benchmarks more often worsened than improved. . . . between the 2006 and 2008 Scorecards."[11]

- And it has a problem of *public confidence*. Opinion polls regularly show most Americans placing the reform of health care high on their domestic political agenda, with significant minorities prepared to put on record their dissatisfaction with the status quo. And not just ordinary Americans – Presidents too, and of both parties: George W. Bush used his 2005 State of the Union Address to tell Congress to "move forward on a comprehensive health care agenda" immediately and with some speed. Barack Obama used his 2009 Address to a Joint Session of Congress to do the same: "Given these facts," he said, "we can no longer afford to put health care reform on hold."

The problem, however, is that this consensus on the *need* for reform does not extend to any agreement on the *nature* of the reforms needed. On the contrary, on the reform agenda the parties are deeply, even negatively, divided. They are divided – in that they disagree with each other on what should be done; and the division is a deep and negative one – in that each side sees in the other's proposals the genuine risk of making a bad situation worse. On health care – arguably the most important political issue touching the daily lives of each of us – deep ideological differences scar the political landscape. Politicians and policy advisers feel passionately about what to do, precisely because the problem with which they struggle is so important to each and every one of us. The Conservative case, broadly speaking, goes something like this.

1. There are serious problems in the US health care system – just not the ones talked about by liberals

There are things wrong with the way in which US health care is currently provided and managed, but we will not correct any of them if we continue to mis-specify what they are. Liberals continually talk the system down. They endlessly make use of meaningless international comparisons, and go on and on about the 40+ million Americans who lack health insurance, when the true figure is only half that.[12] They forget to take out all the uninsured children covered by Medicaid, the adults who are only temporarily without cover, and the many young and healthy Americans who choose to be uninsured. And they tend not to mention that, anyway, the uninsured get emergency care at hospitals whenever they need it, care which the rest of us then pay for in higher insurance premiums. Instead liberals advocate ever more government interven-tion into every aspect of health care, when it is that very intervention which inflates demand and prices across the system, putting health care coverage out of the reach of so many hard-pressed Americans. If people were free to chose health insurance packages appropriate to their circumstances, many more would do so; but they cannot. Government regulations get in the way. The problem here is not the under-regulation of the entire health care industry but its over-regulation. The US health care system is already far too close to socialized medicine for its own good, "with all the increased costs and rationing of care that follow";[13] and it needs to back away.

2. The present situation is untenable and must be changed

The Government already directly finances health care for more than a quarter of the American population, and that "translates into nearly half (44 percent) of all medical care in the United States."[14] In 2005 Medicare and Medicaid cost the federal government more than the cost of national defense. Add spend-ing on Medicaid by state governments, and the bill exceeded that of Social Security. It is a bill that, unless brought under control, is likely to double by 2015. It is currently growing at twice the rate of GDP, and heading for a revenue deficit six times larger than that projected for Social Security. Spend-ing here has its own internal motor of expansion. The federal government has an open-ended commitment to match state Medicaid spending, so states have an incentive to spend on Medicaid to draw down matching funds. The benefi-ciaries of that spending are then sealed from the cost of their own care, which only leads to "increased demand, over-consumption, higher prices, and enor-mous waste."[15]

- *It leads to waste, because the unscrupulous are free to scam the system, and even more honest folk are free to consume medicines that do not actually bring measurable health benefits. (Researchers at Dartmouth College estimated that 20 percent of Medicare spending is so wasted.)*
- *It leads to higher prices, particularly to non-Medicare and non-Medicaid recipients, because the government systems underpay, and medical suppliers cross-compensate by inflating prices elsewhere. (Cato estimates that price inflation on non-Medicaid prescriptions at around 13 percent.[16])*

- *And it leads to increased demand and overconsumption, because removing price sensitivity "induces patients to consume more medical care"[17] (43 percent more in the widely cited RAND experiment designed to test this out).*

3. The problem here is government intervention

Everyone knows that markets work best when prices are left free to reflect individual preferences and needs. This is currently not happening in the US health market because of three different but linked distortions introduced by public policy.

- *By making care free at the point of use, Medicare and Medicaid remove any incentives on the elderly and the poor to ration their use of health care in an appropriate manner. Free coverage also builds up in those groups patterns of welfare dependency of the kind associated with Social Security. The elderly and the poor lose independence. Their capacity to own and to choose their own health care is diminished, as is their propensity to join private insurance schemes that finance better quality care. In fact, extended government coverage of the kind now advocated by President Obama always and inevitably crowds out private coverage.[18] Put a free program in, and you build in incentives for people buying private cover to abandon it. The tax payer then picks up the tab for people who previously picked up their own; and by reducing the pool of risk-spreading customers in private heath insurance, you drive up the costs of those insurances for honest customers who choose not to free-ride on the state. Drawing people into Medicaid who might otherwise provide their own coverage actually reduces the public program's capacity adequately to fund those who genuinely need its help.*
- *By giving tax breaks to employer-sponsored insurance programs, public policy privileges that form of saving for health care over others, significantly distorting the market for health insurance in the United States. Currently this tax break is the largest in the entire tax code – $200 billion annually. The tax break encourages people to hold more health insurance than they might otherwise do. It favors spending on health care over other forms of spending and saving; and it gives employer-provided insurance the edge over other forms of health insurance – so disadvantaging workers in firms too small to participate, and*

people excluded from employment altogether.[19] *It also inflates demand and prices. No less a figure than Milton Friedman reckoned that third party payment systems (private and federal together) inflated per capita spending through the 1990s by a factor of two!*[20] *Which is presumably one of the reasons why John McCain campaigned through 2008 to replace employer-based health insurance with individual health insurance plans, and was prepared to give families a $5,000 tax credit to help finance the switch.*

- *By regulating medical standards in a centralized and bureaucratic manner – through institutions like the FDA – governments add significantly to drug costs and slow down the rate of technological innovation vital to improvements in the long-term quality and efficiency of health care in the United States. By "requiring insurers to cover certain types of care and restricting their ability to set premiums,"*[21] *state regulations inflate costs and price people out of health insurance altogether. A recent Cato analysis "found that the costs of health care regulation outweigh the benefits by two-to-one and make health care insurance unaffordable for roughly 7.5 million Americans."*[22] *Cato estimates that 4,000 more Americans die each year from costs associated with health care regulation than do from lack of health insurance; and that the annual cost of health regulation averages out for each American household at over $1,500 – and all that before the disastrous creation of any kind of Federal Health Board as advocated by, among others, Tom Daschle, President Obama's first choice as "health czar" in his new administration.*[23]

4. Liberals will take us toward socialized medicine

Liberal solutions will only make a difficult situation worse.

- *Further regulation on drug companies will damage both the US health system and the competitiveness of a key sector of the US economy. The toleration of uncapped medical liability suits will line the pockets of trial lawyers, inflate medical costs, and drive doctors (and patients) out of the system altogether. Expansion of "free" government coverage will force taxpayers to bear costs hitherto borne voluntarily by the private sector, and encourage employers to cut back on private health care provision. "It's a shell game" Michael Savage said. "They 'give' you 'free' health care, then enslave you with a tax burden so heavy you go into cardiac arrest from the load."*[24]

- *Moving toward any form of "single payer system" will significantly reduce the freedom of Americans to own and choose their own health care. It will take control away from doctors and patients, and give it to politicians and bureaucrats. The result can only be longer waiting lists for patient care, diminished quality of care, and greater amounts of patient suffering and death. "Socialized medicine requires a culture of submission."*[25] *Socialized medicine "free rides" off the dynamism of market-based health care provision; and must be avoided like the plague. Put it into California, the Pacific Research Institute estimated in 2006, and the number of physicians would drop by 23,000, access to medical technology would diminish, waiting times would lengthen and about $9 billion of "free" health care would be wasted on people who did not really need it.*[26]

- *Even Republican Administrations and Congresses can get this wrong. The Medicare Prescription Drug Coverage was a move in entirely the wrong direction. We cannot afford it. It was poorly targeted. It invites price control. It was slipped through Congress on some pretty dodgy stats; and it is a form of corporate welfare. Once again, legislators were making the hard-pressed young finance the consumption of the privileged old, having taxpayers pick up the tab, and cutting "corporations a check just for providing the drug coverage they [were] already providing."*[27] *In the end everyone suffers: because the new program also reduces savings, puts up drug prices, and even (via its impact on payroll taxes down the line) hits jobs and slows economic growth.*

5. The way forward must be market-based

It is time to get control back into the hands of consumers, by strengthening competitive forces within the health care system and by giving individuals direct control of what they save and what they spend on the protection of their own health. "To control health costs, we must give consumers an incentive to spend money wisely."[28] *Markets have to be allowed to work in health care; and so we must . . .*

- *. . . change Medicare from a system where politicians define benefits to one in which seniors chose the benefits they want. We should give* *them a voucher with which to purchase health coverage from a variety of competing private insurers, or to make a deposit in a health savings account. We should make the voucher bigger if the seniors have expensive medical needs. We should allow retirees to supplement the voucher with their own money if they chose to, and to spend any unused health savings funds on nonmedical items. We should even go so far as to allow current workers to place their Medicare payroll tax in their own personal retirement health savings account.*

- *Introduce 1996-type reforms into Medicaid. We should pass control over spending down to the states by freezing federal funds and distributing them as a block grant. We should allow the states full flexibility on eligibility and benefits in Medicaid programs. We should encourage them to target only the truly needy, by "eliminating eligibility for those most likely to land on their own feet";[29] and we should have them replace open-ended entitlements with vouchers/tax credits, which the poor can then use to buy health coverage and/or create their own health savings accounts.*

- *We should develop savings accounts as the main way of financing health coverage for adults of working age. We should let people become the "stewards of their own health care dollars rather than force [them] to rely on their employer to spend those dollars wisely."[30] A proper system of HSAs, combining personal savings accounts with low-cost, high-deductible health insurance for catastrophic expenses, would be "the opposite of federal control. . . . patient control."[31] Since individuals, not bureaucrats, make the best decisions about their own health needs, empowering them is the best way to bring demand and costs down, and access up.*

- *Finally, we should make out-of-pocket medical expenses tax-deductible (so removing the bias in favor of third-party payers), deregulate the health insurance and pharmaceutical industries, and relax the regulation of medical professionals. We should allow individual patients and medical providers to strike their own agreements on malpractice protection. We should "improve access to health care through incentives to purchase less comprehensive insurance, expand high-risk pool coverage, finance charitable safety net care, and deregulate state insurance regulation."[32] In a word, we should create a system in which people take responsibility for their own health costs, a "genuine free market in healthcare, from cradle to grave."[33]*

A liberal response

That all sounds sensible and reasonable, does it not? So what could possible be wrong with it? This much at least.

1. The key weakness here is "access," not "costs"

Pick up the Cato Institute's flagship "solution" to the crisis of the US health care system – Cannon and Tanner's *Healthy Competition* – and check out what they say are the "real problems" bringing that crisis into being. They turn out to be "costs . . . quality . . . [and] bureaucracy"[34]: but not *access!*[35] Not access, in a health care system, in the richest country on earth, in which one American in seven cannot get any regular health care coverage at all. At 15.3 percent of the population uninsured in 2007, that proportion of the excluded puts the US alongside Mexico and Turkey in the OECD's list of health providers. Virtually every OECD country manages to provide health cover to the vast majority of its citizens: but Mexico, Turkey and we do not.[36] And because we do not, the Institute of Medicine estimated in 2002 that as many as 18,000 unnecessary deaths occur here each and every year.[37] Lack of access to adequate health care is literally killing us. That is *the* problem with which this discussion must begin: the problem of why the most expensive health care system on earth fails to provide even minimum levels of adequate coverage for such a significant portion of its population.

There is a framing issue here. Problems of cost, quality and bureaucracy have to get in line. They are not important to the nearly 46 million Americans who in 2008 were not even in the system[38]; or at least they are only important to those 46 million if they are the prime cause of their lack of access. But they are not. At most, they are a second line of causation, not the first. Americans have problems getting health care primarily because, uniquely here, we treat health care as something to be bought – bought like any other thing we buy. And we treat it as something to be insured against, because when we are really sick, we will need to buy lots of it all at once. Buying health care, and buying health insurance, costs money – lots and lots of money: the critics are correct on that at least. But money is not evenly divided in the United States. If you are poor, you cannot afford health care.[39] If you do not have a job, or if you work for a small employer who is also strapped for cash, you and your employer cannot afford the insurance. And even if you can, if you are young and healthy, there will be a thousand more pressing calls on the money on which you are just getting by. When the OECD ranked countries by equity of access to physician care in 2000, access here turned out to be more sensitive to income *even* than in Mexico.[40] When the scale of *un*met medical needs was mapped in 2001, 15 percent of the uninsured reported such a need against 4 percent of those with medical insurance.[41] Inequality, poverty and inadequate health insurance go together here. They form an iron triangle. To tackle one, you have to tackle the rest. Those who would fully privatize American medicine seem to know that. They simply won't take on the wider inequality issue – at most, insisting that "redistribution issues should be debated separately"[42] – and so they can neither privilege nor solve the problem of unequal access.[43] We, by contrast, must.

2. Separating work and health

As so many commentators have said, in comparative terms "the most striking feature of the American health care system is the absence of a statutory universal health care program and [the presence of] an employment-based fringe benefit in its stead."[44] Unequal access to health care is endemic to such a system: one in which people paid so differently have to rely on employer-provided insurance for the bulk of their health cover. Voluntary safety nets and federally sanctioned access to hospital emergency rooms for the uninsured can at best only ameliorate that inequality, because inequality itself is structured into the system. There is a huge amount of research material out there making two things as clear as it is possible to be. One is that the length, intensity and stress of work in many American factories and offices actually make people sick, such that if we genuinely want to improve American health we will need to improve the terms of American employment as well. The other is that tying health coverage to work does not work well – at least it does not work well for everybody – because employees in small businesses are much less likely to be offered coverage than employees in large companies, because layoffs and job switching often lead to irregular coverage even for those offered it, and because certain categories of worker are prone not to be offered coverage at all: particularly part-time and temporary workers, low-paid and women workers, young workers and those from minority communities.[45]

This access problem is a very deep one in the current health system. It is not just that so many Americans lack secure health coverage, and so miss or delay seeking medication until their illnesses intensify – though that certainly happens.[46] It's also that those with health coverage live perpetually with the fear of its loss: its absolute loss, with unemployment or job change; and its incremental loss, as benefits are eroded in annual reviews or as cover is denied as illnesses become catastrophic.[47] How often do we hear of Americans working full-time for low pay, juggling *which* pills to take of the many they need, and struggling to balance spending on medicine, food and fuel when their incomes will not cover all three? And how often do we hear of even better-paid Americans working on, long past retirement age, for fear of losing their ability to buy the medication that they require? The *stress* and *deprivation* associated with a health system based on the purchasing of health care has to be set against the claim that only through private purchasing do health consumers get genuine *control* and *choice*. Perhaps the Cato people should try it. Put themselves down in rural Tennessee, live on a low wage for a couple of years with a chronic illness, see the state government cut back on its health care plan for the poor and uninsured and then find out exactly how much "personal control of healthcare decisions" they really enjoy.[48] Not much – not much at all. It is oh so easy to type this kind of self-delusory nonsense, but it is so much harder to live it.

3. Focus on supply-side issues, not demand-side ones

The impression so often created by conservative critics of Medicare and Medicaid – and of the tax break given to employer-provided private health insurance – is that the great driver of health costs is the excessive and unnecessary *demand* for medical services and products created by health consumers who do not directly pay for what they get.

But in reality no such over-indulgent inflationary dynamic is currently at work in American medicine. There is simply no evidence of systematic overconsumption of routine medicines by the majority of US health "consumers." On the contrary, at least 80 percent of all the demand flowing into the contemporary American health system comes – entirely legitimately – from the 20 percent of Americans with genuine and serious illnesses. In 2002 "a mere 5 percent of Americans incurred almost half of US medical costs."[49] Americans actually "visit a physician or go to a hospital *less* often than people in other developed countries,"[50] though you would not think so, if all you read are conservative critiques of pill-popping seniors bleeding the rest of us dry through their excessive zeal for unnecessary medicine.[51]

Nor are federal/state provided funds the great triggers to rising costs. Costs are rising in American medicine. That we know; but they are rising primarily for reasons of technology and demography, not politics. Doctors can now do things that they could not do a generation ago; and cutting-edge medicine is increasingly sophisticated and expensive.[52] Both independently and as a consequence of that, we are now living longer than ever before, and gathering ever higher expectations of the doctors who keep us alive and well. What is striking about this much-cited dimension of the US health crisis, however, is that it is not uniquely American at all. Every health system in the advanced world is dealing with a similar cost explosion – there is a cost-containment problem everywhere. Between 1990 and 2004, expenditure on health provision rose faster than GPD in all 30 OECD member countries except Finland, and not just in the United States.[53] What is actually unique about our experience of that general inflationary phenomenon is that we spend more, and get less back for each dollar we spend, than do the best of our equivalents abroad. It is the *expense of what is supplied* in the US health system, rather than the *excess of what is demanded* there, that constitutes – alongside the access issue – the real problem facing us today; and we need to say so.

If you doubt that, just look at the figures. The US tops the list in the technology and sophistication of the medicine being practiced in its health system. It also tops the list in spending on medicine. Overall indeed, although Americans make up less than 5 percent of the world's population, we "account for roughly half the money that goes for doctors, drugs and other health expenses on [the] planet." But "line up the nations in order of longevity or infant mortality . . . and the United States does not even make the top twenty"; and "the places we trail, in addition to the usual suspects – Sweden, Norway, Switzerland and Canada – include Greece, Hong Kong and Martinique."[54] The US currently ranks dead last (13 out of 13) on three, and 12th out of 13 on sixteen, of the main indicators of health status in the advanced capitalist world[55]; and the latest WHO rankings of high-performing health systems lists the US as 33rd, below Costa Rica and just above Cuba! Even the Brits occasionally do better, though they spend way less than the European average on health care provision. When researchers from the US and UK recently compared the health of large samples of men aged between 55 and 64 – men with similar lifestyles and ethnic backgrounds – they found the British to be significantly healthier, even though their American counterparts consumed health care that cost nearly twice as much.[56] It was not a finding that the researchers could explain, but it did point to the capacity of health systems less generously funded than the American to produce outcomes that are measurably better. What you pay for – in health care provision in the United States at least – is not always what you get. There is a "value-for-money" issue here which we need to confront, and soon.

4. "Fragmentation," not "overregulation," is the deepest weakness of all

Conservatives and libertarians like to portray government involvement as *the* problem in American medicine: inflating costs on the demand side by giving free care, and on the supply side by overregulating health providers and insurance companies. This, as we saw, was largely the way advocates of privatization currently explain America's unique lack of access to medical cover by the poor: not that people are disproportionately poor here, but that regulations disproportionately inflate costs. But the converse is actually true. Costs inflate in the US health system faster than in equivalent health systems elsewhere because our system is *less* regulated than theirs are. Not overregulation, but the fragmentation of the system into a myriad of ostensibly competing units, is the extra bit that the US brings to the cost-inflation table. Though the government here "pays directly or indirectly for more than half of the nation's healthcare . . . the actual delivery . . . is undertaken by a crazy quilt of private insurers, for-profit hospitals, and other players who add cost without adding value."[57] Within that "quilt," prices escalate because nobody controls the system as a whole. Doctors do not. Consumers do not. The Government certainly does not. Insurance companies try, but they fail. Indeed, in a real sense, there is no one system for anyone to control. There are just "ten thousand little health care systems," and as such, a veritable "plague of administrative and clinical fragmentation."[58]

That very plague then adds a powerful inflationary dynamic of its own. The well-insured are left free to seek expensive care that guarantees benefits, however small. Hospitals are left free to exploit their local monopoly positions, able to set prices at will; and no one purchaser of any one drug is large enough to constrain the capacity of those supplying it to set whatever price they deem appropriate. The inflationary dynamic at work here is partly one of *defensive medicine* – doctors over-medicating for fear of later litigation if they do not. It's also one of *cost-shifting*. Maybe 2 to 3 million people are now employed to pass the costs of particular treatments from one insurance company to the next, in a paper chase that absorbs maybe 20 percent of the entire health bill.[59] And it is also one of *fee-setting*. Most physicians set their own prices; and until the era of "managed care" the insurers largely paid what the doctors billed without questioning the clinical judgments involved. The 1990s experiment with "managed care" ended that at least – shifting control from doctors to insurers – but only at the cost of an administrative arbitrariness which alienated all of us from the system, and yet still failed to stem the rise in costs. A family of four spent $3,400 a year in 2008 on insurance policies whose average price ($12,700 in 2008) has risen by a staggering 120 percent since 2000, a family contribution that had doubled since 2000![60] The cost of medicine is no longer just a problem for the American poor. Paying for health insurance is becoming a *general middle-class problem* in states as geographically and socially separate as Texas and New York. Little wonder then that, in a recent poll taken by the Center for American Progress, 89 percent of those questioned agreed with the proposition that "the health care system in our country is broken, and we need to make fundamental changes."[61] The question is no longer about the need for change, but only about its direction.

5. A solution focused on demand and regulation will not solve weaknesses rooted in supply and fragmentation

There is much that cannot be known about the future of US medicine, but this much at least is clear. The direction of change favored by both moderate and radical elements within the Republican coalition will simply make that future worse.

To take the moderates first: former president Bush clearly favored the strengthening of portable health savings accounts, medical liability reform and – if his budgets were any guide – financial limits on Medicaid. True, it was his administration that pushed through the Medicare Drug Prescription Bill in the face of opposition from fiscal conservatives and libertarians within his own base – but even that bill was constructed in such a way as to reinforce the incremental drift to privatization. Historically, Medicare offered retirees a choice: let the government pay your medical bills directly, or finance a private plan that will do it for you. Most retirees chose direct payment. This time, however, they were not given that choice. To receive the drug benefit, they *had* to sign up with a private insurer; and remarkably, under the terms of the Republican legislation Medicare was specifically prohibited from using its bulk-purchasing power to help those private plans get lower drug prices! Instead of choosing between Medicare and private insurers, retirees had to choose between a myriad of private insurance providers – more fragmentation, more subsidization of private insurers and drug companies. By privatizing the new drug benefit, the Bush administration created an extra and unnecessary layer of complexity and cost, which then had the usual and entirely predictable consequence – namely a low rate of take-up of the new benefit by the most vulnerable and poverty-stricken groups among the seniors at which it was aimed. More stress for health consumers and more profits for the usual suspects – hardly an adequate way forward.

The Cato Institute's proposal for vouchers to replace Medicare, and the phasing out of federal health care support in favor of individual savings accounts, are just bigger steps in that same wrong direction. Their proposals only make sense if excess demand, caused by the irresponsible use of free medicine, is the prime driver of costs in the American health system; but as we have seen, it is not. The Cato people are not proposing to leave the seriously ill without access to proper medical care unless they can afford it. On the contrary, they are advocating vouchers calibrated by risk: with bigger vouchers for the genuinely ill. But the delivery of that would be a bureaucratic nightmare open to huge abuse – who, after all, would make the final judgment in each case here – and if it is not the patients themselves, then where is the enhanced consumer empowerment that supposedly justifies the proposal in the first place? And since spending on the seriously ill makes up 80 percent of all the spending in the system, where is the gain in reduced demand and lower costs? There would be gain to hard-pressed employers: shifting risk, as with pensions, off their shoulders and on to those of their employees'. But where is the gain to the employees themselves, faced with a plethora of complex plans covering a multitude of medical conditions they currently lack but may one day face? That is much harder to discern.

No, there are simpler and more direct ways of containing health costs than this. As with Social Security, the Cato people are going around the woods rather than moving directly through the trees. A voucher system and individual health savings accounts run the risk of splitting "consumers" in the American health market into the rich and the poor, the young and the old, the healthy and the sick: adding to the premiums and out-of-pocket expenses of the second of the two in each category as they do so. You do not guarantee universal health cover by disaggregating those who need it. You get guaranteed universal cover only by guaranteeing equal access to all, regardless of their status. You get guaranteed universal cover only by *managing* health markets rather than by surrendering to them.

6. The special features of health markets require special kinds of market regulation

Not all markets are the same. We have seen that already (in Chapter 3) in relation to labor markets, and we need to see it now in relation in health ones. Labor markets and markets for baked beans are different because you can leave baked beans unsold on the shelf for months without adverse social consequences, but cannot leave labor unemployed even for a day without those consequences immediately coming into view. And you can go to a number of car companies, and compare prices, or move between gas stations looking for the cheapest fuel, and exercise real (if limited) consumer power in the process. But no two medical operations are the same; and unlike your car, if one does not work you cannot just trade it in for another. Conservatives might argue that "health care is fundamentally no different from any other goods and services. Both consumers and providers react to normal marketplace incentives."[62] But we should not argue anything so ludicrous. Rather, as Charles Morris has said, we should emphasize that

> . . . buying health care, at the end of the day, is not like buying television sets. It is not the affluent, healthy, probing consumer. . . . that accounts for the spending. Mostly, it's people who are sick, frightened and not likely to be thinking clearly. You are in hospital, festooned with stitches and tubes, and your doctor comes into tell you about chemotherapy – do you reach for your laptop?[63]

No, of course you don't.

In economic terms this all comes down to a disagreement about the way prices work as signals in markets. You have a choice. You can go with the right-wing health economists, and argue that by lowering the price of health care at the moment of consumption, insurance (public or private) causes rational economic actors to over-consume. But if you do, you need to realize that your perfect solution – rational consumers making carefully calibrated health choices – will only come into existence if everyone in the market has equal purchasing power as well as equal knowledge, and if you can find some way of enabling people to buy "big" operations (expensive ones) when they need them, even if their income is – in the moment – too small. Income equality, fully informed consumers and risk-pooling are essential prerequisites of your market-based solution; so if you are serious about your kind of health reform, you will need to be serious about them too.

But why go that way at all? What is the sense of even formulating the issue in those terms, when in reality people are often being asked

to make life and death decisions – should I have a heart bypass operation, or will medication be enough – when they cannot know what
each outcome would actually be, and when even the professionals can
only talk in probabilities. The pill may be purple, but is it any good?
How can the general consumer know? And why advocate increased
reliance on private insurance, when by its very nature a private insurance system must shake out high-risk candidates in favor of low-risk
ones, and charge heavier premiums to the ill? Health insurance, after
all, suffers from a particularly acute version of the well-known problem of "adverse selection"[64]; and the famous RAND Corporation
study in the 1970s showed that higher cost-sharing reduced both
necessary and unnecessary medical spending in broadly the same proportions.[65] So why not go the other way: and recognize that given the
inevitability of imperfections in consumer knowledge about medical
conditions and options, and the heavy presence of drug advertising by
pharmaceutical companies dedicated to private profit growth, a free
market of consumers and suppliers is as likely to generate poor decisions as optimal ones.

Public figures in the US tend not to be so bold these days as to
say all this – though in the 1930s they clearly did[66]– but in Europe, it
has lately been a slightly different story. Even parties of the center-
right –Angela Merkel's Christian Democrats in Germany being the
prime recent example – have responded to the pressure of health
costs on employers by absorbing responsibility for health care back
into general taxation. They are beginning to socialize rather than privatize their health systems, in the manner of parties of the center-left.
Indeed on occasion, major figures there have explored in public the
necessary limits to the role of market forces in systems of universal
health care. Gordon Brown – the finance minister of Tony Blair's
much admired "third way" – said this in 2003.

> The free market position which would lead us to privatized hospitals
> and some system of vouchers . . . starts by viewing health care as akin to
> a commodity to be bought and sold like any other through the price
> mechanism. But . . . use of healthcare is unpredictable and can never be
> planned by the consumer in the way that, for example, weekly food
> consumption can. . . . The market for health care is dominated by the
> combination of, on the one hand, chronically imperfect and asymmetric
> information and the potentially catastrophic and irreversible outcome

of healthcare decisions based on that information and, on the other, the necessity of local clusters of medical and surgical specialisms. Take the asymmetry of information between the consumer as patient . . . and the producer. With the consumer unable – as in a conventional market – to seek out the best product at the lowest price, and the information gaps that cannot . . . be satisfactorily bridged, the results of a market failure for the patient can be long-term, catastrophic and irreversible. [Add to that, the fact that] local emergency hospitals are – in large part clusters of essential medical and surgical specialities and have characteristics that make them akin to natural local monopolies . . .

. . . and the conclusion is clear: "in health, price signals don't always work, the consumer is not sovereign, there is potential abuse of monopoly power . . . [and] we risk supplier induced demand."[67] He had a point. In a very real sense the genuinely sick are invariably too ill systematically to shop around; and we would do well to design a health system that has the recognition of that inability at its core.

7. The time for reform is now

We certainly will not get to such a design by over-glorifying the system we have inherited, or by misunderstanding its history. There is nothing quintessentially American about the present arrangements, no matter what right-wing politicians and shock jocks periodically claim. The creation of the contemporary health system has been far too haphazard for that. Employer-provided insurance cover was the accidental product of a class compact struck in the 1940s between strong companies and industrially militant labor unions. Medicare and Medicaid were later add-ons – products of urban unrest *and* Conservative political maneuvering in the 1960s: the first the result of Johnson's War on Poverty, the second the unintended consequence of a conservative move to block it. Progressive social forces extended health coverage down the American social ladder in the 1940s and 1960s, but failed to push that coverage all the way. They failed under Truman in the 1940s, and they failed under Clinton in the 1990s: in both cases because of opposition from the medical community, who feared loss of professional control, and from employers who preferred their own benefit-based system. Throughout the postwar period, that is, "the triple trench" of "weakly organized workers, constrained citizenship rights and the disproportionate power of business and institutional interest groups"[68] combined to block any attempt to create here the kind of universally accessible health care systems emerging in the rest of the advanced industrial world.

But that triple trench is not now the force it once was. The political space for reform is opening again as the current arrangements begin systematically to unravel. That space is reemerging in part because of professional dissatisfaction with managed health care. The private rule of the insurance companies satisfies no one, and certainly not the doctors whose autonomy it erodes.[69] It is emerging because the nation's emergency rooms can no longer easily meet their legal obligation to treat the flood of patients – insured and uninsured – now crowding their corridors.[70] It is also emerging because, in this age of intense international competition, both large and small US companies, and indeed foreign ones like Toyota, are no longer prepared/able to carry the expense of large health benefit packages. Indeed Toyota recently redeployed a car plant to Canada – to single-payer Canada! – because of the burden of health costs here. And it is emerging because the fallout from that corporate retreat – the general shifting of costs and risks to ordinary working Americans through greater co-pays, higher deductibles and the withdrawal of all cover by more and more small US companies – is educating all of us in the need for substantial health care reform. The unreformed American health system is well on its way to the very worst kind of rationing system – rationing health care by excluding the poor while allowing those with insurance to get whatever health care they demand, regardless of its value. The very visibility of that move is making the present arrangements progressively more difficult to defend. We need a better rationing system. The only question is which.

8. Choosing the best way forward

The choice we face is not, as Michael Savage and others would have it, between the free enterprisers and the Marxists/socialists. Nothing stymies clear thinking on this key topic faster than the far too rapid deployment of either *pejorative labels* – "Russian-style" medicine against "American free enterprise" – or *false polarities* – "single-payer systems with long waiting lists" against "market-based systems with none." Those pejorative polarities distort because they obscure. They obscure the fact that all medical systems are regulated. There is always a role for government somewhere. They obscure the fact that all medical systems have greater demands placed upon them that they can immediately meet. There is always rationing. Sometimes rationing in time (someone has to wait). Sometimes rationing by price (someone cannot afford). And they obscure the fact that all medical systems are complex. There are always patients, professionals, suppliers and regulators. The trick is not to play clever labeling games. The trick is to find a set of arrangements that can minimize the rationing and the complexity, and create clear lines of control and accountability that can be democratically accessed. The trick is also to find a set of arrangements capable of maximizing the quantity and quality of medical outcomes without placing excessive cost burdens on the surrounding economy and society. High-quality, high-efficiency, low-cost and publicly accountable medicine should be our target, and the question is how best to get to it.

The real choice we face is between options canvassed by those "who start with a private insurance (individual responsibility) model and try to fix the problems that a competitive market poses for equity and access"; and those who "begin with a public insurance (social justice) model, like Medicare, and try to adapt it to deal with issues such as overall cost or misuse of health care."[71] If the argument here is right, and a more privatized and market-based system can only intensify already existing levels of inequality in health care, then we clearly need to move toward the second of those: because "on balance," as Leif Wellington Haase has so persuasively argued, they "make much more sense."[72] The task we face is therefore two-fold: both to stem the drift towards the incremental marketization of an employer-based insurance system in decline, and to develop a public insurance-based model that is electorally credible. Indeed we will not manage the first of those two tasks if we do not also manage the second; and doing the second will be (and indeed is) extraordinarily difficult in our present political circumstances, given the increasing weight of market orthodoxies in the entirety of American public life over the last two decades – given what Mark Schlesinger has quite properly called "the corrosive power of market thinking."[73] But just because a thing is difficult does not mean that it should not be tried.

9. Progressive alternatives

The most radical reconstruction of the US health system from a social justice point of view would be what Paul Krugman calls a "VA system for everyone": a reconstruction in which federal and state authorities ran the hospitals as well as financed them. A less radical move in a similar direction would be a "Medicare for everyone," some kind of Canadian-style *single-payer* system of universal health coverage financed through general taxation. In a single-payer system, private insurance would be replaced by public insurance, with medical services provided by the existing set of private practitioners: primary care providers, specialists, hospitals and clinics. That would bring at least three huge advantages into play. Everyone would have access to medical services, regardless of their income and employment status. Employers would be free of the cost burden of the insurance they now provide. And because the government alone would administer and purchase services, running costs would be reduced and the capacity to slow the rate of growth of medical and drug costs would be enhanced. Indeed, according to its advocates, the scale of the savings involved by the introduction of a single-payer system here could be so great as actually to reduce overall health spending while extending coverage to all Americans.

The big problem with such a move, however, is the range and number of interests that would mobilize against it. The private insurance companies would be the great losers, and are unlikely to go quietly from the scene. Likewise the big drug companies. The other potential losers – small businesses providing no cover, workers with already established medical benefits and physicians with affluent lifestyles – might be more inclined this time than last to tolerate reform, given the fragility of their current privileged position; but the insurance companies would certainly fight any single-payer proposal, and play on fears of big-government among employers and workers alike. Which is why some *hybrid* scheme – strengthening the role of public insurance alongside existing private insurance coverage – seems to many people on the Left to be a more realistic alternative. The argument here is that the perfect should not be allowed – in the arena of health care at least – to drive out the good. If it is true that "when advocates of market-based solutions and single-payer systems put purism ahead of pragmatism, we get gridlock,"[74] a mixture of the old and the new seems to be essential.[75]

There are lots of schemes out there mixing the old and the new, all now seeking political support.[76]

- There is considerable support in progressive circles for the generalization of the Federal Employee Health Benefits Program – one in which federal employees and their dependents choose coverage from one of a number of federally regulated private insurers and where the membership pool is big enough to keep premiums down. The Center for American Progress is currently canvassing such a generalization,[77] and Tom Daschle, among others, has recently argued that "one of the options under the expanded FEHBP should be a government-run insurance program modeled after Medicare."[78]
- The Century Foundation's Charles Morris has recently suggested a similar scheme: a universally available federally regulated basic health plan, with subsidized premiums for the elderly and the poor.[79] The Foundation has also published a more complex proposal from Leif Wellington Haase, in which the federal government would establish and sponsor three different insurance packages, and make purchase of at least the basic package mandatory: with subsidies again for the old, poor and disabled.[80]
- The Economic Policy Institute (EPI) is currently canvassing what it calls its Health Care for America Plan, one open to any legal US resident who currently lacks good workplace coverage. Under this proposal, the self-employed and employers who are not already providing cover will pay a 6 percent payroll tax to fund Health Care for America coverage for all their employees; and all Americans currently without insurance will be mandated to purchase private coverage or buy into the Health Care for America Plan.[81]
- The issue of mandates divided proposals offered by the two leading Democratic candidates in the 2008 presidential primary race.

Hillary Clinton fought her campaign on the basis of what she called The American Health Choices Plan, which allowed people to either (and only) keep their existing coverage, choose from the same coverage options that members of Congress enjoy, or choose a quality public plan option similar to Medicare. Barack Obama, by contrast, mandated employers to provide coverage or contribute to a fund financing a new national health plan similar to that offered through FEDBP, but did not mandate individuals to purchase it. Both candidates included in their plans measures to prevent adverse selection, to mandate coverage for children, and to expand Medicaid and SCHIP (the State Child Health Insurance Program aimed at families whose incomes fell just above poverty thresholds).[82]

There is therefore quite a choice out there: and the best of the progressive proposals all widen access, lower costs and strengthen quality controls by reinforcing the role of public institutions in the management of what is still a privately provided system. That is certainly the minimum direction in which public policy on health care now needs to go; and it does seem at last to be going in that direction. The new President's first budget set aside $634 billion over 10 years for health care reform, and the *New York Times* (February 20) reported progress in private talks initiated by Senator Kennedy between all major stakeholders in the health debate.[83] We can take some comfort too from the reported principles currently guiding the new administration's pursuit of health care reform, which the *Financial Times* reported this way.[84]

> These include an "aim for universality", an effort to insure the 46 million Americans now without it; a reduction in premiums for Americans who have increasingly expensive insurance; a move to portability which would help loosen the ties between employment and insurance; and an aim to make the reforms pay for themselves by reducing long term health costs.

10. It is time to "go to the mattresses"[85]

We need a move in that direction as a matter of urgency, and we should say so. We should say loud and clear that it is entirely *unacceptable,* in the most affluent society on earth, for 46 million Americans to have no regular health coverage at all, and for perhaps an additional 100 million Americans to be continually worrying about their capacity to sustain adequate coverage. We should also say that it is quite *ridiculous* that access to proper health care should be dependent on the company people work for, on whether they work at all, and on what kind of benefits package they manage to negotiate; and that it is *bad medicine* for those who lack insurance to use hospital emergency rooms as their first and last port of call. We should insist on the *unfairness* of a system denying basic coverage to so many while providing super-profits for insurers and drug companies alike; and we should label as *obscene* any system of health finance under which, the sicker you are, the more expensive cover becomes and the more difficult it is to acquire.

"Health care must be affordable and accessible to all, irrespective of health, age, income or work status."[86] Adequate health cover is not something you should have to buy. It is something you should have by right. It is, after all, one of the major rights guaranteed by the UN's Universal Declaration of Human Rights. In the area of health perhaps more than any other, "no man is an island." The health of each of us is the responsibility of us all. Of course, we also have a responsibility to each other to live a healthy life – there are issues of self-inflicted illness with which any affluent society has to deal – but that is only one of the health responsibilities we carry. We also carry the responsibility to help others to the health care they need, and to create a reasonably level playing field of economic and social rewards on which healthy lives can be easily lived. There is a relationship between poverty and illness at play here, as well as one between affluence and excess, that we need to remember. Inequality actually makes people ill. Inequality also denies to many who are ill the capacity to "buy" back their health. We need therefore to design a health care system free at the point of use, and a society in which that freedom, because shared, is not abused.

Market-based health reform will not give us that system or that society. Conservatives regularly praise markets as instruments of free-dom, and denigrate democratic politics (and politicians) as corrupt and self-seeking. But as earlier chapters have already shown, markets are not instruments of popular control in societies where income is as unequally divided as it is in the United States right now. Market actors do not respond to the totality of human need. They respond only to needs that are linked to purchasing power. So to be very affluent in a privately funded health market is indeed genuinely to have "consumer power"; but it is a power to exclude as well as to consume – a power to lay claim to more than your fair share of limited health resources by pricing those resources out of the hands of those who are less affluent. To be only moderately well-off in a privately funded health market, by contrast, is to have the appearance of consumer power but invariably not its reality – certainly not its full reality – the bureaucrats in the insurance scheme have that, and the insured do not. And of course to be poor in such a system is to have no power at all – just the freedom to know bad health and early death.

Democratic politics, by contrast, does have the potential to be genuinely responsive to the full set of American health needs, if those who care about universal health care can mobilize – as the Obama administration is now trying to mobilize – enough numbers to overcome the defensive leverage of the special interests. The rich and the poor, after all, each only have one vote. American politics is not always democratic, because money gives political leverage and special interests are so entrenched – especially around issues of health reform. But the potential for democratic change is always there. Change is possible, if it can be *made* to happen. It is up to progressive forces in contemporary America to realize that potential, by uniting around a health platform based on universal access and by campaigning for it with vigor and determination. Progressive health reform is there for the taking, but it will have to be taken. There will be a fight – probably a truly enormous fight – which is why, on this issue perhaps more than on any other issue in contemporary domestic politics, it is genuinely time for us to follow the man's advice: time to say "enough already – away with all this right-wing nonsense," time, on this issue at least, to go to the mattresses!

Notes

1. Rush Limbaugh, "Health Care and Automobiles," *Welcome to Rush 24/7*, August 30, 2004. For a similar argument, see Michael Savage, *The Enemy Within*, Nashville, WND Books, 2003, p. 55.

2. $6,700 per head in the US 2006, as against $3,100 for the OECD as a whole (Ben Furnas, *American Health Care since 1994* (Center for American Progress, January 2009, p. 3). Health care spending in 2008 accounted for 10.9 percent of the GDP in Switzerland, 10.7 percent in Germany, 9.7 percent in Canada and 9.5 percent in France, according to the Organization for Economic Cooperation and Development. Those countries provide universal health care. We do not.

3. Commonwealth Fund, *Why Not the Best?*, July 17, 2008, p. 1 of 7.

4. National Coalition on Health Care, *Health Insurance Costs*, www.nchc. org, retrieved March 2, 2009.

5. Furnas, *American Health Care since 1994*, p. 2.

6. Commonwealth Fund, *Why Not the Best?* p. 4 of 7. The 2003 percent had been lower, 35 percent of all working-age adults.

7. The Medicare Trustees estimated (April 2008) that the program's hospital insurance fund would be empty by 2019. With the recession deepening, they now estimate it may be empty by 2016 (*New York Times*, March 2, 2009). The only other form of public expenditure currently rising as rapidly is that on prisons!

8. Jeanne Lambrew, *Testimony: Hearing on Health Care*, Before the Subcommittee on Labor, Health and Human Services, Committee on Appropriations, House of Representatives, March 5, 2007.

9. *Why Not the Best?*; and Niko Karvounis, *The Newest Last-Place Finish for US Health Care*, Washington, DC, The Century Foundation, October 1, 2008.

10. Cited in Leif Wellington Haase, *A New Deal for Health*, The Century Foundation 2005, pp. 2–3.

11. Furnas, *American Health Care since 1994*, p. 4.

12. Both these from Michael Cannon, *Hilary's Worse Nightmare*, Cato Institute Website, May 9, 2004.

13. Michael Cannon, *Kerry Prescribes More Government-Run Health Care*, Cato Institute Website, April 23, 2004.

14. Michael Cannon, "Medicare and Medicaid," *The Cato Handbook on Policy*, The Cato Institute 2004, pp. 85–6.

15. Michael Cannon, "Medicare and Medicaid," p. 86.

16. Michael Cannon, "Welfare Reform's Unfinished Business," Cato Institute Website, May 26, 2005.

17. Ibid.

18. Robert E. Moffitt, *How a Public Health Plan Will Erode Private Care*, Heritage Foundation Backgrounder No. 2224, December 22, 2008.

19. Hence George W. Bush's proposal, in his 2007 State of the Union Address, to, as he put it, "level the playing field for those who do not get health insurance through their job" by providing tax breaks to help

low-income people buy health insurance and tax increases for workers whose health plans cost significantly more than the national average.

20. Cited in Michael Cannon, "Medicare and Medicaid," pp. 86–7.

21. John Cogan, R. Glenn Hubbard and Daniel P. Kessler, *Healthy, Wealthy and Wise*, Washington, DC, The AEI press, 2005, p. 2.

22. Christopher J. Conover, *Health Care Regulation: A $169 Billion Hidden Tax*, Cato Institute, Policy Analysis no. 527, October 4, 2004.

23. For the argument against such a board, see Robert E. Moffitt, *How a Federal Health Board Will Cancel Private Coverage and Care*, Heritage Foundation Backgrounder, No. 2155, December 4, 2008.

24. Michael Savage, *The Enemy Within*, p. 55.

25. Michael Cannon, *Hilary's Worse Nightmare*.

26. National Center for Policy Analysis, *A Single-Payer Health Care System for California*, Daily Policy Digest, June 26, 2006.

27. Michael Cannon, *Eight Reasons to Delay the Imprudent Drug Program*, Cato Website, November 14, 2005. Bruce Bartlett later called the Medicare drug bill "the worst piece of legislation ever enacted" (Bruce Bartlett, *Imposter*, New York, Doubleday, 2006, p. 80).

28. Allen B. Hubbard, Assistant to the president for Economic Policy, *New York Times*, April 3, 2006.

29. Michael Cannon, *Medicaid's Untallied Costs,* Cato Institute Website, July 1, 2005.

30. Michael Cannon, *Hilary's Worse Nightmare*.

31. George W. Bush, quoted in the *New York Times*, January 29, 2006.

32. Tom Miller, "Private Health Care," *Cato Handbook for Congress: Policy Recommendations for the 108th Congress*, Washington, DC, n.d., p. 283.

33. Ibid., p. 293.

34. Michael Cannon and Michael Tanner, *Healthy Competition*, Washington, DC, Cato Institute, 2005, pp. 27–30.

35. "We must shift the health care debate away from its single-minded focus on expanding coverage to the bigger question of how to reduce costs and improve quality" (Michael Tanner, *Leviathan on the Right*, Cato Institute 2007, p. 118).

36. OECD, *Towards High Performing Health Systems*. Paris, 2004, p. 44.

37. Paul Krugman, "Death by Insurance," *New York Times*, May 1, 2006.

38. The Census Bureau figures for 2005 show an increase of 6.8 million in the number of the medically uninsured since 2000. The total includes 8.3 million children – more than one American child in 10 – the first increase in that number since 1998.

39. Broadly speaking, three equally sized groups are currently uninsured in the United States: young healthy adults on more than $50,000 a year;

Medicaid-eligible poor who don't take up private insurance; and workers earning more than the poverty level but less than $50,000 a year – the group referred to in Chapter 3 as the "twice poor" (This, from Cogan et al., *Healthy, Wealthy and Wise*, pp. 18–21).

40. OECD, *Towards High Performing Health Systems*. Paris, 2004, p. 51.

41. Leif Wellington Haase, *A New Deal for Health*, p. 22.

42. Tom Miller, *Rising Health Costs*, The Cato Institute Website, August 13, 2002.

43. The most serious attempt to address access issues from a market perspective can be found in Cogan et al., *Healthy, Wealthy and Wise*, p. 72; where they estimate tax changes could reduce the uninsured by between 6 and 20 million (i.e., up to half). The best Cato has come up is this: "For low income individuals lacking access to health insurance, the better policy solutions include safety net reforms that strengthen state high-risk pools and encourage charitable contributions to provide health services through nonprofit intermediaries . . . In the long run, improving the quality of education that lower-income individuals receive, expanding their personal control of healthcare decisions [*sic*!], and reversing regulatory policies that increase the cost of their heath care will yield even greater returns in improved health outcomes" (*The Cato Handbook for Congress: Policy Recommendations for the 108th Congress*, 2003, p. 291).

44. Susan Giaimo, "Who Pays for Health Care Reform?" in Paul Pierson (editor), *The New Politics of the Welfare State*, Oxford, Oxford University Press, 2001, p. 357.

45. "Low-wage workers are about half as likely as high-wage workers to have employer-provided health insurance from either their own employers or a family member's"; and "women among the low-paid are twice as likely to be without such cover as are low-paid men" (Heather Boushey and Mary Murray Diaz, *Heath Insurance Data Briefs #1: Improving Access to Health Insurance*, Center for Economic and Policy Research, April 13, 2004, p. 2 of 13).

46. Emergency room visits nationwide increased by 20 percent between 1992 and 2001, even though the total number of emergency departments fell by 15 percent in the same period (source: Wellington Haase, *A New Deal for Health*, p. 22).

47. "A recent study by the Urban Institute estimated that 43 percent of low-income workers and 31 percent of middle-income workers would be unable to afford alternative coverage should they lose their employer benefits" (Wellington Haase, *A New Deal for Health*, p. 9).

48. On the Tennessee cutbacks, see Julie Rovner, *Tennessee Health-Care Cuts Roil Poor Community*, NPR, July 5, 2006.

49. Paul Krugman, "Health Economics 101," *New York Times*, November 14, 2005.

50. Wellington Haase, *A New Deal for Health*, pp. 13–14.

51. Virtually the entire growth of Medicare spending is on patients with five or more conditions; many triggered by/associated with obesity. So there are lifestyle issues to discuss on the "demand" side of the medical equation, similar in kind to those surrounding smoking and cancer treatment. (On this, see Kenneth Thorpe and David Howard, "The rise in spending among Medicare Beneficiaries," *Health Affairs*, August 22, 2006.)

52. This is not to say that it is inefficient. Charles Morris's writings regularly stress the *rising* productivity of US medicine. Procedures are now often quicker and cheaper than ever before. As he says, "it is not falling productivity that is driving costs . . . but the expanding basket of effective interventions – both for diseases doctors have always treated, and for a growing list of conditions previously beyond our reach." (Charles Morris, *What's Right with Health Care*, New York, The Century Foundation, March 3, 2006.)

53. Chris Giles, "Healthcare costs rising faster than GDP: OECD," *Financial Times*, June 27, 2006, p. 4.

54. David Williams and James Lardner, "Cold truths About Class, Race and Health," in James Lardner and David A. Smith (editors), *Inequality Matters*, New York, The New Press, 2005, p. 103.

55. Ichiro Kawachi, "Why the United States Is Not Number One in Health," in J. Morone and L. Jacobs, *Healthy, Wealthy and Fair*, New York, Oxford University Press, 2004, p. 20.

56. The details are at NPR, May 3, 2006, and in the corresponding issue of the *Journal of the American Medical Association*.

57. Paul Krugman, "The Health Care Crisis and What to Do About It," *New York Review of Books*, vol. 53, no. 5, March 23, 2006, p. 1 of 14.

58. The description of the system is that of J. D. Kleinke, cited in Wellington Haase, *A New Deal for Health*, p. 24.

59. Krugman puts administrative costs in the US system as 31 percent of total health expenditure, as against 17 percent in the Canadian single-paper system (Paul Krugman, *The Conscience of a Liberal*, W. W. Norton, 2007, p. 222).

60. NCHC, *Health Insurance Costs*, p. 1.

61. Americans for Health Care and Center for American Progress, *If It's Broke, Fix It*, Washington, DC.

62. Michael Tanner, *Leviathan on the Right*, p. 118.

63. Charles Morris, *Apart at the Seams*, New York, The Century Foundation, 2006, p. 51.

64. On this, see Paul Krugman, "The Health Care Crisis . . .," p. 4 of 14.

65. For the latest research showing that imperfect information can lead consumer-driven health care to preempt, not promote, good health, see Jeanne Lambrew, *Consumer-Driven Health Plans May Preempt, Not Promote, Prevention*, Center of American Progress, April 10, 2008; and Niko Karvounis, *Will Consumer-Driven Medicine Really Cut Health Care Costs?* Century Foundation, February 14, 2008.

66. See Schlesinger, "The Danger of the Market Panacea," in Morone and Jacobs, *Healthy, Wealthy and Fair*, New York, Oxford University Press, 2004, p. 96.

67. The Rt. Hon. Gordon Brown MP, Chancellor of the Exchequer, *A Modern Agenda for Prosperity and Social Reform*, speaking to the Social Market Foundation, February 3, 2003.

68. Lawrence Jacobs, "Health Disparities in the Land of Equality," in Morone and Jacobs, *Healthy, Wealthy and Fair*, p. 59.

69. "More than half of US doctors [surveyed] now favor switching to a national health care plan and fewer than a third oppose the idea. . . . The survey suggests that opinions have changed substantially since the last survey in 2002" (*Reuters*, March 31, 2008).

70. 90 million patients in 1990, but 114 million in 2003.

71. Leif Wellington Haase, *Universal Health Coverage: The Problem with Individual Mandates*, The Century Foundation Website, February 14, 2003.

72. Ibid.

73. This, on page 116 of the remarkably valuable essay by Mark Schlesinger, "The Danger of the Market Panacea," in Morone and Jacobs, *Healthy, Wealthy and Fair*, pp. 91–134.

74. Jeanne Lambrew, *Consumer-Driven Health Plans May Preempt, Not Promote, Prevention*, p. 6.

75. Quite how radically to mix them, and with what speed, remains in dispute between progressives. For the argument for speed and radical change, see Paul Krugman, *The Conscience of a Liberal*, p. 233: for the argument for caution and incrementalism, see Henry Aaron, "The Pitfalls of Overreaching in Health Reform," *Health Affairs*, January 2009.

76. Among important ones *not* surveyed here are E. Emanuel, *Healthcare, Guaranteed* (Public Affairs, 2008); and Jason Furman (editor), *Who Has the Cure? Hamilton Project Ideas on Health Care* (Brookings Institution, 2008).

77. Center for American Progress, *Progressive Prescriptions for a Healthy America*, March 2005.

78. Tom Daschle, *Critical: What We Can Do about the Health Care Crisis*, Thomas Dunne Books 2008, p. 144.

79. Charles Morris, *Apart at the Seams*, pp. 57–60.

80. Wellington Haase, *A New Deal for Health*, p. 5.

81. Jacob Hacker, *Health Care for America*, EPI Briefing Paper, January 11, 2007.

82. See Hilary Clinton, *The American Health Choices Plan* and Barack Obama, *Barack Obama's Plan for a Healthy America*.

83. What was not clear at that point, however, was the likely depth of Republican opposition to any reform that moved away from market-based provision to government-supervised provision: that ideological chasm is likely to remain.

84. March 3, 2009, p. 2.

85. An injunction beloved by all fans of "The Godfather" movies!

86. Center for American Progress, *Progressive Prescriptions for a Healthy America*, p. 11.

CHAPTER 7

Immigration Control in a Land of Immigrants

Emma Lazarus's injunction on the base of the Statue of Liberty could not be clearer. "Give me your tired, your poor, your huddled masses yearning to breathe free." It was never so simple, of course. "The wretched refuse of your teaming shore" always had to negotiate their way past Ellis Island. Even in the late nineteenth-century heyday of open borders, one would-be immigrant in every 150 never made it out of there; and as many as one-in-three of those who did eventually chose to return home. And after 1882 the border was never entirely open – not open to first the Chinese, then from 1917 to people from India, Indochina, Arabia and Afghanistan (the so-called Asia-Pacific Triangle), and from 1921/24 to people from countries other than those from which the majority of Americans had already come. Immigration in the United States, that is, has long been regulated, and regulated in ways that traditionally privileged immigration from the western hemisphere.[1]

Being regulated, immigration into the United States has also periodically been "reformed" – sometimes to reinforce that European privileging, as in 1952, or to lessen it, as in 1965 and 1990. Over time, immigration acts have set (and then varied) limits on the totals of immigrants annually allowed in. They have regulated the places from which those immigrants have come, by setting national quotas; and the skills required to come with them, by issuing work visas. They have opened American borders to refugees from political repression and natural disasters, and to family members of people already here. Between 1943 and 1964, Congress even created a guest-worker system for Mexican agricultural laborers, and in 1986 attempted to stem the flood of illegal immigrants, again mainly Mexican, by proposing penalties on those employing undocumented workers. And legislation has periodically altered the terms on which people can visit the United States, study here, or work in American factories and offices on a temporary basis. There has been a lot of immigration legislation.

The big moments in that legislative flood have come in broadly 20-year phases, with each one triggered by the left-over business of the previous ones. We are into another of those phases now, picking up the pieces left in place from 1965 and 1986. Two pieces in particular – the dramatic change in the scale and regional origins of recent immigration (the unexpected legacy of the 1965 Act), and the number of undocumented immigrants now working in the United States (a number whose growth the 1965 Act inadvertently triggered, and which the 1986 Act failed to stem).

- In December 2005, the House of Representatives voted to erect a 700-mile fence along the United States' southwestern border, to increase the number of patrol agents by 10,000 over 5 years, to make illegal immigration a felony and to require employers to identify illegal workers by checking their status against a national database. Driven by strong feelings in the Republican Party base, the House bill incorporated no guest-worker proposals nor any amnesty for immigrants already illegally here. It was an "enforcement-only bill" that "essentially dared the Senate to depart from that tough-minded framework."[2]
- In May 2006 the Senate did precisely that, passing a bipartisan measure whose coverage of the immigration issue was more comprehensive than the legislation passed in the House. The Senate Bill, proposed by Republican Senators Martinez and Hagel, divided illegal immigrants by length of stay. It allowed those here for over five years to pursue citizenship after paying

a fine and back taxes, and passing an English language test and a background check. It sent home illegal immigrants here for less than two years, while allowing those here for more than two years but less than five privileged access to green cards distributed from specially created "ports of entry" back in their home country. The Senate Bill also proposed fence building – 370 miles of it along the Mexican border – and a guest-worker program admitting 400,000 guest-workers a year.

- Between the two, 2006 saw a proposal from the then president Bush to give temporary guest-worker status to 325,000 foreign nationals a year while also sending 6,000 National Guard troops temporarily to the southern border. It saw another, from Senator Arlen Specter, to create a three-year guest-worker program, with workers free to stay for three additional years if they so wished; and yet another – a so-called no amnesty guest-worker program – from Representative Mike Pence, requiring even long-standing "illegals" to briefly leave the country, register as temporary workers, and return: a kind of "self-deportation," with the prospect of US citizenship still there, but way down the line. But eventually it was the House Bill, amended in committee but still with its 700 miles of fence, that was sent to the President for signature in the dying moments of the 109th Congress.

At stake in these various legislative proposals was neither the volume nor the internal composition of *legal* immigration, though the scale and character of that did loom large in the background of this dispute for some of its participants. The hot button issues this time were *illegal immigration* and *border security* – primarily border security to our south. And unlike other debates discussed in this volume, this was not a fight that primarily pitted Republicans against Democrats. Here the major line of cleavage lay, and still lies, inside the parties themselves, particularly inside the Republican Party. On this issue, more than on any other in recent times, right-wing elements within the broad conservative coalition have mobilized *against* their own liberal wing and against their own national leadership. In consequence, this is also a debate in which you find real bitterness – angry accusations of "betrayal," "cowardice" and "sell out" as well as of "error" – from anti-immigration forces whose general argument takes the following shape.

1. The US border is porous, allowing in a flood of immigrants

By common consent, the number of people currently in the US without proper papers and documentation is at least 12 million,[3] with more arriving daily. Perhaps as many as 3 million in 2004 alone, if Michael Savage is right – enough, as he put it, to fill "22,000 Boeing 737-700 airliners, or sixty flights every day for a year."[4] This, in the context of what some are calling "the second great migration": one similar in scale to the wave of immigration around 1900 that created the modern American population profile. The two great migrations are said to be both similar and different. They are said to be similar, in that both altered the number of foreign-born people living here. The current migration has taken that figure from one-in-twenty in 1970 to one-in-eight now. The two are also different, in that the first great migration was regulated in ways that the current one is not. Unlike last time, at least one-third of America's current foreign-born population is here illegally. The flow of illegal immigrants may not be as large as Michael Savage suggests – the average annual figure often cited is nearer 500,000 – but it does have the geographical focus he mentions: namely Mexico. One-third of all foreign-born persons in the US are currently Mexican; "over half of all Mexicans in the United States are illegal immigrants; and in the last decade 80 to 85 percent of the inflow of Mexicans into the US has been illegal."[5]

These people are entering illegally because legal immigration is controlled by tight quotas – quotas of skill, and quotas of global region – that fail to match the number of people from Mexico wanting to move north. Existing legislation allows for 19 million extra legal immigrants over the next two decades. Critics of the Martinez-Hagel Senate Bill say that, had it passed, that number would have risen by a factor of 5: not 19 million by 2026, but probably 103 million.[6] Even bleaker scenarios put the figure higher still – 200 million is sometimes mentioned – but even when more conservative projections prevail, the point is clear. The US is said to be facing demographic change of an unprecedented scale, one that will permanently alter the ethnic and cultural makeup of the entire population. It is also said to be facing a mass challenge to the legality and effectiveness of its immigration codes. In trying to block that change/challenge, critics vary in what they emphasize. All are troubled by the scale of illegal immigration and want it stopped. But many on the Right are concerned about the scale of immigration, period, and want some kind of moratorium on entry to the United States, illegal or otherwise.

2. It is not just a matter of numbers. We are actually letting in the wrong kind of immigrant

Critics concerned with the scale of immigration as well as its legality also worry about the proportion of unskilled workers, relative to skilled ones, in existing immigration flows. They point to the tight limits set on the number of skilled workers allowed into the United States, in a policy mix that allows family members of existing immigrants to enter, regardless of the skills they bring/lack. Where is the economic sense, these critics say, in inflating the pool of the unskilled and the poor, in a world in which economic competitiveness turns on the quality of human capital, and in which social inequality only fuels urban tensions. After all, "if low-skill workers were the key to economic growth, Mexico would be an economic powerhouse, and impoverished Americans would be slipping south over the Rio Grande."[7] Opening doors to what Michael Savage called "a deluge of human flotsam and jetsam"[8] may well have made sense in the past, when manual labor and semiskilled industrial workers were the bedrock of American economic growth. But we now live in a world of intense competition between knowledge-based industries, a world in which the average skill level of a labor force can make the critical difference between global success and failure. Of course, not all the conservative critics of current immigration policy favor privileging even skilled immigrants. Some think the skilled should be excluded too, to give home-grown American scientists a chance;[9] but there is widespread agreement among critics of current immigration policy that leaving the door open to the global poor no longer makes any kind of sense. "H-1B Workers: Highly Skilled, Highly Needed" was how the Heritage Foundation chose to pitch their immigration policy in 2008. Congress should do more than seal the border. It "should raise the cap on H-1B visas."[10]

Shipping in the unskilled does more than undermine competitiveness. It is also said to intensify income inequality. According to Francis Fukuyama at least, "the growing inequality of American income distribution over the past decade is not . . . the result of Reagan-Bush tax policies or the failure of 'trickle-down' economics." It is caused by the excessive immigration of low-skilled Hispanic workers into the base of the US economy, displacing "blacks out of a variety of menial jobs, [and] adding to the woes of an already troubled black community."[11] *The arrival of unskilled labor in such volume is said only to compound problems of urban decay and white flight. Allowing them in no doubt eases the conscience of liberal elites, guilty that the US is so prosperous when the Third World is not; but it does nothing to solve the global income inequality that has liberals so distressed, and it forgets that the US is not responsible for the poverty of others – least of all the Mexicans. On the contrary, as former Congressman J. D. Hayworth had it, "one thing we can say for sure about Mexico's economy is that all of its problems are self-inflicted"; and that we do them, and ourselves, no favors by pretending other-wise. What Mexico needs now is not special privileges but a solid dose of "tough love"!*[12]

3. Such immigration threatens American national unity

Some of those critics – but critically not all of them – then go the extra inch, and raise objections to the places of origin of so many contemporary immi-grants, as well as to their lack of skills.

They argue that more than economics has changed in America, that the political context of immigration has changed as well; and that because it has, the rules of immigration now need to be reset. We live, they say, in a new age of political correctness, an age of multiculturalism, an era in which minorities within the United States have come to expect recognition and rights linked to their minority status rather than to their individual standing as citizens. Older immigrants came mainly from Europe. They left the old country behind, and arrived determined to assimilate, knowing that they had to, and that they would have to wait in line for the benefits of the new society to which they had come. They might not feel those benefits, but their children would. Things are different now. The new immigrants do not arrive from the same places. Nor do they arrive with the same expectations and flexibilities. They come from Asia, bringing completely different cultures and languages with them. They come from Mexico – so many from Mexico – not leaving their country so much as just slipping across its northern border. And these Mexican migrants do not come to assimilate. Many come to work, but many do not. They come to live off our welfare services, or even to recolonize land that was once Mexican: to pull the southern United States back into a Hispanic linguistic and social orbit from which it was wrenched by military force in the 1840s.[13] *They come in search of the good life, and they expect it now.*

In the worst fears of such critics, what we face in the contemporary United States is not the traditional melting pot of cultures subsumed into a common Americanism, but the emergence of an increasingly balkanized society riddled with ethnic tension – "the United States as a Bosnia of continental proportions"[14] – one in which illegal immigrants "get bumped ahead of everybody"[15] and in which Americans no longer even speak the same language. They fear that Mexican immigration without assimilation threatens to end the Anglo-Protestant cultural dominance on which, they claim, American greatness has been built.[16] California is already heavily bilingual. It will soon, Pat Buchanan says, be the United States' Quebec. In such a bleak scenario, "differences between legal and illegal immigrants fade into a generalized belief that a brown-skinned, Spanish-speaking tidal wave is about to swamp the white-skinned population of the United States."[17] This is not immigration, we are told. It is invasion: the creation of a nation within a nation, a gradual transformation of the American Southwest, California and Texas into a veritable "Republica del Norte." What Mexican soldiers could not hold by force in the nineteenth century, Mexican immigrants will take by stealth in the twenty-first. We need to recognize this, and resist it accordingly.

4. Illegal immigrants bring crime, disease and terrorism with them

When the criticism of existing immigration policy switches from issues of scale to issues of legality, the case being made switches with it. Then what we hear is that all illegal immigrants break the law by coming here, and all of them continue to break the law by staying. They are all, in that sense, genuinely criminals. And though the majority of them are not engaged in an active life of crime – most indeed come illegally simply to do honest work – among their number are active criminals, and post 9/11, active terrorists as well. Tom Tancredo has written of "the corruption that is spreading through the United States that is linked to Mexican-based drug cartels and the Mexican mafia . . . Some of the most violent criminals running loose in the United States," he tells us, "are illegal immigrants."[18] *Apparently, we are "in the middle of a mounting epidemic of preventable crime by illegal immigrants . . . Americans murdered, raped and assaulted by criminal illegal aliens."[19] The Mexican drug war is now bringing social carnage to a growing number of American cities.[20] This violence is "one of the largest causes of financial loss to emergency departments around the country," triggered as it is by illegal immigrants who also harbor (and so reintroduce) "fatal illnesses that American medicine fought and vanquished long ago, such as drug-resistant tuberculosis, malaria, leprosy, plague, polio, dengue and Chagas disease."[21]*

We are told that terrorist groups keen to enter the United States face lax security systems both north and south of us – Mexico and Canada both – and that the United States has a uniquely long and open border to police. According to Michael Savage, 190,000 illegal immigrants from countries other than Mexico "melted into the US population . . . during the first nine months of 2004" alone: "people from El Salvador, Nicaragua, Russia, China and Egypt, not to mention Iran and Iraq."[22] So "if Al Qaeda wanted to smuggle in a nuclear weapon, America's southern border is a very inviting place to start."[23] Add to that the proposal in Section 240d of the Senate Bill to prevent local law enforcement agents arresting aliens for civil violations, as distinct from criminal offenses, and the United States is poised to create what the Heritage Foundation's Kris Kobach has called a new "terrorist loophole."[24] Four of the 9/11 hijackers had been stopped for speeding before the attack, and could have been arrested by better-briefed police officers. Why take that law enforcement power away?

5. Illegal immigration costs the rest of us jobs and wages, taxes and space

Do not let anyone tell you that illegal immigrants make the rest of us prosperous by doing the grunt work that other Americans will not do, for wages that other Americans will not accept. The truth is entirely otherwise. Illegal immigrants take the jobs that native-born Americans would gladly do if they were offered to them, at wages that would be higher if immigration was less. Unemployment among adult Americans rose by 2.3 million between 2000 and 2004. The number of employed adult immigrants rose in the same period by exactly the same amount;[25] and even the Clinton Labor Department admitted that half the wage losses experienced by low-income Americans in the 1990s was caused by immigration. Mexican wage rates act as a weight, pulling down the wages of the rest of the labor force. Big agribusiness gets the benefit of cheap labor in its fields, but honest businesses suffer from unfair competition, and other workers suffer too. Their living standards are squeezed by the downward pressure released by illegal immigration on jobs and earnings economy-wide. Over the longer term, those same living standards are held back by slower rates of technological improvement in the industries whose costs low-immigrant wages subsidize. All American workers suffer, and the poor suffer most. Illegal immigration has undermined the capacity of African-Americans to realize the promise of the 1960s;[26] and legal immigrants from Mexico have suffered most of all, with their pace of assimilation and acceptance slowed by the illegal presence of huge numbers of their fellow country-men/women, from whom they find it so hard to differentiate themselves.

Illegal immigration creates poverty, not prosperity. It also overburdens social services and the American welfare state; and it fills up an already crowded American landscape. Illegal aliens and their children cost US taxpayers probably $10 billion a year in Medicaid, uninsured medical costs, aid to schools, food stamps, free school lunches and jail time. "The cost of providing free health care for illegal immigrants is one of the primary reasons the price of US health care continues to rise."[27] "Right now, 34 percent of all LEGAL Mexican immigrants are on welfare, and 25 percent of illegals are getting government assistance."[28] The pressure placed on the school systems and hospitals in areas of high illegal immigration is accordingly daunting. "Every year 65,000 illegal aliens graduate from our nation's schools. . . . who pays for that?" Michael Savage has asked. "The Mexican Government? Sorry Senor, You do and I do. . . . It's all part of the No Illegal Alien Left Behind program"[29] that is bleeding America dry. The folks in Washington might get their grass cut cheaply, and their laundry done, but the rest of us "are owed tens of billions of dollars in reparations from Mexico for feeding, clothing and providing health care for millions of illegal aliens over the last several decades."[30] It is time to stop the rot and get the money back.

6. This is a problem made in Washington, DC, and one that can be solved there

We have lost control of our borders, so the argument runs, because of politics in Washington. Outside the beltway, significant majorities of ordinary Americans want action on illegal immigration, and restrictions on the flow of migrants given green cards to work here legally. But not inside the beltway: there an unholy alliance of corporate interests, labor unions, and politicians seeking immigrant votes regularly combine to pass inadequate laws and to conspire against their full implementation. Border patrolling is regularly underfunded. Companies employing illegal immigrants are systematically ignored. Periodic amnesties for illegal immigrants are either proposed or passed. One passed – under Ronald Reagan himself – in 1986. It was presented as a solution to illegal immigration, but was actually a trigger to even more. Too often in Washington, leftists consumed with guilt about their own affluence turn a blind eye to the illicit arrival of the Mexican poor, and passionate free-traders argue for the dismantling of border controls, not just on goods and capital but on people too.

The Democratic Party has been the great sinner here. It relies heavily on the votes of recent legal migrants, and is unwilling to criminalize their family members by cracking down on those here without proper authorization or papers. Rush Limbaugh for one regularly reminds his listeners of what is afoot. According to him, they are "trying to recruit these people and legalize them on the spot just to make them voters."[31] They are trying to build a new constituency for big government.[32] But elements in the current Republican leadership are proving equally spineless on this matter – "running scared" as Rush Limbaugh has it, "pure cowardice in action":[33] "gutless" "country-club, blue-blood Rockefeller-type."[34] Republicans who also want that migrant vote and are prepared to surrender principle to get it. Not all of them, of course – certainly many House Representatives have an impressive and principled record on border and repatriation issues, and deserve the support of all right-thinking Americans. But since 2000 Senate Republicans have been a different matter. Their ranks have contained maverick and liberal elements with presidential ambitions. For Rush Limbaugh at least, liberal Republican Senators are definitely part of the problem, not part of the solution.

7. Any kind of amnesty is the wrong kind of solution

So what is the solution? Definitely not any kind of amnesty, nothing as soft and spineless as a $2000 fine and a compulsory English class! "Do not accept amnesty as the answer," the Heritage Foundation told the incoming Obama administration. "Those who enter, remain in, and work illegally are in ongoing and extension violation of our laws. This has a corrosive effect on civil society and undermines confidence in the immigration process and the rule-of-law

principles that govern our nation."[35] *To allow illegal immigrants to stay –
either unpunished or only moderately penalized – would send out completely
the wrong kind of signal. Far from ending illegal immigration, it would encourage it. It did in 1986, and it would again.*

*What we have to do is to close the border, stopping illegal immigration
altogether. In the short term, that means deploying the National Guard and
reinforcing border patrols. In the longer term, it means building an actual fence,
all along the United States' southern edge. Some bloggers have even suggested
that the Mexicans be invited to build the wall themselves, as a boost to their
own economy – so increasing the capacity of the Mexican Government "to
offer their people an incentive to stay home. A living wage springs to mind."
(This from Michael Savage.*[36]) *In addition, illegal immigrants already here
must be denied any access to schooling and health care, and the companies that
employ them must be heavily fined. If the demand for illegal labor is cut off in
this way, then the supply will dry up. And it will definitely dry up quicker if
people illegally in the United States are then rounded up and sent home. All
of them rounded up. All of them sent home. Not just those in the border states,
but every single one. Not everyone thinks that is practical – Rush Limbaugh
for one does not; and attrition, not mass deportation, is Pat Buchanan's policy
of choice*[37] – *but Tom Tancredo certainly does, and he is by no means alone in
that belief. "Those who don't go home," he told the House in December 2005,
"you deport."*[38]

A liberal response

So what could possibly by wrong with that? This much at least.

1. You don't have to be a Democrat to disagree with Tom Tancredo

All you have to be is a Republican like George W. Bush, and recognize
that "it is neither wise nor realistic to round up millions of people,
many with deep roots in the United States, and send them across the
border."[39] Not only is it not wise, it is not practical or politically
expedient either. You cannot build a 2,000-mile fence; and even if
you did root out every illegal immigrant, all you would end up with

would be 12 million versions of what Congressman Pence referred to as "the horrific images in the world press the night Elian Gonzalez was taken into custody." Which is why Pence, and many Republicans more liberal than he, believe that "this idea of putting everybody on buses and conducting a mass deportation is a non-starter."[40]

Even if it were not – even if somehow all illegal immigrants could be expelled – the resulting economic fallout would be catastrophic. "The economics are simple," New York City's Republican mayor has argued. "We need more workers than we have,"[41] and we rely on immigration to provide them. According to liberal and libertarian Republicans, there are powerful forces of supply and demand at work here, forces which make border security counterproductive, if used alone. "Coercive efforts to keep willing workers out" have not only "spawned an underground culture of fraud and smuggling," the Cato Institute told the 108th Congress, and "caused hundreds of unnecessary deaths in the desert." They have also "disrupted the traditional circular flow of Mexican migration, perversely *increasing* the stock of illegal Mexican workers and family members in the United States."[42] Michael Bloomberg made the same point even more graphically when appearing before members of the 109th Congress. "It's as if we expect border control agents to do what a century of communism could not: defeat the natural market forces of supply and demand and defeat the natural human desire for freedom and opportunity. You might as well sit on your beach chair and tell the tide not to come in."[43]

In any event, the tide is currently going out. Of late, the demand and supply conditions surrounding illegal immigration have changed significantly. The industries habitually employing illegal workers – construction, leisure and agriculture – have all been severely affected by the financial meltdown. Demand for illegal workers is currently falling. Unemployment among even legal Latino immigrants is currently rising sharply. The Pew Hispanic Center reported Latino unemployment up by 2.9 percentage points in 2008, as against a 2.0 percentage point rise for the US labor force as a whole.[44] Pew researchers also reported illegal immigration numbers as down and falling: a flow of 500,000 in 2007, as compared to an annual average rate of 800,000 earlier in the decade; and by August 2008 possibly a 1.3 million reduction in the overall total of illegal immigrants here – a reduction of 11 percent from the August 2007 peak.[45] The volume of dollar remittances back to Mexico is a good proxy for the number of illegal Latino immigrant workers in the United States. Those remittances slowed substantially in the first half of 2008,[46] and presumably slowed even more as general unemployment rose sharply in the wake of the September 2008 credit crisis.

2. Patrolling the border of Pat Buchanan's mind?

None of that satisfies Pat Buchanan, of course, because he sees amnesty lurking in the detail of any guest-worker program, and "loss of country," as he puts it, in any proposal for comprehensive immigration reform. But then Pat Buchanan has a very particular view of what is actually going on here, a view that can and should be challenged in at least the following ways.

The present immigration situation is neither as threatening nor as novel as he would have it. Certainly in terms of scale the proportion of foreign-born people in the United States – at 12.7 percent in 2004 – is still lower than in 1890, when that included several of Pat Buchanan's German and Scots/Irish ancestors.[47] The United States has survived this scale of immigration before – it survived the arrival of the Buchanans, after all – and it will do so again. Moreover, there is nothing unusual in people coming to work in the United States, and then going home. That was a common feature of Mexican immigration in particular, from the end of the Mexican–American War right through to the passing of the 1965 Act. It was that act's specification, for the first time, of a quota for Mexican migrants that inadvertently triggered this new phenomenon of the illegal Mexican immigrant. Pat Buchanan would have us understand this flow of predominantly Latin American migration as something intensely alien to an American culture rooted in Western values; yet in reality the bulk of those migrants come from former Spanish colonies. They come, like him, with Roman Catholicism as their religion.[48] They come with strong family values and a powerful work ethic. Pat Buchanan is also highly critical of the decline of US morality and popular culture, and yet criticizes immigrants for not assimilating into it. He would surely do better, from a conservative perspective, to welcome this addition to the bloc of social forces uneasy with abortion on demand, gay rights and explicit sexuality. What Mexican immigration brings isn't "alien behavior. It's admirable behavior, the antidote to the excessive individualism that social conservatives decry."[49] How else did Prop 8 pass in California in November 2008, except with the solid support of Latino voters?

3. Getting the history right

To those who would contrast an old-style melting pot America with a future of Balkanized ethnic tension, we should ask for the restraint of historical accuracy. Ethnic – and indeed racial – tension has been, and remains, central to the American story. Try asking Native-Americans if the old-style melting pot was one in which the newly arrived Europeans assimilated into existing native Indian culture. Try asking the descendants of African slaves if those who arrived first set the cultural tone for those who arrived later. After all, Black America was here long before Irish America, Italian America or Polish America: and the very choice of those three major ethnic groups in the United States should remind us that, to the degree that Samuel Huntington and others describe American culture as Anglo-Saxon and Protestant, they write out of the American story, among other things, Catholicism, the Romance languages and European Jewry.[50] There is nothing new in this nativist fear of cultural change linked to immigration, or in the politics of "last man in, shut the door." Benjamin Franklin expressed that same fear in 1751 about the arrival of Germans in Philadelphia.[51] But they assimilated. They did not initially speak English, but within three generations they were bilingual. In fact, German settlers in the mid-west reportedly maintained bilingual public school systems until World War I made it impolitic to do so; and by that measure, current immigrants and their children are actually learning English "faster than their predecessors [did] a hundred years ago."[52]

Mexican immigrants are not qualitatively different in this regard, just newer in the immigration cycle. The data we have does suggest higher rates of bilingualism among current second-generation Hispanic immigrants than among European immigrants of the first great wave; but it also shows that by the third generation, English-speaking predominates in all Hispanic households.[53] People at the bottom of

English-speaking social structures *have* to learn English to make progress up them. The German immigrants certainly did. The Mexicans will no doubt follow suit. The only thing that will block the rapid assimilation of Mexican immigrants into mainstream American life − if that is the outcome we want − is the very hostility to their presence here that the politics of the Right encourage. The only thing that will hold more of them here than actually wish to remain is the difficulty of going back and forth across the very wall being built to keep the rest out; and the only thing that will keep them poor − and a burden on the welfare state − is discrimination against them in American labor markets. If we want the new wave of immigrants to assimilate, all we have to do is to let them: and as we do so, we too will change. Streets run in two directions, after all, and they always work best when their lanes are open to traffic moving both ways. What would America be today if an earlier generation of Pat Buchanans had frozen US culture in the mind-set of the 1840s? At the very least, it would be racist, homophobic, anti-Catholic and anti-Semitic. Immigration is one of the things America does best, and cultural change is one of the *positive* benefits of the American immigration story. We need to recognize that, and celebrate it.

4. Framing the issue the Columbus way!

Mexican immigrants − at least in the hands of the more strident defenders of the American border − stand condemned for bringing disease, crime and terror to the American heartland; as though *guns, germs and steel*[54] are not central to the entire American story. Christopher Columbus was not a legal immigrant, as far as I'm aware; and though he went back to Spain twice after "discovering" America − a pattern of return of which many "no amnesty" advocates would doubtless approve − he did not leave these shores because he could not get a green card. He went home to restock, the better to seize more American land in the name of Imperial Spain when next he returned. Indeed there is something particularly ridiculous about the current claim of an impending Mexican "Reconqista" when you think back to what has actually happened in North America since Columbus turned up. Over that intervening period, the USA was

expanded by conquest and held united by war. From the very beginning, "the building of America" was a national project with a fair
degree of ethnic cleansing at its core, not to mention a large slice
of slavery on the side. Anyway, there is just no credible evidence of
any Mexican plan to retake the American southwest – historically, the
urban and rural poor have never been an independent imperial force,
and Mexican workers are unlikely to break that pattern – but the
rhetoric which sometimes surfaces among Mexican radicals is understandable nonetheless. The American southwest *is* itself a product of
conquest; and we would do well to at least acknowledge that, before
raising the fear of an impending invasion by forces that actually exist
only in the imagination of the paranoid few.

As for disease and terror, how more American could the story be?
When the Mayflower arrived off Cape Cod in November 1620, its
capacity successfully to land its tiny band of exhausted pilgrims was
entirely the product of the prior arrival of European diseases which
had all but decimated the local Indian forces that might otherwise
have repelled them.[55] And as we now know – but tend not to mention in polite conversation – in the century and a half after 1492, a
staggering 95 percent of the pre-Columbian native American population fell victim to deadly European diseases – either by direct contact or indirectly via contact with infected tribes[56] – so that European
settlement largely expanded into areas left empty by American versions
of the Black Death.[57] True, European settlers brought superior weap-
onry, and that was important; but the most vital thing they brought
were killer illnesses. They traded smallpox, measles, influenza, typhus,
even bubonic plague – for syphilis. Not a pleasant trade, it must be
said, but a trade on such a scale as to render current claims about
Mexican immigrants overusing local hospitals trivial by contrast.

Moreover, it is neither legitimate nor helpful to collapse together
the Mexican drug war and the issue of illegal immigration from
Mexico, or to suggest that building a wall to keep out illegal immigrants will keep out Mexican drug cartels as well. It will not. Drugs,
drug-related crime and drug-linked gang membership collectively
constitute a growing American problem, one of concern both to
indigenous law enforcement here in the United States and to the
leaders of recently arrived Latino communities. But it is a problem
which is predominantly *indigenous* in origin, and whose drivers cannot

be reduced to anything so simple as one country's drug cartels, however ghastly those cartels may be. For drugs do not arrive here by accident. Not are they forced on a reluctant American population. On the contrary, as Hillary Clinton said so clearly in Mexico City in March 2009, it is "our insatiable demand for illegal drugs [that] fuels the drug trade" and it is "our inability to prevent weapons from being illegally smuggled across the border to arm these criminals [that] causes the deaths of police officers, soldiers and civilians."[58] To stop the drug trade, we need to stop the illegal demand for drugs from legal US citizens. To stop fueling the drug war, we need to cut off the illegal flow of American guns supplied by legal US citizens. There is illegality here. There is a flow across the border; but the illegality is anchored more in American demand and American guns than it is in Mexican immigration; and the flow is one that begins with demand and guns moving south before the drugs move north. The forces creating the drug problem are predominantly home grown ones. They will not be terminated by demonizing the flow of hardworking, nondrug-taking Mexican immigrants into the base of the American labor market, and we need to say so.

5. Let's not be so quick to discount the benefits of immigration

Michael Savage would have us believe that the Mexican Government owes ordinary Americans a big reparation check, because of all the expenses imposed on the rest of us by the presence of so many immigrants, legal or otherwise. But this really is to count with one eye open and one eye shut. Ledgers always have two columns, and before we can judge the debit side, we need a list of assets too.

There is a clear scholarly consensus – even among economists troubled by the impact of immigration on wage levels – that in overall terms immigration brings positive benefits to the society in total. Quite how much is hard to quantify: the National Academy of Sciences in 1997 thought it might be a $1–10 billion gain in an $8 trillion economy.[59] No serious argument is currently circulating that immigration by professionals and skilled workers is other than entirely desirable. Roy Beck apart, the general consensus seems to be that their presence here directly enhances the competitiveness of US industry, and contributes to technological growth, labor productivity and rising general standards of life. Illegal immigration is more problematic, of course: but at the very least, it visibly provides labor to a number of important American industries which would otherwise experience serious labor shortages, and industries whose costs are significantly reduced by the immigrant presence.[60] The American consumer clearly benefits from these lower costs: cheaper housing costs, food costs, costs of domestic service. The bigger question is whether those benefits come with a price: the price of higher unemployment and lower wages for that section of the native-born labor force whose skills and employment prospects are similar to the immigrants' own.

In periods of rapid growth – such as those enjoyed by the US economy in the 1990s – that question tends to be buried, as immigration, rising real wages and falling unemployment all go easily together. But in periods of recession and jobless growth it tends to reappear, and the argument is heard again that immigrants take American jobs. But the best research data we have would suggest that the concern, though understandable, is misplaced: because the kinds of jobs on which competition is fiercest are likely to remain plentiful over time, and because the skill sets of immigrants and native-born workers are likely to continue to be different. The Labor Department's own employment projections anticipate the creation of an additional 7.7 million unskilled jobs in the US economy in the first decade of the new century, with more to come in the decades to follow.[61] Those will be decades in which the indigenous population will continue to age and become more educated, and for both those reasons become less willing and less suitable to fill jobs at the bottom of the employment food chain. That unwillingness and lack of suitability is already in place: currently there is a significant mismatch between the skills of unemployed Americans and the skill-requirements of the jobs taken by undocumented Mexican workers.[62] That mismatch is likely to continue, because in general the shape of the skill distribution among immigrants is hour-glassed: immigrants arrive with either very high skills or very low ones. The skills of most native-born

Americans are, and are likely to remain, more middle-range in kind. Immigration doesn't threaten that indigenous skill pattern. It actually complements it.

6. The thorny question of wages

The issue of immigration and wages is more difficult to resolve. Here there is a genuine academic dispute. It is not a dispute about the impact of high-skill immigrants on professional wages. Immigrants with professional skills tend to be among America's highest earners. No, the argument is focused elsewhere: on the impact of the presence of so many unskilled workers on the earning capacity of indigenous labor, similarly unskilled. The most quoted study here – by George Borjas and colleagues at Harvard – suggests a 3 percent reduction in average wages between 1980 and 2000 because of immigration; and a cut in wages for high-school dropouts of around 8 percent.[63] But such calculations have long been questioned by economists using different methodologies and data, and "many studies continue to find no effect or only weak negative effects of immigration on low-skilled workers or workers in general."[64] David Card's early work, for example, on the Mariel Boatlift – the unexpected influx of 125,000 Cubans into southern Florida in 1980 – found no adverse impact on Miami wages, even among earlier unskilled Cuban arrivals. His later research confirmed his general thesis: "overall, evidence that immigrants have harmed the opportunities of less educated natives is scant."[65] Gianmarco Ottaviano and Giovanni Peri, in a recent and widely cited research paper, have the impact of immigration on American wages as actually *positive*. Counterintuitive as it may seem, they calculated that in the 1990s the average wage of native-born workers increased by 2–2.5 percent because of immigration, that the inflow lowered the real wage of native workers without a high-school [diploma] by 1 percent, but increased the real wage of native workers with at least a high-school [diploma] by as much as 3–4 percent overall.[66]

Factor in the extra demand created by the wages of illegal workers. Factor in additions to the capital stock. Factor in the high concentration of illegal labor in just a limited number of industries; and suddenly the general impact of immigration on indigenous wages begins to look more benign. The most we can safely say here is that if the flow of illegal immigrants does indeed hit the earning capacity of the indigenous unskilled, it does so only at the margin, and only in specific industries. And if we are concerned about that margin – and we ought to be, since we're talking about the poorest of all American workers – then excluding immigrants is definitely not the quickest way to fix it. The quickest way to fix poverty, among both indigenous and immigrant American labor alike, is to raise significantly the minimum wage and to improve by legislation the working conditions of the very low-paid.

Ultimately there is only one certain way to determine whether illegal immigrants are, or are not, doing jobs that native-born Americans would want for themselves if those jobs were properly rewarded; and that is to ensure that those jobs *are* indeed properly paid. Raise the minimum wage. Send in the factory inspectors. Block off the super-exploitation of both illegal immigrants and the indigenous poor simultaneously; and do it, not by criminalizing immigrants, but by criminalizing those who so cruelly exploit both groups of vulnerable workers. Epiphanies are always wonderful things to watch: so seeing the Republican Right suddenly concerned with the wages of the lowest paid – particularly the wages of African-American men – is genuinely touching! But let us see just how deep and genuine that concern actually is. Let us see Republicans bringing in or supporting legislation that really will stop illegal immigrants undercutting local wages: legislation, that is, that fines/jails the employers who pay less than a much-improved minimum wage,[67] rather than attacking people struggling to keep body and soul together as they work long hours in appalling conditions for a mere pittance.

7. Illegal immigration and the welfare burden?

Conservative critics of the current influx of particularly Spanish-speaking immigrant labor regularly bewail the impact of that influx on America's social infrastructure – particularly on its hospitals, its schools and its jails. You remember Michael Savage's question – about who pays for all this "welfare." His answer, of course, was that we do – that the tab is picked up by honest American taxpayers. He was partially correct. Only partially: he was quite wrong on jails. The Latino population is *underrepresented* in the US prison population, relative to its proportion in the US population as a whole. But on schools – yes: right now the children of immigrants from Mexico do get more help with school meals and medical cover than the American average: and there is more going out from public coffers to support their families than the immigrants are putting in. But that imbalance is not primarily the result of them being here illegally, or being Mexican. It exists because they are newly arrived, badly paid and poor; and there is nothing particularly new or shocking in that.

The newly arrived have always been poor in the US immigration story. When the Irish, the Italians, the Germans and the Poles arrived – they too arrived poor. Their children avoided burdening the US welfare state not because there was something particularly superior about late nineteenth-century European immigrants, or something particularly feckless about contemporary Mexican ones. The earlier generations of the immigrant poor did not burden the US welfare state because there was *no* welfare state to burden. They and their children lived initially in levels of squalor that none of us ought now to wish upon anyone; dependent on charities and political parties for help with employment, housing and health because no public institutions existed to provide those vital early supports to them. No doubt there was an imbalance of payment then too – the charities giving more to the newly arrived poor than the poor gave back to them. But over time – through education and individual effort – those immigrants and their children raised their skill levels and their earning capacity. Over time they did get to a point at which they could begin to contribute more to the welfare-support of others than they took in welfare-support for themselves. That is already happening again now, among the second generation of this most recent influx of poor immigrants; and it will go on happening. If Mexican-Americans currently draw slightly more heavily on the US welfare system than do Americans in general, that is a temporary condition. Assimilation and spreading affluence among the newcomers will solve it. The denial of basic services, and mass deportations, most definitely will not.

In any case, many conservative critics of excessive immigration also regularly bewail the absence of sufficient workers to sustain the baby boomers in their retirement. Yet immigration – both legal and illegal – is by far the most effective source of that extra necessary labor. Tom Tancredo blames illegal immigrants for rising health costs. The claim is, at best, shortsighted. The immediate burden illegal immigrants place on local welfare services, though undeniably heavy in certain localized areas, is both temporary and solvable with federal help.[68] The long-term assistance those same immigrants can provide to those same welfare services will be permanent and more general. For the median age of American workers is currently 34. By 2025 it will be 43; as former Commerce Secretary Gutierrez recently put it, "every 60 seconds, a baby boomer turns 60." We are running out of workers, and in this we are not alone. All developed industrial societies currently need more labor, and more babies. All of them – the European Union and Japan alike – are recalibrating their immigration laws to meet that need; and as Gutierrez said, relative to them, "we have an incredible advantage here. We can stand out from the pack by using our well-honed skills from 230 years of assimilating immigrants."[69] Between 2000 and 2004, the US population grew by 12 million. More than 5 million of those were immigrants. The age and fertility profile of those immigrants was significantly younger and more active than that of America as a whole; and the skill levels and educational performance of their children is already on the rise.[70] Their presence here offers the promise of an enhanced stock of able-bodied workers in the decades to come; so if Republican legislators also try to shut them out as they bewail the welfare crisis, it is hard to avoid the conclusion that – though the critics of Mexican immigration presumably want, like the rest of us, more workers and babies to sustain them in their old age – they want that sustenance to be provided by workers with a particular color of skin.

8. Shades of Ross Perot

The Michael Savages of this world are naive to propose, as a solution to the flow of Mexican labor, that the Mexican Government give their people a living wage; and they are also misguided if they imply that only corruption in Mexican politics is preventing that from happening. Leaving aside the inconsistency of argument here – with

Michael Savage advocating more government management of the Mexican economy while decrying government interference with the economy at home – the whole proposal ignores the legacy of two centuries of economic underdevelopment. Contemporary Mexican politicians and workers, like their equivalents everywhere, are constrained by the past. Living standards in Mexico and the US were not that different in 1776, but they are now because the nineteenth-century Mexican economy failed to grow as fast as the American one. No one alive today is to blame for that nineteenth-century failure. They just have to operate within the limited amount of industrialization and infrastructure that it left in place, an amount that all through the twentieth century triggered a regular and steady flow of Mexican labor north, to work in the agricultural businesses of the American Southwest. That flow of labor was genuinely migratory, in the main coming north and going south with the seasons.[71] It was also a flow that paid the real price of underdevelopment: destitution at home, and appalling working conditions on the road. Those leading the charge against contemporary Mexican migration often present the US worker or taxpayer as the real loser in the immigration story. They should try being a Latino migrant working long hours for low wages in an American chicken factory, or a Mexican child left behind by parents going north in search of a better life.[72] Losing a tax dollar is one thing, losing a parent is quite another!

Anyway, Mexican workers do not hold the prime responsibility for the changed pattern and volume of their migration into North America. That responsibility lies with the North American Free Trade Agreement (NAFTA). The Mexican economy had been a success story in the 1950s and 1960s – growing *faster* even than the Japanese economy for most of that period – behind policies of import-substitution and oil exploration. But by the later 1980s Mexico had gone through a major oil-based debt crisis and a policy shift to free trade – one that culminated in Mexican participation in the NAFTA in 1994. That agreement (among other things) progressively and incrementally exposed modestly subsidized Mexican agriculture to competition from heavily subsidized US agribusiness.[73] In 2002 Oxfam estimated the average rural subsidy/farmer in Mexico to be just $720 a year, whereas in the United States it was $20,800;[74] and as the two subsidy systems interacted, the Mexican elite may have benefited, but in general Mexican farm incomes began to fall. They fell at a rate of 4.3 percent per year throughout the 1990s.[75] A new iron triangle then opened up. Tax dollars flowed out from Washington to the American West – $180 billion dollars worth in the 2002 Agriculture Bill alone, mainly going to big companies.[76] Ever greater volumes of their subsidized agrarian produce then flowed south across the border, threatening the living standards of the 20+ percent of the Mexican population still working in agriculture; and in consequence Mexican workers left the countryside in ever greater numbers – maybe 2 million in total since 1994 – with some then finding work in US factories at the border, but others moving even further north, unable to sustain themselves at home.

We need to remember that the great flows of permanent immigration from Mexico that so concern Pat Buchanan are of very recent origin. In the 1980s, before the signing of NAFTA, illegal migration from Mexico averaged about 140,000 people a year, and the total undocumented population was fairly stable, at around 2.7 million. People came, and people went home. After the signing, by contrast, illegal immigration averaged anywhere between 500,000 and 800,000 people a year – the vast majority of whom did not go home. On the contrary, they stayed, to take the total number of illegal immigrants now in the United States up to its present level (of probably 11–12 million). *Two-thirds* of all undocumented workers now here actually arrived after 1994.[77] If the American Right want those flows to slow, and the Mexican economy to sustain (and retain) its own people, then the policy weapon to achieve it is in their hands. Instead of building a wall to keep Mexicans out, they should help the Obama administration turn off the tap: stop the subsidies to US farming that brings so many Mexicans here in the first place.[78] The Right doesn't like giveaways. So stop giving it away. Turn off the largesse given by Republican politicians to the agribusiness interests that sustain them. Live up to the Right's traditional antigovernment stance, and stop the public funding of *all* American industries, including the agrarian one. Then see what happens, over time, to migration flows. Successful farmers don't migrate – American farmers certainly don't, so why should Mexican ones!

9. Try not to make a bad situation worse

The golden rule of politics is normally this: if you are in a hole, the first thing you should do is stop digging. That rule needs to be applied here because we are genuinely in a hole. The critics of illegal immigration are entirely correct on that. Illegal immigration does present us with a cluster of genuine problems which public policy must at the very least *not* make worse. It is clearly undesirable to have 12 million people in the United States without authorization and proper documentation. Their presence does indeed call into question the effectiveness and legitimacy of the entire legal system. But it is also clearly undesirable to see those same people then exposed, as a result of their illegal status, to terrible wages and working conditions, open to super-exploitation by unscrupulous employers and forced to live a subterranean life without adequate access to legal protection for themselves and their families. Nor should we be happy with a situation in which heavy pressure is placed on schools and hospitals in border states, and on honest taxpayers there; or with people waiting abroad for green cards being passed in line by those who slipped across the border undetected. And since those illegal immigrants are generally paid so badly, we should not be happy either with a situation in which they are forced to live in poverty, and in which their willingness to work for so little then makes whatever contribution it does – big or small – to poverty wages for others. As Michael Dukakis has recently noted, currently "millions of illegal immigrants work for minimum and even sub-minimum wages in workplaces that don't come close to meeting health and safety standards."[79] That is clearly something that we need to end.

Illegality, exploitation, differential welfare-use, wage pressure and queue-jumping are all real problems. They are just not problems that will be solved by criminalizing the people caught up in them. Putting up a wall will not stop the flow. People can always get round walls. It certainly will not keep out terrorists. None of the 9/11 terrorists slipped into the United States across the Rio Grande, and there is no reason to suppose that the next lot will either. Anyway, only half of all illegal immigrants entering the United States do so across the Mexican border, so how many walls are we proposing to build?[80] All a wall, or a set of walls, would do is cost a very large amount of money,[81] and break the circularity of migration by stopping those already here from easily returning home. Criminalizing illegal immigration, and deporting illegal immigrants whenever they are found, would simply add to those costs[82] while driving those immigrants further underground. It would add hugely to the fear and stresses they already carry, and it would leave them even more vulnerable to exploitation by their employers. And any mass deportation would almost inevitably backfire, and at some speed – certainly in public relations terms, but probably in economic ones as well. In a place like Arizona, for example, the spending power of illegal immigrants is already a significant component in the local structure of demand for goods and services – outstripping that of even highly paid physicians by a factor of 2.5:1 – and across the country as a whole, large-scale deportations would inevitably create acute labor shortages (and associated price hikes) in industries as disparate as leisure and entertainment, construction and agriculture, cleaning and food preparation.

To then compound the mass deportation of illegal immigrants by also denying basic welfare services to their children and dependents would be simply inhumane and profoundly un-American. Is anyone actually proposing that hospitals literally dump people without papers on the streets? Any guest-worker system put in place in the wake of that dumping would run counter to the American tradition of granting eventual citizenship to those who enter legally and work. Indeed, if that new guest-worker system tied workers to specific jobs, and made eventual citizenship dependent on employer support, it would only increase guest-worker vulnerability to exploitation. And if it were to be applied to Mexican immigrants alone – if it became a kind of second *Bracero* program – its creation would only institutionalize and exacerbate the racism that is currently slowing the assimilation of existing Latino immigrants. You cannot split the Mexican-American population into two, and force one half to go back to Mexico, without turning the other half into second-class citizens in the country from which you have just expelled their important family members: so it would be entirely counterproductive to try.

10. So what should we do?

The only way out of this impasse is to separate its immediate participants from the processes generating their contemporary plight, and then to deal with each half of the problem in different ways.[83]

We should start by celebrating the contribution made by even illegal immigrants to contemporary American prosperity. We should celebrate their capacity for the hard work that sustains basic services, their willingness to live in (and revive) depressed urban areas, their propensity to spread out beyond the normal "big six" immigrant states into every corner of the United States,[84] and their commitment to the building of strong families, powerful churches and stable communities of a traditional American kind. We should accordingly support programs of registration that allow immigrants already here to build up entitlements to citizenship – that is, we should support a general amnesty – paralleling that with a quickening and expansion of the flow of legal immigration from Latin America during the period through which the amnesty holds. And we should protect the integrity of the amnesty by limiting the flow of family members allowed in after citizenship to immediate relatives, and by setting a clear end point: a moment after which anyone unregistered would be deported, and any employer giving work to the unregistered would be heavily penalized. In other words, we should bring the existing flow of illegal migrants into the orbit of law, and use the legal system to turn off *demand* for such illegal workers in the future. Walls will not keep people out, but a properly funded and adequately computerized system of social security numbers certainly can. Its creation should be a common rallying point for all the nonracist players in the contemporary immigration drama – since it is visibly in the common interests of honest employers, native-born workers and legalized immigrants alike.

But that is not all we should do. To get rid of an underclass – Mexican or otherwise – we have to do more than influence the social background and national origins of the people occupying its lowly positions in any particular generation. We have to get rid of the lowly positions themselves. To stop people competing for poverty wages, we need to do more than simply half the number of competitors, by sending those here illegally home. We also need to remove the poverty wages over which they compete when here, and the super-poverty wages from which those coming illegally are trying to escape. The first of those is easier to tackle than the second, but we need integrated programs that are capable of addressing them both. Poverty wages in the United States have to be legislated away by raising (and then enforcing) the national minimum wage, and by requiring that even workers on temporary work visas are paid no less than the prevailing wage paid to their native-born equivalents.[85] And over time, poverty wages back in Mexico have to be eased by removing any US-induced pressure to keep them down. At the very least, we need a significant reduction in public subsidies to large US agricultural companies, a reduction which will free public funds for much-needed antipoverty programs at home. Higher wages here will, of course, be a spur to further illegal immigration. That is why penalizing employers who use illegal immigrants will be so vital. But higher wages will also remove the need for a migrant labor force which survives by trading its low skills for low pay, and create instead an entirely different dynamic at the base of the US labor market. Putting a solid floor under the wages of low-skilled native-born *and* immigrant workers will enable the living standards of both groups to grow together, with all the positive social consequences of generalized affluence over time. The only way to protect the American Dream is to share it; and the best way to share it is to design public policy that allows everyone to dream together.

Notes

1. For a fuller discussion of the issues raised in this chapter, see David Coates and Peter Siavelis (editors), *Getting Immigration Right: What Every American Needs to Know*, Dulles, VA, Potomac Books, 2009.
2. David Martin, "Eight Myths about Immigration Enforcement," *Legislation and Public Policy*, vol. 10, no. 3, p. 528.
3. The estimates do vary, and the numbers are controversial. The Immigration service put the figure at 7 million for 2003; the US Census Bureau at 8.7 million for 2000; the Pew Hispanic Center estimates 11.5–12.0 million; Bear Stearns Asset Management had it at 20 million. For a fuller discussion, see Coates and Siavelis, *Getting Immigration Right*, pp. 3–6.
4. Michael Savage, *Liberalism is a Mental Disorder*, New York, Nelson Current, 2003, p. 60.
5. Robert Rector, "Amnesty and Continued Low-Skill Immigration Will Substantially Raise welfare Costs and Poverty," The Heritage Foundation *Backgrounder* No. 1936, May 16, 2006, p. 2.

6. Robert Rector, *Senate Immigration Bill* . . . The Heritage Foundation, Web memo 1076, May 15, 2006. The Cato Institute, by contrast, dismisses these numbers as not even passing the "laugh test." Cato's argument is that the Heritage Foundation is exaggerating the numbers of temporary workers who will stay, and draw relatives after them. (For the disagreement, see the Cato Website May 30, 2006, and the Heritage Foundation Website June 5, 2006: also chapters 11 and 12 of Coates and Siavelis, *Getting Immigration Right*)

7. *Welcome to Rush 24/7*, April 4, 2006.

8. Michael Savage, *Liberalism is a Mental Disorder*, p. 60.

9. See, for example, Roy Beck, *The Case against Immigration*, New York, W. W. Norton, 1996, pp. 136–55. It is significant in this regard that early in 2009 Senator Chuck Grassley (R-Iowa) urged Microsoft to first dismiss foreign workers on H1B visas if down-sizing became necessary, saying that "Microsoft has a moral obligation to protect . . . American workers by putting them first during these difficult economic times" (*Financial Times*, February 2, 2009, p. 2).

10. Heritage Foundation Web memo no. 1916, May 6, 2008. The cap on such visas in 2007 was 65,000 – well down on the 195,000 cap in 2000. Issued on a single day in 2007, they attracted over 120,000 applicants!

11. Francis Fukuyama, "Immigration and Family Values," in Nicolaus Mills, *Arguing Immigration*, New York, Simon and Schuster, 1994, p. 166.

12. J. D. Hayworth, *Whatever It Takes: Illegal Immigration, Border Security and the War on Terror*, Washington, DC, Regnery Publishing Inc, 2006, p. 85.

13. Pat Buchanan calls it "La Reconqista" (see his *The Death of the West*, New York, Thomas Dunne books, 2002, p. 123).

14. Peter Duignan and Lewis Gann, *The Debate in the United States over Immigration*, Stanford, Hoover Institution Press, 1998, p. 38.

15. *Welcome to Rush 24/7*, March 31, 2006.

16. The key source here is academic rather than popular: Samuel Huntington's *Who Are We? The Challenge to America's National Identity*, New York, Simon and Schuster, 2004.

17. Leonard Zeskind, "The New Nativism," *American Prospect*, November 2005, p. A15.

18. Tom Tancredo, *In Mortal Danger*, Nashville, WND Books, 2006, pp. 82 and 157.

19. J. D. Hayworth, *Whatever It Takes*, p. 28.

20. Chuck Norris, *Mexico, Mafias and Baggy Borders*, Human Events Website, posted March 25, 2009.

21. Tom Tancredo, *In Mortal Danger*, p. 165, citing the research data of Madeleine Pelner Cosman.

22. Michael Savage, *Liberalism is a Mental Disorder*, pp. 61–2.
23. La Shawn Barber, reviewing J. D. Hayworth's *Whatever It Takes*, Townhall.com, February 21, 2006.
24. This in Robert D. Novak, *Immigration and Terrorism*, Townhall.com, July 6, 2006.
25. *Welcome to Rush 24/7*, May 5, 2005.
26. On this, see Roy Beck, *The Case against Immigration*, chapter 8.
27. Tom Tancredo, *In Mortal Danger*, p. 163.
28. BillOReilly.com, May 4, 2006.
29. Michael Savage, *Liberalism is a Mental Disorder*, p. 71.
30. Ibid., p. 84.
31. *Welcome to Rush 24/7*, April 12, 2006.
32. *Welcome to Rush 24/7*, May 26, 2005.
33. *Welcome to Rush 24/7*, April 3, 2006.
34. *Welcome to Rush 24/7*, June 21, 2006.
35. Jena Baker McNeill and James Jay Carafano, *Fixing Border Security and Immigration: A Memo to President-elect Obama*, Washington, DC, The Heritage Foundation, December 18, 2008.
36. Michael Savage, *Liberalism is a Mental Disorder*, p. 84.
37. Buchanan's "crucial steps" are these: "Build a fence along the 2,000-mile border to stop the flood. End welfare benefits to illegal aliens, except emergency medical treatment. Vigorously prosecute employers who hire illegals. Cease granting automatic citizenship to 'anchor babies' of illegals who sneak across the border to have them. Take care of mother and child; then put them on a bus back home. Turn off the magnets, and the illegals will not come. Cut off the benefits, and they will not stay. In five years, the crisis will be over" (Patrick J. Buchanan, *The Stealth Amnesty of Rep. Mike Pence*, WorldNetDaily, June 13, 2006).
38. Quoted on *BBC News*, December 17, 2005.
39. *Address to the Nation on Immigration Reform*, May 15, 2006.
40. Quoted in Lee P. Butler, *It's Amnesty Only if We Say It's Amnesty*, OpinionEditorials.com, June 28, 2006.
41. Michael Bloomberg, quoted in the *Washington Post*, July 6, 2006.
42. Cato Handbook for Congress, Cato Institute 2004, p. 638.
43. Quoted in the *New York Times*, July 20, 2006.
44. Pew Research Center, February 12, 2009.
45. For this data, see *New York Times*, July 31, 2008 and *Financial Times*, February 2, 2009.
46. Emily Garr, *As US Construction Slows, Remittances to Families in Mexico Decline*, Economic Policy Institute Snapshots, July 9, 2008.

47. It peaked at 14.7 percent in 1910 (see Coates and Siavelis, *Getting Immigration Right*, p. 3).

48. Pat Buchanan and the Pope are not together on this. When the Pope visited the US in April 2008 and urged protection for immigrant families, Tom Tancredo, for one, dismissed his remarks as "faith-based marketing" that "may have less to do with spreading the Gospel than they do about recruiting new members of the Church." Tancredo said it was "not in the Pope's job description to engage in American politics" (cited in the *New York Times*, April 20, 2008).

49. David Brooks, "Immigrants to be Proud of," *New York Times*, March 30, 2006.

50. On this, see Luis Frega and Gary Segura, "Culture clash? Contesting Notions of American Identity and the Effects of Latin American Immigration," APSR, *Perspectives on Politics*, vol. 4, no. 2, June 2006 , pp. 281–3.

51. See Luis Fraga and Gary Segura, "Latinos, Latino Immigrants and American National identity," in Coates and Siavelis, *Getting Immigration Right*, p. 63.

52. James Lindsay and Aubrey Singer, *Changing Faces: Immigrants and Diversity in the Twenty-First Century*, Washington, DC, Brookings Institution, 2003, p. 232.

53. For the data, see Richard Alba, "Mexican Americans and the American Dream," APSR, *Perspectives on Politics*, vol. 4, no. 2, June 2006, p. 291; Fraga and Segura, "Latinos, Latino Immigrants and American National identity," pp. 63–79; and Jacob Vigdor, *Measuring Immigration Assimilation in the United States*, Brownsville, Texas, Center for Civic Engagement, May 2008.

54. The title of Jared Diamond's prize-winning book, first published by W. W. Norton in 1997.

55. "From 1616 to 1619 what may have been bubonic plague introduced by European fishermen in modern Maine spread south along the Atlantic seaboard . . . killing as many as 90 percent of the region's inhabitants. Portals of coastal New England that had once been as densely populated as Western Europe were suddenly empty of people" (Nathaniel Philbrick, *Mayflower*, New York, Viking, 2006, p. 48).

56. Jared Diamond, *Guns, Germs and Steel*, New York, W. W. Norton, 2005, p. 78. See also Charles Mann, *1491*, New York, Knopf, 2005, pp. 100–4.

57. "Indian populations were falling almost everywhere: European diseases and European disruptions did deadly work, and a population estimated at 4 to 5 million before 1492 was tumbling toward half a million by the end of the eighteenth century" (Colin Calloway, *The Scratch of a Pen: 1763 and the Transformation of North America*, New York, Oxford University Press, 2006, p. 24).

58. Quoted in the *New York Times*, March 26, 2009.
59. For this, see David Coates, "The Economic Impact of Immigration," in Coates and Siavelis, p. 95.
60. Between 2000 and 2005, according to estimates from the Pew Hispanic Center, there were more than 1.4 million unauthorized workers in the construction industry, 1.2 million in leisure and hospitality. Agriculture had 110,000 (*The Labor Force Status of Short-Term Unauthorized Workers*, Fact Sheet, April 13, 2006). Unauthorized migrants made up 24 percent of all agricultural workers in 2005, 17 percent of all cleaners, 14 percent of all construction workers and 12 percent of all those employed in food preparation. Collectively, unauthorized migrants made up 4.9 percent of the civilian labor force in March 2005, some 7.2 million workers out of a total of 148 million (same source, March 7, 2006). An earlier study published by the Pew Hispanic Center put the number of unauthorized workers in agriculture much higher: at 1.2 million, or 47 percent of all wage-earners in the industry (this, by Philip Martin, March 21, 2002). Either way, the evidence suggests a big dependency in certain industries on undocumented labor, which then impacts costs in a way beneficial to consumers: lowering housing costs in North Carolina, for example, by an estimated 10 percent (*Winston-Salem Journal*, January 10, 2006, p. 1).
61. "Thousands of new jobs each year for low-skilled workers . . . in retail sales, food preparation, cleaning and janitorial services . . . agriculture, construction, and landscaping and grounds-keeping" (Daniel Griswold, *American Needs Real Immigration Reform*, Cato Institute Website, May 18, 2006).
62. The latest findings here are in David A. Jaeger, *Replacing the Undocumented Work Force*, Washington, DC, Center for American Progress, March 2006.
63. See George Borjas, *Heaven's Door: Immigration Policy and the American Economy*, Princeton, Princeton University Press, 1999; and George Borjas and Lawrence Katz, *The Evolution of the Mexican-born Workforce in the United States*, National Bureau of Economic Research, Working Paper 11281, April 2005.
64. Julie Murray, Jeanne Batalova and Michael Fix, *The Impact of Immigration on Native Workers: A Fresh Look at the Evidence* (Washington, DC: Migration Policy Institute, Insight, no. 18, July 2006), p. 4.
65. David Card, *Is the New Immigration Really so Bad?* (NBER Working Paper No. 11547, August 2005), p. 1.
66. Gianmarco Ottaviano and Giovanni Peri, *Rethinking the Gains from Immigration: Theory and Evidence from the US* (NBER Working Paper 11672, September 2005), p. 4. (See also their later NBER Working Paper 14188, July 2008.)

67. This of course would be a huge change of policy. The US economy has more than 6 million workplaces. In 1999, 417 employers were fined for hiring undocumented workers. In 2004 that number was down to 3!

68. See Audrey Singer, *Communities with New Immigrants Deserve Federal Aid*, The Brookings Institution, July 8, 2008.

69. Guitierrez, speech to the Cato Institute, August 1, 2006.

70. For details, see Lindsay Lovell and Roberto Suro, *The Improving Educational Profile of Latino Immigrants* (Pew Hispanic Center, 2006); and Fraga and Segura, "Latinos, Latino Immigrants and American National identity," p. 71.

71. See Ronald Mize, "Mexican Contract Workers and the US Capitalist Agricultural Labor Process: The Formative Era 1942–1964," *Rural Sociology*, vol. 71, no. 1, March 2006. 85–107.

72. See Rosa Maria Aguilera-Guzman, V. Nelly Salgade de Snyder, Martha Romero and Maria Elena Medina-Mora et al., "Paternal Absence and International Migration: Stressors and Compensators Associated with the Mental Health of Mexican Teenagers of Rural Origin," *Adolescence*, vol. 39, no. 156, Winter 2004, 711–23.

73. NAFTA phased out tariffs on agricultural produce between the USA and Mexico over a 15-year period, ending in 2008. Agricultural exports grew during those years in both directions – doubling in a decade in the Mexican case, but increasing by more than 15 percent a year from the American side. Rice, cattle, pigs, corn, dairy and fruit products have gone south in such volume that by 2001 Mexico's agricultural trade deficit with the US was running at over $4 billion a year (source: *Business Week*, Nov 18, 2002). Corn imports, for example, from the US into Mexico increased a staggering 18-fold between 1994 and 2002, affecting 3 million Mexican farmers, and triggering rural unemployment. The *Los Angeles Times* cited a Mexican hog farmer who, because of US competition, laid off 35 workers, 17 of whom then entered the US illegally. Hog exports from the US to Mexico doubled between 1994 and 2002. Mexican exports of hogs to the US halved! (October 26, 2002, p. A11)

74. These figures, and those later in this paragraph on rural unemployment, are from Bill Weinberg, "NATFA at ten: Tragic Toll for Mexican Maize," *Native Americas*, vol. XXI, no. 2, June 2004, 52–3.

75. John Judis, "Immigration Confusion: Illegal Substance," *The New Republic Online*, April 6, 2006, p. 1.

76. Those subsidies cover crops such as cotton, corn, rice and soy beans. The US farm program paid growers an average of $15.3 billion a year between 1996 and 2001, and $23 billion in 2005. (These figures are

from C. Ford Runge, "Agrivation: The farm bill from hell," *The National Interest*, Issue 72, Summer 2003, pp. 85–93.) By contrast, Mexican farm subsidies totaled only about 6.8 billion pesos in 1996, running at about one-third the OECD average for agricultural support (*OECD Observer*, June/July 1997).

77. See the Pew Hispanic Center report, *Unauthorized Migrants: Numbers and Characteristics*, June 14, 2005.

78. The 2009 Obama budget proposed a $5 billion reduction in payments to agribusiness and to farmers with more than $500,000 annual revenues.

79. Michael Dukakis and Daniel Mitchell, "Raise Wages, Not Walls," *New York Times*, July 25, 2006.

80. The Pew Hispanic Center estimate that "40 to 50% of the total [unauthorized migrant population] entered the country through legal ports of entry" – that is, are overstayers on visitor and student visas, or on temporary work permits (*Modes of Entry for the Unauthorized Migrant Population*, Fact Sheet, May 22, 2006).

81. The Congressional Budget Office estimated that the building and maintenance of 870 miles of fencing would cost $3.3 billion (This, in the *Washington Post*, August 22, 2006, p. A01).

82. The Center for American Progress estimates the cost of deporting 10 million illegal immigrants over a five-year period at $206–230 billion, or at least $41.2 billion annually. That's twice the current cost of military operations in Afghanistan, and half the annual cost of the war in Iraq (See David A. Jaeger, *Deporting the Undocumented: A Cost Assessment*, Washington, DC, Center for American Progress, July 2005).

83. For a fuller statement, see David Coates, "Options for Action, Strategies for Change," in Coates and Siavelis, *Getting Immigration Right*, pp. 219–33.

84. The big six are California, Texas, Florida, New York, Arizona and Illinois. New Jersey and North Carolina are also big recipients of Mexican migration, and the diaspora is now countrywide (For details, see William Frey, *Diversity Spreads Out*, Washington, DC, The Brookings Institution, March 2006).

85. The Economic Policy Institute currently proposes that they be paid no less than 150 percent of minimum wage. For the argument, see Ross Eisenbrey, "The H-2 Visa Programs: Real Need for Reform," in Coates and Siavelis, *Getting Immigration Right*, p. 216.

CHAPTER 8

Is God Necessarily Conservative?

You would definitely think so, if all you listened to were the radio programs of the Christian Right. And there are lots of such radio programs around these days – so many indeed that you have to work rather hard to avoid them – radio programs that all push a particular and a similar message. It is a message that links public policy to a set of religious values. It is one that sees those values as everywhere under challenge and in retreat. It is one that treats the major social ills of contemporary America as the consequence of that challenge; and it's one that urges people of faith to fight back. It tells them to bring their own conservative social agenda to the political table, and to hold the Republican Party responsible for its implementation.

It was not always so. In the past, as now, the attitudes of the American electorate were heavily shaped by religious convictions; but historically those convictions were as often liberal as conservative. Indeed, from the very moment they arrived in the United States, most Irish, Italian and Polish Catholics voted Democrat rather than Republican, and the candidates they supported were invariably progressive on economic issues if not always on social ones. White southern Baptists voted Democratic too – they did so pretty consistently from Reconstruction to Civil Rights – though their Democrats were invariably on the conservative, even racist, wing of the party; and the bulk of the Jewish vote – certainly in the Northeast – was solidly in the New Deal camp after 1932. So there is nothing new about the linkage between religion and politics in the United States. What is new is the way in which, of late, the political face of American religion has been monopolized by the Right. What is new is the conservative impact on national politics of a rising tide of Evangelical Protestantism.

Though the history of Evangelical Protestantism is as old as that of the United States itself, it is normal to link its recent political history to the organizational initiatives of two men – Jerry Falwell and Pat Robertson – the first setting up the predominantly Baptist *Moral Majority* in 1978, the second hosting the more ecumenical *700 Club* television program before creating the *Christian Coalition of America* in 1989. What they began, others then copied, putting into place organizations of a bewildering number and complexity. Not all the Christian organizations now politically active on the American Right are evangelical, Protestant and white. There are Catholic players here too, and a number of conservative organizations/individuals rooted in the African-American community. But white evangelical Protestantism is the main force behind many of the leading organizations now seeking to speak on social issues for Christian America: among the more influential of which are Focus on the Family, Concerned Women for America, The American Family Association, The Family Research Council, The Traditional Values Coalition, The Campaign for Working Families, The Free Congress Foundation, The Center for Moral Clarity, The Ethics and Public Policy Center and The Discovery Institute. For the purposes of this chapter, it is these organizations to which we will refer collectively as "the Christian Right."

Between them, they and their supporters now command a vast array of radio stations, their own television networks and news agency, a host of think tanks and several universities. Their reach and impact is correspondingly remarkable. Reportedly, "the radio commentaries of *Focus on the Family*'s James C. Dobson alone are heard by more than two hundred million people every day in ninety-nine countries on more than five thousand radio outlets."[1] So not surprisingly perhaps, a Gallup poll taken in 2005 found that 41 percent of Americans classified themselves as "born again" or Evangelical Christians; and 59 percent of Americans said that "religion can solve all or most of today's problems."[2] More significant still for our purposes here, four out of every five white Evangelicals voted for George W. Bush in 2004, and made up more than a third of his entire electorate; and even in 2008, when evangelical enthusiasm for the Republican candidate was far weaker – though for his vice-presidential pick, quite ecstatic[3] – John McCain outscored Barack Obama among white evangelicals 74 percent to 24 percent, among white mainline Protestants 65 percent to 34 percent and among white Catholics 52 percent to 47 percent.[4] What Christian Conservatives think is therefore very important to Republican politicians – and through them, to the rest of us – and what their leaders say they think is broadly of the following kind.[5]

1. America as "a city upon a hill"

The uniqueness of America lies in its Christian character. America was created by men and women of faith, refugees from religious persecution. They came to these shores "to do justly, to love mercy, to walk humbly with our God," believing that if they dealt falsely with that god, they would ultimately by "consumed out of the good land" on which they had landed.[6] There was a subordinate Catholic strand in that early American story, but nonetheless the values to which all decent Americans now adhere are understood as predominantly Protestant in origin: values such as individualism, freedom of thought and conscience, equality, and self-improvement. America prospered, so the argument goes, because it was a society built on these Christian values. The separation of church and state established in the revolutionary settlement guaranteed the right of every American to worship as he or she thought fit, but that separation was not designed to divorce religion from politics. On the contrary, religious values were from the beginning of the American story – as they must now remain – a vital source of guidance for the design of public policy, with the Bible itself as the main repository of those values. Indeed, according to Beverley LaHaye of Concerned Women for America, "politicians who do not use the Bible to guide their public and private lives do not belong in office."[7]

Conservative Christians differ on whether the New Testament should be treated as simply the main or as actually the only source of guidance on political issues. The more fundamentalist and evangelical such Christians are, the more the Bible is taken as the literal Word of God, and as such entirely true, complete and definitive in its own terms. The Bible is everywhere in the promotional literature of the Christian Right. The self-proclaimed mission of Concerned Women for America, for example, is to "protect and promote Biblical values among all citizens – first through prayer, then education, and finally by influencing our society."[8] The Traditional Values Coalition is similarly committed to "living, as far as is possible, by the moral precepts taught by Jesus Christ and by the whole counsel of God as revealed in the Bible."[9] So whether or not they are actually committed to the view that the Bible contains the full and authoritative word of God – when polled in 2004, 53 percent of all Americans and 83 percent of all evangelicals believed that the Bible was literally true[10] – all the major Christian think tanks and campaign organizations agree that Christian religious teaching has an importance, a legitimacy and a priority that no other source of values can command. For daily guidance, they say, go to the Bible; and if in crisis, turn once more to Jesus. Indeed, being "born again" is, for evangelical Christians at least, an essential stage in the personal journey back to a better and (for many) a more conservative politics.

2. The social ills of secularism

Many leading conservative Christians are convinced that most modern social ills are the direct consequence of the inability or refusal of many people to be born again in that fashion. They treat themselves and their churches as a persecuted and misunderstood minority. They insist that their religious convictions are regularly dismissed and derided by liberal policy makers and media pundits. They see their influence blocked by policies that deny the presence of scripture in public buildings or prayer in public schools – to America's great and continuing cost. This "de-Christianizing of America" is, for Pat Buchanan at least, a key element in a more general "death of the West" that he uses to explain our current moral malaise;[11] and he is not alone in that view. The taking of prayer out of schools in 1962 was condemned as recently as 2002 by the evangelist Joyce Meyer as nothing less than "a violent assault against the future of the kingdom of God." "Satan knew," she told the delegates to the Christian Coalition convention, "that if he could take spirituality away from children . . . the next generation would not be able to do the kingdom of darkness any damage."[12] Indeed, taking prayers out of public schools in this way is seen by many on the Christian Right as simply one example of that *"constant attempt to strip our Judeo-Christian roots out of every nook and cranny of American life"*[13] *that has so eroded American values over the last half-century.*

Such socially conservative Christians often assert a direct causal link between a multiplicity of modern general and specific ills and the secularization of American public life since 1960, a secularization they blame entirely on liberals. They explain the rise in crime in this fashion. They understand the upward trend in teenage pregnancies in a similar way. They lay much of the blame for declining moral standards on pornography and the entertainment industry, and see both as driven by liberal Hollywood elites. Some conservative Christians – at the more extreme fringe of their coalition – even link things like Hurricane Katrina,[14] *the scandal at Abu Ghraib*[15] *and the attacks on 9/11*[16] *to this retreat from core religious convictions in American social life. Many leading Christian Conservatives regularly describe modern America as a country without a proper moral compass; and insist that the reestablishment of that compass, by the reintroduction of religious values into US public life, is the political task of the age. It is a task, moreover, that the vast majority of them seem to believe can only be achieved by the election of Republican-dominated Congresses and "born again" Republican Presidents. No Democrats here, only Republicans: because on their conservative reading of the Bible, Jesus Christ's political color was clearly red, not blue!*[17]

3. Marriage as "the union of a man and a woman"

Christian Conservatives are aware that the transmission of solid religious values is no automatic process. It requires institutional support, particularly in times of moral crisis as they believe these to be. Many focus on the importance of schooling in that institutional support system, and seek to influence the content and delivery of the educational curriculum. Others see the mass media as a huge negative influence, and seek ways to offset its impact – particularly on the young – by developing media outlets of their own. Most see a vital role for the courts in the protection of traditional practices, and attach overwhelming importance to the selection of conservative judges. But the key institution to which the vast majority of conservative Christians look for the transmission of values is the family – understood as a permanent union between a man and a woman, sanctified by and before God – and the intensity of Christian Right politics now is, in large measure, a reflection of the extent to which they see the traditional family as everywhere in meltdown.

Many leading Christian Conservatives feel that the American family is under challenge on two fronts. They see it threatened by the prevalence and toleration of sexual relations outside marriage — both premarital sex and marital infidelity — so that many of them actively campaign for sexual abstinence, abhor divorce, set their face against the distribution of family planning advice/equipment to the young, and oppose foreign aid packages that fight AIDS by distributing condoms.[18] They also see the institution of the traditional family as threatened by the prevalence and toleration of homosexuality in the wider community. Indeed the wedge issue here for the Christian Right in the first decades of the twenty-first century is less sexual promiscuity of a heterosexual kind than non-promiscuous sexual activity of the homosexual variety.[19] The Christian Right treats homosexual acts as a sin, and their defense as a left-wing practice. They see homosexuality as a socially learned form of deviant behavior, proscribed by God; and they campaign vigorously against its receipt of any form of social recognition/acceptance. In particular and of late, they have set their face firmly against any extension to gay couples of the legal rights and privileges associated with marriage. They have argued that recent judicial decisions extending equal rights to gay and heterosexual couples actively undermine the sanctity of marriage as an institution, put at risk the stability of the wider society, and endanger the moral conduct of future generations of young Americans.[20] Many of them joined President Bush in 2006 in demanding a constitutional amendment defining marriage as a union between a man and a woman; and the enshrinement of that definition in Californian law by the passing of Proposition 8 in November 2008 they hailed as a huge victory for their cause. Mormon money reportedly played a significant part in the funding of the campaign for Proposition 8.

4. The horrors of abortion and feminism

The other wedge issue on which many Christian Conservatives have actively campaigned since the 1970s is that of abortion. Organizations speaking for the Christian Right are unambiguously "pro-life" and entirely opposed to the rights granted to pregnant women by Roe v. Wade. Not for them, a woman's right to choose. They plant their flag firmly on the side of the embryo: insisting that life begins at conception, and that abortion is literally murder. They vary in the degree to which they are prepared to take direct, even illegal, action to stop this murder. There are fringe groups within their number who are prepared physically to attack the abortion clinics and the staff who work there. The majority of the organizations of the Christian Right, however, are not. Their focus is elsewhere – on the election of legislators willing to restrict or eliminate the right to abortions, and on the selection of judges prepared to give any pro-abortion legislation the narrowest of interpretations. This narrowness is vital, so Christian Conservatives contend, because only unwarranted judicial activism since the 1970s has allowed the scale of abortions to grow to its present holocaust-like proportions: to such a scale indeed, at 30–40 million aborted fetuses, as to make this the time for Christians "unashamedly [to take] up the cause of pre-born children in the name of Jesus Christ."[21]

The antiabortion campaign, so central to the contemporary politics of the Christian Right, then sits alongside other campaigns of a related kind. The Traditional Values Coalition, for example, has also been active opposing the "murder of the elderly through active euthanasia";[22] *and many socially conservative Christians have been equally active opponents of embryonic stem cell research, on the grounds that it too constitutes the slaughter of "innocent life at its earliest stages."*[23] *But oddly, antipathy to murder does not always translate into opposition by organizations of the Christian Right to the taking of life by the state. On the contrary, The Traditional Values Coalition, for one, makes a specific exception to its general pro-life argument in the case of the death penalty. The Coalition supports the death penalty – indeed it actively advocates it – on the grounds that the Bible is clear on the responsibility of government "to provide peace and security for its people," a responsibility the Coalition interprets as giving "the government the power to take the lives of those who murder others and to wage war against our enemies."*[24]

What the pro-life position does often translate into is a generalized antifeminism, and a desire for the restoration of more traditional gender roles. James Dobson of Focus on the Family, for example, and Beverley LaHaye of Concerned Women for America, have both long been strong advocates of the patriarchal family and the stay-at-home mom: consistently arguing that women have a divine obligation to submit themselves to their husband's authority, and that whenever women leave the home for paid work, their children suffer. "Careerism may satisfy for a while," Janice Shaw Crouse has argued, but "nature will not forever be denied; women are beginning to see the costs of imbibing the unnatural cocktail of self-centeredness served up by radical feminism."[25] *Pat Robertson, of the Christian Coalition, has been more explicit still. Strident antifeminism is God's Work, he has said, because "the feminist agenda is not about equal rights for women. It is about a social-ist, anti-family political movement that encourages women to leave their husbands, kill their children, practice witchcraft, destroy capitalism and become lesbians."*[26]

5. The need for a new crusade

The great claim of the Christian Right is that the United States needs to rediscover its traditional values, and to live by them. To do that, so the argu-ment runs, political loyalties must be determined by the positions that potential legislators take on social and moral issues rather than on economic and mate-rial ones. There's a culture war going on – "a battle over values, beliefs and the cultural basis of western civilization"[27] *– one in which people must vote their conscience, not their pocketbook.*

Domestically that means supporting candidates who oppose gay marriage and a woman's right to choose. It also means supporting candidates who are economic conservatives. Leading figures on the Christian Right tend to interpret traditional American values as meaning low taxes and limited gov-ernment rather than any modern version of the New Deal. God, apparently "never authorized government to tax in order to provide matters such as housing, food, child-care [and] health-care." He required governments, no less than individuals, to obey the eighth commandment – "thou shalt not steal" – and that holy injunction stretches out to taxes! Domestically, the key require-ment therefore is for America to "return to its moorings, once again embracing the biblical concept of limited government"[28]*: which is presumably one reason why, in 2004, "the Christian Coalition of America listed making the Bush tax cuts for the rich permanent its number one legislative priority"*[29] *and in 2008 threw its support behind the McCain-Palin ticket.*

In foreign policy, taking the proper side in the global culture war meant for most conservative evangelicals – during the Bush years at least – support-ing Israel and the invasion of Iraq.[30] *The obligation on the Christian Right to support the state of Israel and its current hard-line stance against the Palestinians is rooted in the force of Old Testament arguments about Jewish rights in the Holy Land. "I have many Palestinian friends," the Reverend Franklin Graham has said, "and my heart breaks for them . . . But I have to look at the Scriptures. Whose land is it? God created this earth." Palestine "was God's and He gave it to the Jews."[31] Likewise the vast majority of the Christian Right are committed supporters of the war in Iraq, because – to varying degrees – they see the United States as engaged in some kind of holy war. Moderate elements within the Christian Coalition do recognize the right of Muslims to worship as they choose, but even moderates believe in the superiority of Christian teaching to that of Islam, and see the only route to salvation as that through Jesus Christ. More radically evangelical Christians, of course, go the extra inch – and condemn Islam as not only misguided but as evil.[32] And if it is evil, it has to be fought.*

A liberal response

So what should a liberal answer be to arguments of that kind? Maybe something like this.

1. The hijacking of evangelical Protestantism

The Christian Right likes to present itself as the voice of an older, safer, more traditional America, and uses a literal reading of the Bible to sustain its positions. The impression given is of continuity and conservatism that stretches back through time – certainly down the decades, and even the millennia. But the impression is a false one, and the reading of the Bible made to support it is highly selective. The conservative politicization of contemporary evangelical Christianity is actually very modern, dating back only to the 1970s. And in spite of how conservative evangelicals now choose to understand their own history, the issue that initially galvanized the modern Christian Right was actually not abortion, or even homosexuality. *Roe v. Wade* was initially welcomed by some leading evangelical ministers, and met with silence by most.[33] The fight-back on this issue came initially from Catholics, not Evangelicals. It was the 1975 decision of the IRS to take away tax exemption from the Bob Jones University that really triggered the Christian Right into life;[34] and certainly there was as much racism and anti-communism as homophobia in the early politics of the modern movement.[35] If Balmer is right, the stand against abortion was something added in the early 1980s, and added consciously, to reinforce a segregationist message: and added initially almost as an afterthought.[36] So there is no tradition here. What is now presented as the necessarily conservative politics of evangelicalism is a modern and a very recent construct; and we should say so.

We should say too, as so many liberal evangelicals now do, that what was constructed in the 1970s and 1980s by the leaders of the Christian Right constituted a sharp break from the main lines of social teaching normally associated with evangelical Protestantism. It is worth remembering that "the last two Democratic liberals to be presidents of the United States were Southern Baptists – and by their lights devout ones!"[37] It is also worth remembering that early generations of evangelicals were as likely to campaign for progressive causes as for conservative ones. Many evangelical Protestants opposed slavery. They fought for civil rights. They wanted better labor conditions, even votes for women. They certainly wanted a strong wall between church and state, the very wall that modern conservative evangelicals are so keen to take down. And they were generally ecumenical in their attitude to other Christian nominations, and to people of other faiths. The extreme wing of the contemporary conservative evangelical movement can say, with Randall Terry, that "we are called on by God to conquer this country. We don't want equal time. We don't want pluralism";[38] but that intolerance is not what evangelical Protestants traditionally preached. For them, the church was like a bird. It had a left wing and a right wing; and it flew best when combining the strength of both.[39] So before we deal in detail with the politics of the Christian Right, it is worth saying to its modern rank and file that the general right-wing stance of the contemporary evangelical movement is an *add-on*. So add it on if you want to, but don't for a minute imagine that right-wing politics has always gone hand in hand with the religious beliefs you hold so dear. It hasn't, and it needn't again.

2. The dangers of religious fundamentalism

With President Carter, it is also worth pointing out that religious fundamentalism always sits uneasily with the civil liberties of a democratic system, even if that fundamentalism is Christian.[40] The Religious Right has no difficulty spotting the authoritarianism of Islamic fundamentalism. It does it all the time; but many conservative Christians appear to be less sensitive to the authoritarianism implicit in their own certainty of faith. At the very least, being convinced that you alone have a direct line to God means that you must see the religious beliefs of others as in some way inferior to your own. At the worst, being convinced of the certainty of your religious position must predispose you to treat people of other religious faiths as essentially wrong – certainly misguided and possibly evil.[41] Either way, a commitment to religious certainty sits ill with the central democratic value of freedom of conscience. It puts an inescapable tension into the politics of the Religious Right. They want both to be free to worship as they wish *and* simultaneously to have their religious icons placed at the center of the public school and court systems. But where is the freedom in that, for those of other faiths or of no faith at all. There is none. There is only what President Carter saw in the new breed of fundamentalism within the church to which he remains so dedicated: "rigidity, domination and exclusion."[42]

Fundamentalists of all religious stripes seem reluctant to concede the necessarily conditional nature of true faith. We need to remind them that had they been born in a different time and place their religion would doubtless have been very different, but no less true to them for that. We need to argue that the ultimate questions of the human condition cannot be "known" in any literal sense, and certainly not from the textual evidence of a bible whose construction was a highly politicized process spread over a number of centuries. We need to insist that the quality of a religious faith is to be judged by the seriousness with which it is pursued, not by the dogmatism with which it is asserted. And we need to say that it is perfectly possible to lead a fully moral life without anchoring that moral code in any religious philosophy; and that many of us do. The humanistic values that shape civilized social practice in modern democracies are no monopoly of any particular church, or of people of faith taken together. Those values have come down to us from the Enlightenment and are the common property of all democratic people, religious or otherwise; and they need to be understood and defended as such.

3. The limits of religious reductionism

There is something particularly frustrating in the propensity of the Religious Right to talk of themselves as a persecuted and ignored minority in a society that is overwhelmingly Christian, and to have them explain the persistence of social ills as the product of that minority status. It is just so easy to look at the crime figures, the number of teenage pregnancies, the spread of HIV/Aids and the like, and to see them all as the inevitable consequence of a generalized retreat from religion in this country. Oh that that was so. The solution would then be so straightforward. All we would have to do would be to go back to church. But churchgoing in the United States is already at a remarkably high level when set against the religiosity of other industrial democracies; and yet the United States remains much more prone than they are to the set of social ills that so distress conservatives. The United States is a very religious society. It is also very crime-ridden; and by treating crime as the direct and unmediated consequence of dwindling religious values, the Christian Right blocks off the systematic analysis of any potential causes that are of a more secular kind.

It is all very well for the Gary Bauers of this world to go into simple denial, insisting that "the horrifying violence in American life has little to do with the availability of guns and everything to do with our growing virtue deficit." They are also certainly at liberty to reduce everything back to abortion if they want to, as he does.[43] But what the Christian Right is not at liberty to do is then to deny the legitimacy of other people – "liberals" no doubt – questioning and empirically testing the adequacy of so direct and unmediated a linkage between values and social behavior. After all, that linkage is not just a matter of assertion – of some blind statement of faith. There is real data out there that we need to look at, and real questions that we need to ask. Might it be, for example, that gun crime in the United States is more common than elsewhere in the advanced industrial world because all Americans claim the right to bear arms: that we have more gun crime here because we have more guns? Might it be that criminality has increased since the 1960s because so too has income inequality in a society preoccupied with material wealth? And might the excessive sexuality of contemporary culture be a product, not of the perennial endeavors of Satan and the forces of darkness, but of the deregulation of the media industry in the wake of the Reaganite revolution? Those are certainly questions worth asking; but it is not possible to explore them in any systematic and open-ended way if, from the pulpit, each of them is immediately and entirely explained – Sunday after Sunday – by reference to the actions of a slothful congregation and a wrathful God.

4. "Forsaking all others for as long as you both shall live"

The Christian Right would have us believe that gay marriage threatens straight marriage, and that homosexuality itself is proscribed by Scripture. Yet all the recent research data tells us that the US heterosexual family remains remarkably strong in spite of all this "liberal" advocacy of gay rights;[44] and that what is actually prescribed by Scripture, and what really threatens marriage in its traditional sense, is not gay marriage. It is heterosexual infidelity and divorce. The Bible is very clear on that; and many of us are guilty of that sin – including a significant number of leading figures on the Christian Right itself. By contrast, the New Testament is almost entirely silent on the issue of homosexuality – the Gospels entirely so, the Epistles only briefly – and though silence does not imply approval, it also does not imply its reverse. So if biblical fundamentalists were really as concerned as they claim to be about the future of marriage in the United States, and if the adverse impact on children of parental separation was genuinely their number one worry, then the weight of their campaigning would surely be directed against adultery and divorce, in the manner of the far more traditional Catholic Church. But it is not.

Sexual orientation may be genetically transmitted, or it may be learned behavior. There is scope for dispute on that. But what is not in dispute is that adultery and divorce cannot be explained away genetically. There is no divorce gene. Yet it is homosexuality, not infidelity, that is singled out by the Christian Right for particular attention, and it is the legal rights and social recognition of gay couples, not divorced ones, that stand condemned. But gay couples, no less than heterosexual ones, set high store by fidelity and stability in relationships over time. Children flourish well in stable gay households, just as they do in stable heterosexual ones.[45] So if stable relationships between loving adults are what a solid social order requires, the recognition of the rights of gay couples should be a paramount goal of conservatives everywhere, rather than their prime target. As the conservative thinker Jonathan Raunch has rightly argued, communities everywhere have long "believed that marriage is a powerful stabilizing force: that it disciplines and channels crazy-making love and troublemaking libido." This "belief is a deeply conservative one, based on the age-old wisdom that love and sex and marriage go together and are severed at society's peril." So the question, then, boils down to this. Why, if that is true, as it undoubtedly is, "should homosexuals be the one exception?"[46]

5. "For richer or poorer, in sickness and in health"

Anyway, think about it. How can a gay relationship – between a couple living privately down the road from you, as you live privately in your heterosexual relationship, if that is what you do – how can that relationship undermine yours by its mere existence? It cannot, and it does not. What actually undermines marriages these days – heterosexual or otherwise – aren't private things like that. They are all the public ones – "toxic forces," Myers and Scanzoni call them[47] – that breed instability and stress in so much of modern life. Divorce rates are actually higher in the Bible belt than they are in New England. So too are teenage pregnancies. That not only puts paid to many of the claims made about the importance of religious faith to family stability. It also directs our attention to what else is higher in the Bible belt than in New England: poverty, low wages, long working hours, alcoholism and a culture of male patriarchy and sexual violence. Try tackling those, and family stability will no doubt grow as a by-product. Happy and contented people leave each other far less often than do those strapped for money, prospects and hope. Marriages hung together in the 1950s not because they were happier but because divorce was so difficult. It was less a golden age of happy families than an age in which the agonies of failed marriages had to be privately endured. We do not want to go back to that. We want to go on; and we will not do that by developing some "domino theory" about gay marriage – that it is the thin end of a wedge that will destroy marriage in general. A wedge can be used to prop open a door or to seal it shut. Which consequence it has depends on where the wedge is placed, not on the wedge itself. We need to place it on the open side, the one that welcomes stable marriages, straight or otherwise.

By hounding gay couples as they do, the Religious Right help to destabilize the very private relationships and civil liberties that they claim to value most. You cannot bash gays and protect civil liberties at one and the same time. It just is not possible. You cannot restrict marriage simply to heterosexual couples and still say that in this society "all men are created equal, and are endowed by their Creator with certain unalienable rights, and that among these are life, liberty and the pursuit of happiness." How can "all [wo]men" only mean "heterosexual [wo]men." It cannot.[48] It cannot, not even if you advocate different terminology: "marriage" for straights and "civil unions" for gays. Separate but equal is not equal. Ask African-Americans if Jim Crow worked for them? No, of course it did not; and it will not for the gay community either. If people are genuinely equal, then they are equally entitled to marry; and if the entitlement is equal, why then do we need another word?[49] We do not.

6. Respecting a woman's right to choose

When the Religious Right turns its fire onto the issue of abortion, it moves onto firmer ground. Abortion is not an easy issue for any of us, liberal or conservative; and the United States is not alone among modern industrial democracies in struggling with the moral agendas involved. Catholic democracies in particular – France, Ireland and Spain – have legal codes that are more restrictive of abortion than that created by *Roe v. Wade*; and even industrial democracies whose legal codes set the limits wider than we do, do nonetheless set limits. "So forget the fiery rhetoric of the far Right. Nobody is pro-abortion."[50] Few of us can be comfortable with time limits than allow abortion after the fetus is viable. Few of us can be comfortable with barriers that give women rights in one state but not in another. But nor should we be supportive of a total ban on abortions under all circumstances, for that would take away entirely a woman's right to choose.

It would deny women the right to abort in the wake of rape and incest; and it would simply drive the practice back underground, there to endanger the lives and health of the women involved, with all the inconsistencies of exposure to danger associated with income and racial inequalities among the women themselves. Working-class women, women of color and girls of a particularly young age, all would suffer disproportionate amounts of personal danger if abortions were to be banned entirely. We should say that. We should cite the many religious organizations that support abortion and planned parenthood.[51] We should point out that the number of abortions fell through the 1990s, even with a Democrat in the White House.[52] We should say that the US legal code has now narrowed the right to abortion to an already dangerous level; and we should fight for a woman's right to choose, within the limits of the law as set. And overwhelmingly, we should put the weight of our case on the prevention of conception, as part of a pro-choice position that wants abortion to be "safe, rare and legal."[53]

But we should do more as well. We should fight, as inconsistent and self-defeating, the objections of the Christian Right to the dissemination among the young of information about birth control and access to effective contraception. Providing easy access to contraception increases individual rights. No embryos are desecrated because none are created; and no rights are infringed, because contraception is merely offered, not imposed. It is the denial of that access that erodes freedom and needs to be resisted. In any event, to advocate abstinence rather than contraception is not a solution. Campaigning for sexual abstinence before marriage did not prevent teenage pregnancies in the past, and in the sexually soaked culture of the modern age it will not do so again. Sexual activity rates among the American young are no higher than those among their Canadian and Western European equivalents. But the rate of teenage pregnancy is.[54] The rate of teenage abortion is. The rate of sexually transmitted disease is: all because access by the young to contraception is significantly lower here. Leading figures on the Christian Right actually help to intensify the problem they respond to, by blocking secular solutions that offend their morality; and they need to stop. We have to equip the young to manage their own sexual practices in ways that prevent unwanted pregnancies and the transmission of sexual disease, rather than lecture them on the wickedness of premarital sexual activity. Management rather than repression, and condoms rather than sermons, should be the order of the day.

7. Suffer the little children to flourish, and their mothers too

There are so many double standards at play in the arguments of the Christian Right that it is hard to know where best to begin. They are ferocious in their defense of the rights of unborn children, but they do not show the same level of campaigning intensity for the children themselves, once born. We are still waiting for a right-wing Christian-inspired campaign against child poverty[55] – even though poverty is the main factor triggering abortions in the contemporary United States – or against the inadequacies of a health care system that leaves so many poor people, young and old, without adequate and equal coverage. True, the Christian Right has its own educational agenda: but it is one about access to prayer and biblical studies, not about general standards or equality of access. Indeed, the social conservatism of the Christian Right invariably goes hand in hand with an economic equivalent that leaves the distribution of income to market forces and gaps in welfare provision to voluntary charity. The result of that, generation on generation, is that vast numbers of American children are born into social deprivation from which escape is progressively more difficult: but such social deprivation apparently does not appear to offend the leading organizations of the Christian Right with anything like the intensity that abortion does. The poor are always with us, we're told. Like the weather, they are an inescapable fact of life. Why a God that loves us all should then leave some of us poor and others rich is not something that the Christian Right seem keen to discuss;[56] but unless they believe that income is an index of virtue – and that the poor deserve their poverty – then at the very least they ought to balance their defense of the interests of the unborn child with a parallel defense of the interests of the child once born. But they don't.

We should resist too the antifeminism that so often accompanies the attack on abortion and gay rights, and the reactionary nature of so much of the Christian Right's response to the possibilities opened up by contemporary medical research. Modern science has given women the capacity to control their own fertility just as it has given men (and women) the ability to avoid tuberculosis, polio and a hundred other previous killers. The human condition has been qualitatively improved by that science, and will be so again if research on embryos is allowed to continue. Leading figures on the Christian Right are way too prone to fantasize about a golden age of traditional family roles – before the "evil liberalism" of the 1960s – but that golden age is a myth. Women have been liberated from much of the misogyny and hidden domestic violence of the prepill period: and that set of social freedoms must not be surrendered on the antiabortion altar. James Dobson may want a world in which women obey their men; but we should not. Better he – and we – learn to live in equal partnership with those we love. Adequate methods of birth control are an essential prerequisite of that equal partnership; and we should say so.

8. Reframing the moral agenda

We also need to challenge the *narrowness* of the moral agenda that the Christian Right choose to pursue, and to question the *adequacy* of the political party they have anointed to deliver it.

We have to say to the Christian Right that homosexuality and abortion do not exhaust the moral agenda of the modern world. Far from it. The issues of life and death caught up in the abortion issue do demand moral reflection – no sane person would deny that – but the private sexual practices of consenting adults most definitely do not. If those who want political debate to be dominated by moral issues insist on restricting that debate to questions of sexuality and sexual practice, then homosexuality is surely less pressing a moral issue than say child pornography, or the sexual harassment of minors, or domestic violence. And that agenda in its turn, unpleasant as it is, has no claim to precedence over a whole range of other moral outrages that also demand our response: genocide in Africa, slavery on a global scale, massive poverty internationally and at home, environmental degradation, inadequate health care . . . the list is potentially endless. So we must say to the Christian Right: if morality is your benchmark, come and join us in fighting all of these; and indeed sections of the Christian Right are now beginning to be so engaged. Even the new leadership of the Christian Coalition of America is attempting such a widening of its campaigning focus. But as it does so, it is noticeable that the more conservative elements within the coalition are breaking away. Which raises the bigger question: do the majority of Christian Conservatives oppose homosexuality on moral grounds or because they are acutely homophobic? If the latter, they should say so, and drop the moralizing. We have to lift the moral debate up and away from this prurient preoccupation with other people's crotches.

We also need to challenge the view that the only political party interested in moral issues is the Republican one. Why not also the Democrats – whose record on "most of the great moral battles in our nation's history – the fight for civil rights, a living wage, aid to the poor, disabled and homeless, health care, protection of the environment"[57] is actually superior to its Republican alternative? "Am I the only person in America," Randall Balmer has written, "who finds it curious that" even with Republican control of the House from 1995, the Presidency from 2001 and the Senate in 2003, "these conservatives have made no serious attempt to outlaw abortion, their stated goal?"[58] Could it be that they are playing politics with this question – using it as a wedge issue – keeping the prospect of reform alive (and therefore their base mobilized) by *not* outlawing it? It is surely significant in this regard that many liberal evangelicals are currently finding a home, not inside the GOP, but with the Democrats, and that a new generation of Democratic politicians is also beginning to speak openly of its faith – Barack Obama for one – breaking with the party's older tradition of keeping politics and religion apart. A generation ago, it was enough for John Kennedy to say that "I do not speak for my church on public matters and the church does not speak for me." But today, after two decades of activity by the Christian Right, that declaration is no longer enough. On its own, it only reinforces the Conservative claim that the Republicans alone are the party of God. So Democrats need to talk freely about the sources of their values, and to make a virtue of those sources being, for many them (including the new president), religious ones. The moral high ground in

American politics is not automatically red. It can just as easily be blue, and we need to say so.

9. Contrary to popular opinion, Jesus was probably not a Republican[59]

We would also do well to remember that, for such a supposedly conservative man, Jesus Christ met an extremely unpleasant death at the hands of the Roman authorities. So perhaps He was not such a conservative after all. He certainly irritated the power structure of his day – they feared Him for good reason – it is certainly very hard to see the Conservative in the man who preached the Sermon on the Mount; just as it is also very hard to see the logic of those on low incomes voting for a party that systematically denies them adequate welfare or a higher minimum wage. We need to say to poor white evangelicals that they are being sold a bill of goods, they are being fooled into voting for a party that will not help them, a party whose leaders apparently even privately roll their eyes at the excesses of the evangelical case.[60] Sunday on Sunday, evangelical congregations are being urged to attach more importance, when they vote, to social issues (of sexual orientation and abortion) that hardly touch their lives at all, instead of economic issues (wages, health care costs and pensions) that touch them directly – and where is the sense in that? Jesus taught that it was harder for a rich man to enter the Kingdom of God than it was for a camel to pass through the eye of a needle (Matt. 19:24), and that "if you want to be perfect, go, sell your possessions and give to the poor, and you will have treasure in heaven." (Matt. 19:21) So whatever else He believed in, He visibly did not believe in trickle-down economics. This man may have been many things, including the Son of God: but an economic conservative – never.

The Christian Right continually asserts that its social views encapsulate the essence of a true Christian faith, as though it is not possible to be both a proper Christian and a liberal. Yet in reality it is, and always has been, possible to combine a faith in Jesus Christ with a commitment to progressive causes. There is a Christian Left as well as a Christian Right in contemporary America; not to mention a very large – and politically very "soggy" – Christian Center. "According to the National Opinion Research Center," for example, "the number of conservative Protestants who oppose abortion under all circumstances is a whopping 14 percent, less than the 22 percent who are consistently pro-choice."[61] The Christian community in the United States, like the Christian community in the rest of the globe, is a *politically divided* one: and from a democratic perspective, healthily so. And it is divided, as is secular America, by all the usual drivers of voting loyalty: divided by race, class, education, age, region and gender. The typical (or perhaps more properly, stereotypical) white, southern, middle-class male evangelical Christian may be a rock-solid Republican voter, but his black, northern, working-class female equivalent most definitely is not;[62] and even rock-solid support can and does slip, as the Republican Party found to its cost in 2006 and 2008.[63]

Even if you can somehow twist things about, and interpret Christ's instruction to "render unto Caesar the things that are Caesar's" as one of political quietude, there are clear inconsistencies in the wider message of the Christian Right on which we need to dwell. With what sort of Biblical authority, for example, can the pro-life injunction to stop abortions not also extend to the question of the death penalty? A consistent ethic of life would say that if taking life is wrong, then surely it is always wrong. Cherry-picking which lives can be taken, and which cannot, is just that. It is cherry-picking. Selective literalism is still selective. At the very least, it requires an *active* process of biblical interpretation. It is not that the Bible tells us so. It is that leading figures on the Christian Right *choose* to give the Bible a conservative spin; and if they can make that choice, then liberal Christians have exactly the same right to interpret the Bible in the opposite direction.

Too often the leaders of the Christian Right hide behind their God. They put their words into His mouth, and then tell us that we must follow Him when they mean that we must follow them. There is a profound dishonesty here. People have the right to disagree on value issues, and to engage in dialogue with each other about those disagreements; but the leaders of the Christian Right appear to want more than that. They want to stack the deck in their favor by creating, not a level playing field between informed citizens, but a slippery slope in which dissension is the work of the Devil. That should not cut any ice with any of us, whether we are religious or not. If the Christian Right has a political case that stands up to examination in the normal way, then let us hear it. Let them come down from the pulpit and move out onto the hustings. Let them keep God out of this. He is much too important to be used as anybody's cheerleader, no matter how good the intentions are of those who would use Him in that way – and we should say so.

10. Holy wars are always to be avoided – even ours!

The dangers of religious fundamentalism are real enough when all that is at stake are matters of public policy in the domestic arena: child care, health services, law and order, and the like. But they get really scary when fundamentalism and foreign policy interact, and they always have. Crusades, jihads, holy wars – think how many people have been slaughtered in the name of one God or another. Religions become dangerous only when they become evil; and they become evil, following Charles Kimball's argument, when they begin to talk the language of holy war.[64] Well, we are back into holy war time again, and this time not just with swords and scimitars. This time, the fundamentalists can – if they chose – fight each other with weapons of mass destruction. The fusion of fundamentalism and nuclear weapons is the new nightmare of the age.

This is therefore not the moment to fight fire with fire. Islamic fundamentalism poses new and genuine security issues for the United States – issues that we will discuss in the next chapter. Those security threats are real. They are frightening; and they have to be addressed. But addressing them by matching them would be a disaster. A Christian jihad, to roll back an Islamic one – as canvassed by a number of US military figures of an evangelical and fundamentalist predisposition – would still be a jihad. The world is currently so scarred by the legacy of previous religiously legitimated imperial projects that it hardly needs another. The Spanish, the British, even the Germans under Hitler – all of them rearranged other people's political furniture on behalf of a Christian God, and always at great cost to the people so rearranged! Regime change is not a new element in the global political equation. It's what imperial powers do for a living – to others, of course, never tolerating it for themselves.

So now it is time to say "Enough. We don't need an American version of this old and worn out tale." We have to insist repeatedly, to ourselves and to others, that this world will become safe again only when religious fundamentalism in all its forms – Islamic, Judaic and Christian – begins to fade away: not into an amorphous secularism, but into a genuine respect for the serious religious convictions of others: into what Charles Kimball has rightly called "a twofold mandate to love God and to love our neighbor."[65] He has always been puzzled and saddened, he tells us, "by people who make clear that they couldn't be very happy in heaven unless hell was full to over-flowing with people who disagree with their particular theology"[66]; and so have I. We have a huge security interest, as well as a huge democratic one, in preaching the importance of tolerance, respect and the pleasures of diversity; and we cannot preach that abroad if we do not practice it at home. Practicing and preaching go together: so let's all of us begin again to practice what we preach – freedom of conscience, freedom of speech and freedom to disagree. Not fundamentalism with a capital "*f*" but democracy with a small "*d*."

Notes

1. Dan Wakefield, *The Hijacking of Jesus*, New York, Nation Books, 2006, p. 16.
2. Ryan Sager, *The Elephant in the Room*, Hoboken, NJ, John Wiley and Sons Inc., 2006, p. 146.
3. On this, see Michelle Goldberg, "Palin's Party: The GOP's veep nominee has become the ultimate Christian-right success story," *Nation*, October 13, 2008, pp. 11–14.
4. Data from *The 2008 Evangelical Vote: A Retrospective*: jakebouma.com, November 8, 2008.
5. There is immense complexity here, difficult to capture in a short chapter; and one huge anomaly: namely that African-American socially conservative Protestants vote overwhelmingly for the Democrats. Our focus here is on the arguments of organizations/leaders claiming to speak for Conservative Christians. For what Conservative Christians in contemporary America actually think, see Andrew Greeley and Michael Hout,

The Truth about Conservative Christians, Chicago, IL, University of Chicago Press, 2006.

6. John Winthrop, *City Upon a Hill*, 1630.

7. Quoted on the Website of *People for the American Way*, the entry for the CWA.

8. Concerned Women for America, *About CWA*, at www.cwfa.org/about. asp. That Website also gives a statement of faith. "We believe the Bible to be the verbally inspired inerrant Word of God and the final authority on faith and practice. We believe Jesus Christ is the divine Son of God, was born of a virgin, lived a sinless life, died a sacrificial death, rose bodily from the dead on the third day and ascended into Heaven from where He will come again to receive all believers unto Himself. We believe all men are fallen creatures of Adam's race and in need of salvation by grace through personal faith in the Lord Jesus Christ. We believe it is our duty to serve God to the best of our ability and to pray for a moral and spiritual revival that will return this nation to the traditional values on which it was founded."

9. Traditional Values Coalition, *Traditional Values Defined*, www.traditional-values.org/defined.asp.

10. Kevin Philips, *American Theocracy*, New York, Viking, 2006, p. 102.

11. Pat Buchanan, *The Death of the West*, New York, Thomas Dunne Books, 2002, p. 179.

12. Cited in Joseph L. Conn, "The Christian Coalition born again?" *Church and State*, vol. 55, issue 10, 2002, p. 13.

13. Gary Bauer, *Why We Always Lose,* American Values homepage, February 20, 2004.

14. It was at Jerry Falwell's church in October 2005 that the Rev. Franklin Graham reportedly responded to Hurricane Katrina by saying of New Orleans, "there's been satanic worship. There's been sexual perversion. God is going to use that storm to bring revival. God has a plan. God has a purpose." (This in Robert Keyes, *Franklin Graham Sees Hurricane Katrina as Judgment of God*, www.americanchronicle.com/artices September 27, 2006.)

15. Robert Knight, *Iraq Scandal is 'Perfect Storm' of American Culture*, Concerned Women for America, May 12, 2004.

16. Jerry Falwell reacted to the attacks on 9/11 by saying to Pat Robertson on his *700 Club* that "I really believe that the pagans and the abortionists, and the feminists, and the gays and the lesbians who are actively trying to make that an alternative lifestyle, the ACLU, People for the American Way, all of them who have tried to secularize America. I point the finger in their face and say 'you helped this happen'." He later

retracted his statement to this degree at least – confirming that the hijackers alone bore direct responsibility for the attacks, but remaining of the view that the ACLU and others "have removed our nation from its relationship with Christ on which it was founded" and so "created an environment which possibly has caused God to lift the veil of protection which has allowed no one to attack America on our soil since 1812." (This, on the CNN Website, September 14, 2001.)

17. Not that the support is unconditional. In the run up to the 2006 midterm elections, evidence abounded that evangelical voters were increasingly disturbed by the involvement of leading Republicans in the Abramoff bribery scandal and the Foley sex scandal. As the late Paul Weyrich of the *Free Congress Foundation* put it in September 2006, "at the grass roots, among ordinary people, the enthusiasm is not there." He put that down to unfulfilled promises on abortion restrictions and a constitutional amendment banning same-sex marriages (quoted in the *New York Times*, September 25, 2006).

18. Under their influence, the law financing US global AIDS efforts was amended by the Bush administration to ensure that a full third of all prevention funds had to be directed to programs advocating abstinence before marriage and fidelity within it; and that no health care provider receiving US funds could counsel women on abortion. That last restriction was removed by President Obama by Executive Order in January 2009.

19. The Pew Research Center for the People and the Press found in 2003 that two-thirds of evangelical Protestants heard their ministers speak out from the pulpit against homosexuality on at least a monthly basis, compared to only one-third of mainline Protestants (Pew Website November 10, 2003, for details).

20. Some of them are very homophobic – indeed Jerry Falwell once went so far as to describe the AIDS epidemic as "the wrath of a just God against homosexuals"; such that "to oppose it would be like an Israelite jumping into the Red Sea to save one of Pharoah's charioteers" (Cited in Clint Willis and Nate Hardcastle (editors), *Jesus is Not a Republican*, New York, Thunder's Mouth Press, 2005).

21. www.operationsaveamerica.org/misc/misc/purpose.html.

22. Traditional Values Coalition, *Traditional Values Defined*.

23. This, from the Rev. Mark H. Creech, on the Website of the *American Family Association*, October 4, 2006.

24. Traditional Values Coalition, *Traditional Values Defined*.

25. Janice Shaw Crouse, *Post-Modern Thinking: How It Has Betrayed American Women*, Data Digest, Beverly LaHaye Institute, Volume VI, Number 2, April–May 2005, p. 2.

26. Cited on the Website of *People for the American Way*, under the section on *Family Research Council*.

27. Louis Sheldon of the *Traditional Values Coalition*, at a hearing on the NEA, April 1991.

28. The Rev. Mark H. Creech, Website of the *American Family Association*.

29. Bill Press, *How the Republicans Stole Christmas*, New York, Doubleday, 2005, p. 27.

30. When polled in 2002, evangelical Christians proved to be the biggest backers of Israel and of what was then the planned invasion of Iraq. Sixty-nine percent of evangelical Christians declared themselves in favor of military action against Saddam Hussein, at a time when the figure for the population was 10 percentage points lower (see Jim Lobe, *Conservative Christians Biggest Backers of Iraq War*, Common Dreams News Center, October 10, 2002). By 2007, however, 30 more liberal evangelicals wrote to President Bush that both Israelis and Palestinians had "legitimate rights stretching back for millennia to the lands of Israel/Palestine" (quoted in the *New York Times*, July 29, 2007). This initiative did not go down well with leading conservative evangelicals. For the detail of their relationship with the state of Israel, see Zev Chafets, *A Match Made in Heaven*, New York, HarperCollins, 2007.

31. Interviewed by Deborah Caldwell, on beliefnet.com/story/111/story_1117.html. See also Stephen Zunes, *The Influence of the Christian Right on US Middle East Policy*, Foreign Policy in Focus Report, June 28, 2004.

32. For a representative sample of comments of this kind, from Jerry Falwell, Franklin Graham and Pat Robertson among others, see the Website of the Ontario Consultants on Religious Tolerance, www.religioustolerance.org/reac_ter18b.html.

33. In 1971 delegates to the Southern Baptist Convention actually adopted a resolution calling "on Southern Baptists to work for legislation that will allow the possibility of abortion under such conditions as rape, incest, clear evidence of severe fetal deformity, and carefully ascertained evidence of the likelihood of damage to the emotional, mental and physical health of the mother" (cited in Randall Balmer, *Thy Kingdom Come*, New York, Basic Books, 2006, p. 12).

34. Randall Balmer quotes Paul Weyrich as saying that "the IRS threat to segregated schools was what initially enraged the Christian Community" (ibid., p. 16). Paul Weyrich was a major figure on the American Right until his death in 2009.

35. Jerry Falwell, for example, opposed civil rights in the 1960s, and a decade later visited South Africa and denounced Nelson Mandela as a communist.

36. Randall Balmer argues that the claim that the movement began as a reaction to *Roe v. Wade* is the real "abortion myth" (*Thy Kingdom Come*, pp. 11–14). Ed Dobson, Falwell's colleague in the Moral Majority, is quoted by Blamer as saying "I frankly do not remember abortion ever being mentioned as a reason why we ought to do something" (*Thy Kingdom Come*, p. 16).

37. Greeley and Hout, *The Truth about Conservative Christians*, p. 2.

38. Cited in Clint Willis and Nate Hardcastle, *Jesus is Not a Republican*, New York, Thunder's Mouth Press, 2005, p. 240.

39. This wonderful image is not mine. It has been shamelessly and gratefully borrowed from David G. Myers and Letha Dawson Scanzoni, *What God Has Put Together: The Christian Case for Gay Marriage*, New York, HarperCollins, 2005, p. 135.

40. In his *Our Endangered Values*, New York, Simon and Schuster, 2005, President Carter calls on Christians to resist the rise of fundamentalism within their own ranks, and to "encompass people who are different from us with our care, generosity, forgiveness, compassion and unselfish love" (p. 31).

41. The clearest and most powerful recent statement of this argument can be found in Charles Kimball's *When Religion Becomes Evil* (San Francisco, Harper Collins, 2002).

42. Jimmy Carter, *Our Endangered Values: America's Moral Crisis*, New York, Simon and Schuster, 2005, p. 34.

43. ". . . of course back in the '50s and early '60s we had not yet seen the undermining of the sanctity of human life that was unleashed in the early '70s by *Roe v Wade* . . . there are consequences when you tell young women they have a 'right' to take innocent human life. Can we be surprised when some young men conclude life is cheap?" (Gary Bauer, *Doing Things Right*, Nashville, Word Publishing, 2001, pp. 23–4).

44. Census data released in January 2008 had 7 American children in 10 living with two parents, and about 6 in 10 living with *both* biological parents. These figures were little changed from 1990. The big "collapse" of the US family occurred in the two decades before 1990, not in the two decades after it.

45. The considerable body of research evidence on this is surveyed in Elizabeth Cantor, "Gays and Lesbians as Parents and Partners: The Psychological Evidence," Donald J. Cantor, Elizabeth Cantor, James C. Black and Campbell D. Barrett (editors) *Same-Sex Marriage: The Legal and Psychological Evolution in America*, Middletown, CT, Wesleyan University Press, 2006, pp. 47–80.

46. Jonathan Raunch, *Gay Marriage: Why It Is Good for Gays, Good for Straights, and Good for America*, New York, Time Books, Henry Holt and Company, 2004, pp. 5–6, 81–2.

47. *What God Has Put Together*, p. 38.

48. And in practice it doesn't. Being married brings a whole coterie of financial, legal, social and psychological advantages denied to the unmarried, however long and civil their union. For a list of these, see Davina Kotulski, *Why You Should Give a Damn about Gay Marriage*, Los Angeles, Advocate Books, 2004; or R. Claire Synder, *Gay Marriage and Democracy*, Lanham, MA Rowman and Littlefield, 2006.

49. Evan Wolfson, *Why Marriage Matters*, New York, Simon and Schuster, 2004, p. 144.

50. Bill Press, *How the Republicans Stole Christmas*, p. 143.

51. Abortion divides churches from each other rather than dividing the religious world from the secular. For pro-choice religious views, see the Website of *Concerned Clergy for Choice* and that of *The Religious Coalition on Reproductive Choice*: www.RCRC.org – which lists the many churches affiliated to it.

52. 1.6 million in 1992, but 1.3 million in 2000.

53. This case has been argued again of late by Hillary Clinton, and is defended persuasively by Bill Press, among others, in his *How the Republicans Stole Christmas*.

54. And it's rising: up 3 percent for teenagers 15–19 in 2006, the first increase since 1991. So much for the effectiveness of abstinence teaching! (details in the *New York Times*, December 6, 2007)

55. For Pastor Rick Warren's conversion on the issue of poverty – one reason, no doubt, for his invitation to participate in the inauguration of Barack Obama, see David van Biema, "The Global Ambition of Rick Warren," *Time*, August 8, 2008, p. 39.

56. For a fascinating discussion of evangelical attitudes to wealth, see "Does God Want You to be Rich?" *Time*, September 18, 2006.

57. Press, *How the Republicans Stole Christmas*, p. 233.

58. *Thy Kingdom Come*, p. 23.

59. Though maybe St Paul was! For the relevant arguments, see Clint Willis and Nate Hardcastle (editors), *Jesus is Not a Republican*, pp. 294–306.

60. This claim is in the book by David Kuo, a former official in the Faith-Based Initiatives Program based in the White House, *Tempting Faith: An Inside Story of Political Seduction*, New York, Simon and Schuster, 2006.

61. Eyal Press, "In God's Country," *Nation*, November 20, 2006, p. 34.

62. On this, see Andrew Greeley and Michael Hout, *The Truth about Conservative Christians*, 91–102.

63. The number of evangelicals with a favorable view of the Republican Party fell from 74 percent to 54 percent between 2004 and 2006, according to the Pew Research Center. On the "soggy center," see the exchange between James Davison Hunter and Alan Wolfe in *Is There a Culture War?* Washington, DC, Brookings Institution, 2006. On the tensions between evangelicals and libertarians inside the Republican "big tent," see Ryan Sager, *The Elephant in the Room*, passim.

64. Charles Kimball, *When Religion Becomes Evil*, pp. 154–85.

65. Ibid., p. 213.

66. Ibid., p. 208.

CHAPTER 9

The Wisdom of the War in Iraq?

The Iraq War is likely to go down in history as one of the longest military engagements in the history of the American Republic. It is also likely to go down as one of the most disastrous.

Currently the US military presence in Iraq is being scaled back. Even the Bush administration which launched the war signed an eleventh-hour agreement with the Iraqi government to pull all US troops out by the end of 2011 and to have them out of Iraqi towns and villages by June 2009. The Obama administration – led by a president who had opposed the war from the outset – then shortened the timetable of complete withdrawal to August 2010, for US combat troops at least. In 2008 Bush the invader agreed to pull out. In 2009 Obama the opposer agreed to stay in: both signs of the extent to which an invasion whose mission was announced as accomplished only 42 days after it began had turned itself over time into a quagmire in which accomplishment of any kind of mission – military or otherwise – became increasingly difficult. Getting into Iraq was easy. Getting out is proving extraordinarily hard.

We are stuck therefore with a paradox. Years and years after the horrendous events of 9/11, Osama bin Laden remains alive and free while Saddam Hussein does not. As late as March 2009 we had yet to capture the man who orchestrated the attacks of that day, and we had yet to extricate our troops from a country whose government did not attack us on 9/11 but which we overthrew anyway! Quite how we arrived at that paradox remains a live issue in contemporary US politics. The argument that got us there goes something like this.

1. Iraq and terrorism

The invasion of Iraq was initially presented to the American people as an essential step in the fight against al-Qaeda. The United States had been attacked without warning or justification. The lives of innocent Americans had been taken. A new kind of war had opened up between Islamic fundamentalists and the United States: "not a voluntary war . . . not an optional war . . . a war that was imposed upon us on 9/11," a war in which "we have to go wherever we find a terrorist, wherever we think a threat exists."[1] Oceans no longer protect us, so we cannot sit behind them, deciding whether or not to address threats that are based far away. Now those threats come directly at us — they come invisible and unannounced — in a new kind of war in which preemptive military action is vital to success. It is a war which leaves no room for neutrality, no space to respect the territorial integrity of states sponsoring terrorism and no place for rogue states unwilling to abide by international law. Iraq under Saddam Hussein was such a rogue state.

- *It was a rogue state because of its own past practices and ambitions. Its regime was particularly vindictive toward its own people, particularly hostile to Israel, and particularly ambitious for regional power. The government of Saddam Hussein had used chemical weapons against the Kurds. It had twice invaded its immediate neighbors without provocation. It had developed its own long-range missile capacity and associated weapons of mass destruction. It had systematically blocked UN inspection of its weapons programs, as mandated by the settlement ending the first Gulf War; and in 2002 was refusing to allow full access to its facilities by the international inspectorate.*
- *The Iraq of Saddam Hussein was also a rogue state because it had a record of direct senior-level contacts with known al-Qaeda militants.[2] It was harboring the worst of those militants — particularly Abu Musab al-Zarqawi. It allowed Islamic fundamentalists to undertake military*

training on its territory; and it welcomed and financed the killing of innocent Israeli citizens by Palestinian suicide bombers. Denials of such linkages, Colin Powell told the UN General Assembly in February 2003, were "simply not credible": such that the removal of Saddam Hussein from power would "remove an ally of al-Qaeda and cut off a source of terrorist funding."[3]

- *These two features of its politics, George Bush told us in his 2003 State of the Union Address, then made Iraq a key member of a broader "axis of evil," a group of pariah states – Iran and North Korea as well as Iraq – that possessed stocks of lethal weapons in defiance of existing international agreements. Iraq was a particularly dangerous member of that axis because of its support of terrorists actively engaged in strikes against the United States, and because of the associated likelihood that its weapons of mass destruction would fall into their hands. "Simply stated," Dick Cheney told the Veterans of Foreign Wars in August 2002, "there is no doubt that Saddam Hussein now has weapons of mass destruction" and that "he is amassing them to use against our friends, against our allies and against us."*[4]

- *The invasion of March 2003 was justified under the terms of international law, and made necessary by Saddam Hussein's refusal to comply with UN resolutions on the inspection of his weapon systems. In fact, military action against Islamic-inspired terrorism had been necessary since the first attack on the World Trade Center in 1993, and possibly even earlier than that. Had the Clinton administration been more decisive in 1998, bin Laden could have been taken out then; but the moment was lost through political weakness or worse.*[5] *George Bush, unlike Bill Clinton, did not waste the moment. He was a genuine war president, prepared to act, and act decisively, before any further attack, firm in the knowledge that only through externally imposed regime change in Baghdad could the US be made safe from further terrorist atrocities. Al-Qaeda had to be shown again, as it had already been shown in Afghanistan, that it had no place to hide.*

2. Iraq and the fight for democratic freedoms

Those initial justifications for the preemptive invasion of Iraq were never entirely abandoned, but the way in which the Iraqi War was justified by the people who had initiated it did definitely change. Initially, the sequence of points in the standard defense of the war went antiterrorism first and freedom second. Later the order was reversed: freedom first, with antiterrorism as a fortunate by-product. When George W. Bush spoke about Iraq in the latter half of his term in office, in sharp contrast to the way he spoke about it immediately before and after the invasion, his emphasis was less on the need to make America safe, and more on the need to set the Iraqis free.

- *So, for example, in London as early as November 2003, George W. Bush defended the Iraq War in the context of the "three pillars of security" then said to be driving US foreign policy. Pillar 1 and Pillar 2 required the international community to prevent the proliferation of WMD, if need be by the use of military force. They were entirely in tune with the original justifications for the invasion. But Pillar 3 – the one on which he concentrated most when speaking in London – was not. Pillar 3 required a renewed commitment by the international community to the global expansion of democracy, starting with Iraq. "Our mission in Iraq is noble and it is necessary. Our coalition came to Iraq as liberators and we will depart as liberators," he told his London audience.[6] "Our aim is a democratic peace," he said later,[7] "a peace founded upon the dignity and rights of every man and woman." "We have no desire to dominate, no ambitions of empire." On the contrary, "this great Republic will lead the cause of freedom." The invasion of Iraq was now to be understood, that is, less as an antidote to terrorism than as the trigger to a more general democratization of the Middle East.*
- *George Bush's London audience was left in no doubt that in leading this great crusade for democracy US motives were both altruistic and self-serving. Altruistic, because democracy spreads freedom; but also self-serving, and legitimately so, because democracy brings hope, justice and progress to counterbalance the instability, hatred and terror on which Islamic radicalism feeds. Soft power, as well as hard power, was in play here. "We cannot rely exclusively on military power to assure our long-term security," the then president said in 2003. "Lasting peace is gained as justice and democracy advance." And in the wake of 9/11, the stakes could not be higher. As George W. Bush put it in London, "if the Middle East remains a place where freedom does not flourish, it will remain a place of stagnation and anger and violence for export. . . . No distance on the map will [then] protect our lives and way of life." The spreading of democracy rather than the suppression of*

rogue states — the "opposing of tyranny wherever it is found" — had become America's best hope for its own national security; and it had become that because the failure of democracy in Iraq would not only "throw its people back into misery," it would also "turn that country over to terrorists who wish to destroy us."[8]

3. Iraq as the new battleground in the fight between democracy and fanaticism

Immediately after 9/11 the Bush administration made the critical decision to frame the tragic events of that day in a broad way — not simply as the work of a few misguided fanatics, but as a defining moment in a wider war on terrorism. The target thereafter was set both narrow and wide. It was set narrow: either simply al-Qaeda or something slightly bigger, "Islamofascism." It was also set wider. It was set against terrorism in general — against any antistate group willing to use unannounced violence in the pursuit of its political ends, including Hamas and Hezbollah, groups engaged in armed struggle against Israel. By 2004 the great claim for the war in Iraq was that that country was now the central front in both this narrow and this wider conflict.

- *It was the central front in the narrow conflict, in that the Bush administration was convinced that the continuing insurgency in Iraq drew its strength from the arrival there of foreign fighters, keen to engage in jihad. "They attacked us not for what we've done wrong, but for what we do right," became the standard conservative explanation of the events of 9/11.[9] "Better we fight terrorists far from home, so that we don't have to face them on our own streets," became the Bush administration's response to those who accused them of creating the insurgency by invading a country unconnected to the events of 9/11. And "better we win than lose, regardless of why we went in," became the standard argument against those who persisted in questioning the wisdom of the original invasion. In London in 2003, George Bush had been gracious enough to admit that there could be "good-faith disagreements . . . over the course and timing of military action." But whatever had "come before," he said, "we now have only two options: to keep our word or to break our word." It was his intention to keep his: "to meet our responsibilities in Afghanistan and in Iraq by finishing the work of democracy we have begun,"[10] in that way to starve the fundamentalists of the social and economic fuel they needed to recruit and prosper.*

- *Iraq was also presented as the central front in a wider battle between tyranny and freedom, a genuine clash of cultures with the defense of Israel as a key additional element. It was not a clash of entire religious cultures. Only extreme elements on the Christian Right labeled the entire Muslim world, or Islam as a religion, as inherently anti-Semitic and hostile to freedom. The Bush administration did not. It defined the problem not as one of an entire religion, but as "the perversion by the few of a noble faith into an ideology of terror and death."[11] In the manner of his great ally in London, Tony Blair, George W. Bush presented the war in Iraq as a fight between civilized and uncivilized people, and as a fight between democrats and fanatics. He regularly insisted that the terrorists were inspired by beliefs and goals that were clear and focused, evil but not insane. He also talked regularly of their genuine hatred for America and for freedom, a hatred that was not triggered by any specific act on our part or grievance on theirs – the ones they listed he dismissed as simply excuses for the violence they were determined to inflict upon us – and so a hatred that could not be appeased away by concessions or bribery. What was at stake in the ongoing battle to stabilize post-Hussein Iraq, so the argument went, was not the presence or absence of American troops. At stake were modern values against premodern tyrannies: democracy against theocracy, the rights of women against the rulings of the Shari'a and religious pluralism against Islamic orthodoxy.*

- *Al-Qaeda sees itself engaged in a holy war, to sweep the entire Muslim world free of Western institutions and practices; and in countering that the Bush administration occasionally also talked the language of religion and war. George W. Bush even said on one occasion that God told him to invade Iraq.[12] But more normally, administration figures talked the language of universal values under threat. They told us that we were engaged in "the decisive ideological struggle of the 21st century."[13] They presented the fight in Iraq as one designed to strengthen moderate Arab forces in their struggle with fundamentalism. They characterized the insurgents as Islamic fascists, united by a desire to kill Jews and damage America[14] – as "thugs and gangsters who seek to intimidate through violence and through terror."[15] They presented the enemy as one that viewed the whole world as its battlefield, one intent on winning regional power in the Middle East in order later to threaten and intimidate the entire non-Muslim world. Dick Cheney called it "their dark vision."*[16] *So he and his president presented the fight in Iraq not "as a clash of civilizations" but as "a struggle for civilization" itself: a fight "to maintain the way of life enjoyed by free nations," so that "good and decent people across the Middle East can raise up societies based on freedom and tolerance and personal dignity."*[17]

4. Iraq as a success story, slowly unfolding

Right through to the dying days of the Bush administration, its senior figures also presented the fighting in Iraq as a slowly unfolding story of success.

- *Initially, the administration announced major combat operations successfully over in May 2003, when they still equated the defeat of Saddam Hussein's army in the field with success in the invasion itself. They expected — and told the American people to expect — that coalition troops would be "greeted as liberators"; that the entire exercise would be a "cakewalk"; and that later when it was not, that even so "they're in the last throws, if you will, of the insurgency."*[18] *Senior administration figures even initially anticipated a smoother ride, post-Hussein, than the UN peacekeeping mission had experienced in the Balkans: on the premise that, to quote Paul Wolfowitz a month before the invasion, "there's been none of the record in Iraq of ethnic militias fighting one another that produced so much bloodshed and permanent scars in Bosnia."*[19]

- *It did not work out that way, of course; and leading members of the Bush administration were soon obliged to alter their timescale and to moderate their claims. By June 2005 Donald Rumsfeld was talking about an insurgency that could go on "five, six, eight, ten, twelve years."*[20] *But even then he was still insisting — as administration figures continued to do thereafter — that slowly the US and its internal Iraqi allies were winning the war in Iraq. To say otherwise is "flat wrong," he told NBC. "We are not losing in Iraq." On the contrary, in less than two-and-a-half years, as he earlier testified to the Senate and House Armed Forces Committees, the US military had enjoyed unprecedented success in the war on terror. American arms had overthrown two terrorist regimes, liberated 50 million people, captured Saddam*

Hussein and the majority of his senior aides, hunted down thousands of terrorists, disrupted terrorist cells on most continents, prevented a number of terrorist attacks and captured or killed close to two-thirds of all known senior al-Qaeda operatives.[21] *As late as October 2006, George W. Bush was still insisting that "absolutely, we're winning."*[22] *It was only in December 2006 that both he and his new Defense Secretary publicly conceded for the first time that the war in Iraq was actually not being won: and even then they made that admission of previous failure only to justify an increase in US troop levels that would bring, they claimed, future success. The subsequent surge, and the counterinsurgency strategy it made possible, were then hailed as a total success story, one permitting the scaling down of the US troop presence to lower than pre-surge levels by 2009.*

- *We were also regularly told by senior figures in the Bush administration that things are also going well in the war against terror inside the US itself. A major example of this came in September 2006 when the White House released an updated National Strategy for Combating Terrorism whose conclusion – widely cited at the time – was that America was safer than in 2001 but not yet fully safe. The US was safer because "we have made substantial progress in degrading the al-Qaeda network, killing or capturing key lieutenants, eliminating safe-havens, and disrupting existing lines of support."*[23] *But the US mainland remains unsafe because, as George W. Bush said on an earlier occasion, in a very real sense the war on terror could never fully be won.*[24] *Liberty from terrorism, like liberty on so many other things, required eternal vigilance. However, it was a vigilance made easier in this case by much of the indirect fallout from the continuing demonstration of US military determination in Iraq: not least, the coming to heel of Libya and the isolation of Syria (two of the region's other rogue states); the freezing of terrorist assets in bank accounts worldwide; and the widespread recognition in terrorist circles that, unlike in the 1990s, the US would this time stay the course and see the business done.*

5. Iraq has become a beacon of liberty from which we must not cut and run

The only way we could lose this thing, the Bush people insisted, was by not staying the course; and the only thing that undermined our military stance in

*Iraq, and hence our security at home, was criticism from leading political fig-
ures in the United States – Barack Obama included – criticism that carried
with it the hidden message that we will eventually "cut and run."*

- *To cut and run would be a disaster. It would embolden Islamic fundamentalism across the entire Muslim world, reinforcing their view of
  Western weakness.*[25] *It would undermine the staying power of secular
  and moderate Islamic forces in the Middle East. It would expose Israel
  to even higher levels of terrorist attack. It would shift power and influence within the region toward Iran. It would leave key oil fields under
  the control of fundamentalist regimes ideologically opposed to the
  United States; and it would provide Islamic terrorist groups with new
  havens of support and finance. Far from bringing US troops home as
  a way of increasing domestic security, pulling them back from forward
  positions abroad would actually endanger that security in the middle
  and long term. We have seen appeasement before. We saw in the 1930s,
  and the dreadful consequences that followed. Appeasing fascists only
  delays the moment of confrontation. It does not avoid it. It just makes
  it worse when it has to be faced, and it weakens those who have to face
  it. Terrorists kill, and they kill indiscriminately. They kill "because
  they're trying to shake our will." They know what they are about, and
  we need to know it too. "They're trying to drive free nations out of
  parts of the world,"*[26] *and we must not let them. In fact we have no
  choice: "the dream of some," as Condoleezza Rice put it, "that we
  could avoid this conflict, that we do not have to take sides in this
  battle in the Middle East, that dream was abolished on September the
  11th."*[27]
- *Setting arbitrary dates for troop withdrawal was also dismissed, for
  most of the Bush years, as inherently defeatist, "dangerous, reckless,
  and shameless,"*[28] *Rush Limbaugh regularly reminded his listeners
  that it just was not possible to support the troops without also supporting the mission. To question the original reasons for the invasion of Iraq
  was to say, to those who had lost loved ones because of that invasion,
  that their family members had died in vain. To talk of Iraq as another
  Vietnam was simply to give hope and succor to the insurgents. It told
  them that, if they bombed and maimed enough American soldiers,
  they would get what they wanted: a destroyed Iraq within which they
  could build a fundamentalist Islamic regime, and from which – down
  the line – they could launch attack after attack on a United States*

> *without backbone or character. To denigrate the war was to play politics at home while brave men and women died abroad. It was to put party before country, and short-term advantage before principle. "For the sake of our security," Dick Cheney argued, "this nation must reject any strategy of resignation and defeatism in the face of determined enemies."*[29] *"We cannot fall prey to pessimism about how this will come out," Condoleezza Rice once said: "the really devastating problem for the world would be if America loses its will."*[30]

- *The responsibility now is Obama's. "As Mr. Bush leaves office," his chief speechwriter said, "Iraq is a unified and free country, and our enemies there have suffered a devastating defeat. If his successor does not squander that victory, a free Iraq will one day be to the Middle east what a free South Korea has been to Asia . . . the victory in Iraq is Obama's to lose."*[31]

A liberal response

So how then to counter arguments of that kind: by saying at least this.

1. This was a war of choice – a very bad choice

No matter how often major figures from the Bush administration would have us believe otherwise, the invasion of Iraq in 2003, *un*like that of Afghanistan in 2001, was not a war of necessity. It was a war of choice. It was a war chosen by an administration disproportionately influenced by a group of neoconservative ideologues, and justified by a set of claims that no longer stand up to close public scrutiny.[32]

- We were told that invading Iraq, and at such speed – remember the rush, going to war in March 2003 when the UN weapon inspectors were asking for a delay of only several months, and the Iraqi's were desperately seeking a last-minute deal – was vital because Iraq had weapons of mass destruction that it would either use or hand over to terrorists. Colin Powell put that argument to the General Assembly in February 2003; but he was wrong.[33] Iraq had no such weapons. No such handover ever occurred or had been contemplated.[34] North Korea did have such weapons, of course, and Iran was also said to be developing them; but again it was Iraq alone of the "axis of evil" states which was singled out for invasion.

- We were told that invading Iraq was essential because of links between Saddam Hussein's regime and leading members of al-Qaeda. But in truth, no such links existed, direct or otherwise.[35] On the contrary, the evidence quickly emerged that relationships between the prewar Iraqi government and Islamic fundamentalists were antagonistic and mutually suspicious.[36] Evidence built up too – even more shocking in its way – that US security agencies were aware of those antagonisms and suspicions *before* the invasion, but did not pass that information on. What was widely known at the time, however, and was definitely passed on, was the extent of Saudi funding of Islamic fundamentalism, and of Pakistani support for the Taliban; and yet it was Iraq, not Saudi Arabia or Pakistan, which then received the full force of US and UK military might.

- We were told that the invasion was justified under existing UN resolutions because of Iraqi noncompliance, and was therefore essential to the maintenance of the UN's own credibility. Yet we set no such requirement on Israel as it regularly defied other UN resolutions; and the UN itself felt that it was the invasion, not the Iraqis, that undermined its credibility: to the point indeed that by September 2004 the Secretary-General was prepared to declare the US and UK action illegal under international law.[37]

- We were also told that invading Iraq was vital to save Iraqi citizens from the wrath of a dictatorial regime, and to spread democracy there. Yet clear evidence quickly emerged of a double standard in US foreign policy on Arab democracy over time. It was apparently conveniently forgotten in Washington that Saddam Hussein had committed most of the atrocities used to justify the invasion when actually an ally of the United States against Islamic fundamentalism in Tehran. As central an architect of the war as Donald Rumsfeld had readily met with him as late as 1983, immediately after the Iraqi regime had used, and was known to have used, chemical weapons against the Iranians and the Kurds.[38] The first Bush administration had initially stood idly by as Saddam Hussein had butchered Kurdish and Shia opposition to his rule in the wake of the first Gulf War; and the second Bush administration remained fully in support of authoritarian regimes elsewhere in the region (from Saudi Arabia to Pakistan) even as it preached the cause of democracy for Iraq.

- Finally, we were regularly told that ultimate responsibility for the continued potency of Osama bin Laden lay at the feet of the Clinton administration – who had blown the opportunity to kill him in 1998. Yet evidence quickly emerged of similar Bush administration failings: a steady stream of warnings about an attack to come that failed to produce a response from the Bush people in the days and weeks before 9/11.[39] We were led to believe that the invasion of Iraq was triggered by those events. Yet we now know that there was no Iraqi involvement in either the planning or the execution of the attacks on the World Trade Center and the Pentagon that day. We also know that – in key sections of the administration – the desire to invade Iraq predated 9/11.[40] Paul Wolfowitz, one of those enthusiasts, even conceded later that Iraq's weapons of mass destruction had been singled out for emphasis only because the administration judged it likely to be the best argument they could use to win popular support for an invasion to which they were committed, weapons of mass destruction or not.[41]

There can be no doubt. This was not a war of necessity. It was a war of choice, one designed to a goal – regime change in Baghdad – long wanted by key figures within the administration.[42] Given 9/11, the United States had to go after the Taliban. It did not have to go after Saddam Hussein; and yet it did.

2. They know it really. Read the small print, and find the admissions of error

When reflecting on the appropriateness of the invasion of Iraq, key figures from the Bush administration continued regularly to glide over this gap between justification and reality.[43] George W. Bush was still indirectly linking 9/11 to Iraq in his memorial address five years later; and his vice president regularly listed legitimate responses to 9/11, and placed the invasion of Iraq high on that list.[44] When challenged however, key spokespeople for the Bush administration did not just glide in that fashion. They also asserted the primacy of the "democratizing Iraq" objective, as though that had been the dominant driving motive from the outset. They placed the blame for the lack of fit between claim and evidence squarely back on the shoulders of faulty intelligence, and said that everyone believed that intelligence at the time. They talked of a world made safer by Hussein's fortuitous removal from power, and downplayed the current relevance of any of the arguments originally used to justify his removal. They then asked if we would be safer, or less safe, if a future Iraq was ruled by men intent on the destruction of the United States;[45] and, most terrifying of all, they tried to move us on – shifting the focus of fear onto Syria and Iran – framing the next phase of their crazy neocon drive for US military dominance in the Middle East by replaying their old arguments on a new enemy.

To which our response needs to be twofold. The first response has to be *skepticism bordering on irritation*. After all, governing is all these people did for a living, and if they could not get vital information right before launching a major invasion, perhaps it is as well that they are no longer in charge, and that more competent people now govern us instead. They certainly also need to be reminded that extensive doubts existed well before the invasion about the validity of the intelligence used to justify the rush to the war. Those doubts were both public and private. Public doubts: not least from the chief UN weapons inspector and from a range of major governments, including the Russian and the French. And private ones: doubts widely disseminated inside the State Department, the CIA and other security agencies in both the US and the UK. The UK's joint intelligence committee even warned Tony Blair in February 2003 that the threat posed by al-Qaeda "would be heightened by military action against Iraq."[46] It was a warning he chose to ignore. For what is clear now is that in the critical months leading up to the invasion, the hawks in the Bush administration leaned on the security services – and leaned heavily – to give them the information they required. What is also clear is that those hawks gave disproportionate weight to information from émigré groups with their own political agendas, information which turned out to be particularly inaccurate. And not just hawks in Washington. The UK Government too was accused of "sexing up" some of the data it published in the build up to the invasion. That data was then recycled in Washington to further justify the rush to war; as senior administration figures began to use tactics to discredit their critics that would later land some of them in court, and may yet land others.[47] If those who governed us in both Washington and London in 2003 were misled by inadequate intelligence, as they subsequently claimed, then they were foolish to be so. If they distorted that information to cover up a decision already made, as they now deny, then they were treacherous.[48] Our choice appears to be restricted to that between "knaves or fools" – and what an impoverished choice that is.

The other response has to be one of *disclosure*. Yet for all the implied Iraq-9/11 linking they continued to make in their set speeches, many of the key players in this drama did quietly concede, when pushed, that the original justifications that took us to war were false. Condoleezza Rice did so in 2006, admitting that Saddam Hussein, "as far as we know, did not order September 11, may not even have known of September 11."[49] Colin Powell did it too: telling reporters in January 2004 that he had seen "no smoking gun, concrete evidence about the connection" of Iraq to al-Qaeda. He later called his February 2003 UN speech "a lasting blot on his record" and his neocon colleagues in the Bush cabinet "fucking crazies."[50] When Tim Russett asked the then vice president in 2006 if "we have any evidence linking Saddam Hussein or Iraqis" to 9/11, Dick Cheney said simply "no . . . we've never been able to confirm any connection between Iraq and 9/11."[51] Scott McClellan, White House Press Secretary for much of the war and an ardent defender of it when in post, wrote in 2008 that war should only be waged when necessary, and the Iraq War was not necessary. Both George Bush and Tony Blair eventually conceded that they too had been misinformed about Iraq's weapons of mass destruction.[52] George W. Bush even tried to make a joke of it in March 2005, lampooning himself, pretending to look under pieces of furniture in the Oval Office for WMD[53]; and he had this remarkable exchange with a reporter as late as August 2006. Asked "what did Iraq have to do with the attack on the World Trade Center" he immediately said "nothing. . . . nobody has ever suggested that the attacks of September the 11th were ordered by Iraq."[54] Really? Nobody? Not even Donald Rumsfeld, who famously announced just 15 days after the attack that he had "bulletproof evidence of ties between Saddam and al-Qaeda."[55] Bulletproof evidence. 15 days. Really? No suggestion at all? No slam-dunk evidence at all? Amazing!

3. Wars like this are both self-fulfilling and self-defeating

Invading Iraq was a terrible mistake. It was a blunder of monumental proportions; and we need to recognize that. It was not just any old policy mistake. It was, and remains, a catastrophe – possibly the worst foreign policy blunder in the history of the Republic – certainly one under whose shadow we will all have to operate for decades to come. The lives of our children will be threatened by this idiocy, because its most likely outcome will be the emergence of exactly the world that it was designed to avoid. Policy failure does not come more total than that.

At the very least, invading Iraq dissipated the huge amount of global support and goodwill evident after 9/11. Conservatives like to remind us of Palestinians cheering in the street as the towers fell, and of Saddam Hussein's official approval of the attack. But they were the exceptions, not the rule, in the immediate aftermath of the collapse of the twin towers. World anger at al-Qaeda was general in September 2001. Seventeen countries willingly sent troops to fight alongside the US in Afghanistan, and 70 more sent logistical support: but not any more. World opinion shifted massively against America in the last years of the Bush administration. All that goodwill was lost. All the fine words about reconstructing Afghanistan were betrayed as energies, focus and resources were moved south to Baghdad; a shift in focus that al-Qaeda then followed. The US military estimated a steady flow of foreign fighters into Iraq in 2007 – a monthly rate that varied between 40 and a 100 – the bulk of whom, ironically, came from America's major allies in the region, particularly from Saudi Arabia.[56]

For by invading Iraq in 2003 the US military did al-Qaeda's work for it: overthrowing a secular modernizer despised by Islamic funda-mentalists, and laying the ground for the emergence of a theocratic

Iraq that al-Qaeda alone could never have delivered. In Iraq, the presence of US troops recruited support for terrorism faster than those troops could kill or capture the terrorists so recruited. Tragically, the invasion created the very phenomenon that the Bush administration claimed was there before but was not. Iraq *is* now is a terrorist haven. It was not before but it is now. George Bush and Tony Blair made it so, by invading a country unconnected to 9/11, and by redirecting resources away from military action and social reconstruction in the one country – Afghanistan – that was. The invasion of Iraq in March 2003 put in place the very things to which it was supposed to be a response. It *created* the link between Saddam Hussein's supporters and Islamic jihadists that it was supposed to destroy;[57] and it *created* the danger against which the Bush administration continued to warn us: namely that if we pull out, Iraq will fall into the hands of men bent upon our destruction. The evidence is now overwhelming that by invading Iraq the Bush administration increased the threat of terrorism and fueled Islamic radicalism worldwide. Their own intelligence agencies told them this as recently as September 2006.[58] Invading Iraq has not completed the job begun by invading Afghanistan. It has negated it; and we need to say so.

4. The costs of the Iraq War have been horrendous and must not be forgotten

The costs of this war almost defy imagination: costs in lives, costs in money and costs in alternatives forgone. Three costs in particular stand out as particularly awful.

The first is the cost in *human life*. American and British military casualties are known and can be calculated with some certainty. At least 4,000 US soldiers have died in Iraq since the war began, and at least 30,000 have been wounded, many seriously.[59] The longer-term cost in mental fatigue, family breakdown and other forms of post-stress disorder are less quantifiable, but no doubt larger still. The soldiers and families who fought this war will go on paying for it, year after year, long after the war itself has been brought to some sort of closure. The cost in Iraqi lives is far harder to calculate, but it is quite literally huge. Initially the military did not count civilian deaths; and when later it did, its figures were invariably lessened by problematic categorizations – limiting its data to killings that were visibly sectarian in nature.[60] NGOs and other external monitors have offered far larger civilian casualty figures. The Iraq Body Count estimated that just under 90,000 Iraqi civilians had died in the conflict as of March 2008.[61] It is at least possible that the death toll in Iraq had been higher still: the UK Medical journal *The Lancet* estimated the total war dead in Iraq by 2006 as 655,000: one Iraqi in 40!;[62] with in addition a significant escalation in internal and external emigration, as people fled the troubles as they happened or fled the sectarian power structures that opened up in their wake.

Then there is the actual *money* cost of this war, to US and allied taxpayers. The Bush administration hid lots of that expenditure away in special pieces of legislation, outside the normal budgeting process. The Obama administration, by contrast, does not. The latest figures available to us on the monetary cost of the war, from the Congressional Budget office in 2007, put that figure at $2.4 trillion by 2013; Joseph Stiglitz, taking the longer view and including the medical costs for veterans, has it costing maybe $3 trillion by the time it is done. Military expenditure by the Bush administration reached $572 billion in 2007, "more than the combined GDPs of Sweden and Thailand, and eight times federal spending on education."[63] The daily cost of the war was enough in 2008 to have provided an additional 58,000 Head Start places, or Pell Grants for 160,000 additional college students, or the salary of 10,000 new Border Patrol agents.[64] Add to that the cost to the *international reputation* of the United States as a bastion of freedom and law, and you begin to see that the lives lost and money spent were twice wasted. They were wasted in pursuit of a goal that was beyond them, and their very expenditure eroded the standing of the society that they paid so dearly to defend.

5. Policy that grows terrorists abroad cannot make us safer at home

So it is surely time to argue that invading Iraq without UN approval was exactly the *wrong* response to the terrorist attacks launched upon us in September 2001. It is time to recognize that, if winning the war on terrorism was the real goal of US foreign policy in March 2003, invading Iraq in so unilateral a manner actually made winning that war harder. It is perhaps even time to see that, if reducing the threat posed by radical Islam to US homeland security was the aim, no policy could have been invented which was less likely to succeed in the long term than that of using predominantly US troops to depose an Arab dictator. George Bush may have seen himself as political Islam's greatest opponent. The reality was that he was nothing of the kind. He was actually their star "recruiting sergeant."[65]

In the process of digging the US military deeper and deeper into an Iraqi hole, George W. Bush also dug the mainland US into a hole that was *less* safe rather than more. If you doubt that, try asking the British, after their 7/7 – the London bombings on July 7, 2005 – if the presence of UK troops in Iraq has increased the safety of UK citizens on the street?[66] Or ask the commuters in Madrid a similar question. This war is costing precious US lives. It is also costing precious US dollars: lives and dollars that could be better spent on genuine and extensive security at home.[67] You do not put out a fire by pouring oil on it. You do not make yourself fireproof by shipping your best firefighters overseas. You do not protect yourself from a ring of potential enemies by picking off the weakest and allowing the others to flourish; and you do not strengthen your capacity for rapid response by bogging down the bulk of your military capacity in a quagmire of your own making. We need to bring the troops – all the troops – home, and quickly. We need to argue, and argue strongly, that bringing the troops home is not only the best way of keeping them safe, but also the best way of keeping us safe: by lowering the capacity of US arms, by their very presence abroad, to stimulate the flow of young disaffected Arab men into the ranks of fundamentalist Islam; and by increasing the presence of US soldiers back here in the United States, able to defend in depth our borders, our air space and our food supplies.

6. There is an element of "blowback" in play here, whether we like it or not

Nothing justified 9/11. Americans of a progressive persuasion were no less outraged by the events of that day than were their conservative equivalents; and conservative political forces must not be allowed to monopolize the flag on this one. The invasion of Afghanistan was entirely legitimate and necessary, and we need to keep saying so. We need to keep saying too that progressives are as determined as conservatives to see al-Qaeda finished, and as committed to homeland security and core American values as was the Bush administration. But though nothing justifies what happened on 9/11, certain things do help to explain the terrible events of that day; and in that explanatory mix, there is an important role for "blowback" – for problems created for America now by foreign policy decisions taken long ago. We need to understand that this is so, the better to eradicate any features of our current policy and practices that could feed a similar blowback in the future.

Conservatives like to tell themselves, and us, that we were attacked on 9/11, not for what we have done wrong but what we have done right. Oh that it was that simple; but it was not. We need to understand why Islamic fundamentalists hate America. We also need to understand how what we do now, unless we are very careful and principled in our foreign policy, can only fuel that hatred. Islamic fundamentalists hate the United States because American policy is a presence in their region, sustaining institutions and states to which they take principled objection. They object to the state of Israel, and to its treatment of the Palestinians. They object to the religiously moderate and invariably *un*democratic Islamic regimes that American money sustains; and they object to the presence of US military personnel on Arab soil. The United States cannot and must not abandon Israel; but the slowness and character of Tel Aviv's response to genuine Palestinian grievances only feeds anti-American sentiment in the region, as well as anti-Semitism there. We have a powerful interest in resetting our relationship with Israel, to speed the creation of a viable Palestinian state; and we have a powerful interest in pursuing the democratization of Arab governments in Egypt and in Saudi Arabia. It cannot be one rule for Israel and one for the rest. Nor can it be one political imperative for Iraq but another for coalition partners willing to fight the insurgency with us. When the US explodes militarily outside its borders in search of terrorists, it gives the green light to Israel to do the same; and when the Bush administration accepted repressive regimes in the Islamic part of the former Soviet Union as allies because of the military bases they provided, that choice of allies sent out the very strong signal that what really matters to Washington is regional control, not democratic development. None of those messages make us safer. They just grow support for al-Qaeda.

Which is why, at the very least, how we comport ourselves in the contemporary Middle East must not add to this existing stock of grievances. The shame of Abu Ghraib, the holding of enemy combatants at Guantánamo Bay, the rendition of terrorist suspects to secret CIA jails, the use and defense of questionable "interrogation techniques," the choice of allies who themselves regularly torture and murder their opponents: none of these help the American case. They simply attract criticism from NGOs like Amnesty International, and even the UN itself: and rightly so. "Water-boarding" is an unacceptable technique of interrogation, whether administered by the intelligence services of dictators or those of democracies; and we must say so. Thank goodness that at last we have an administration in power in Washington that realizes this, and is prepared to make the necessary policy changes. We can only hope that those policy changes are both fundamental and permanent. They are certainly necessary.

7. Not "cut and run," but definitely "cutting losses"

We need to remember that retreating from an impossible position takes not cowardice but courage; and that repeating folly is idiocy, not statecraft. We need, as a matter of urgency, to reframe this debate from one of *win or lose* in a war between good and evil – the Bush framing of our choices that has cost us so much – to one of *how best to contain the damage* done by the Iraq War to the global struggle between moderates and fundamentalists in the Islamic world. No matter how often former Bush people tell us otherwise, you don't defeat fanaticism by force of arms. You contain it by eternal vigilance, and you stunt its growth by identifying (and eradicating) the conditions that recruit for it. Islamic fundamentalism will need to be contained, not by American arms, but by more moderate forces within the Islamic world; while our military and security efforts will need to be brought home and directed to the protection of our borders. Being simultaneously tough on terrorism and tough on the causes of terrorism requires a sophistication of policy that was literally beyond the Bush administration to deliver, and which the Obama administration must now develop and deploy.

The way forward has to be twin tracked: back to the war on terrorism, and out of Iraq.

- *The War on Terrorism*: We do live in new times, and those new times do require new foreign policies. For the first time, the United States does face groups of determined men and women, willing to sacrifice themselves in what they understand as a holy cause, willing to hit Western targets (and especially American ones) without warning or mercy.[68] There are also dreadful weapons out there for them to use, weapons capable of genuinely mass destruction. We therefore have an overwhelming security interest in locating and disarming those people. We also have an overwhelming security interest in locating and containing the dissemination of those weapons. And we have an overwhelming security interest in doing both those things with the full support and cooperation of others. Why in cooperation with others? Because local sources invariably have better knowledge of homegrown radicals than do external sources. Because international agencies are better at regulating weapons of mass destruction than are individual nation-states, however powerful; and because the greater legitimacy of multilateral action is bound to lessen the adverse fall out – in new radicals recruited – whenever a terrorist cell is located and captured. We clearly need a consistent, sustained and broadly based "war" against any organization that is planning acts of violence directed at us, and at us alone. But what we do not need is a widely diffused and unilaterally implemented "war" against any state or non-state actor whom we just do not happen to like. Well-funded homeland security, plus action abroad focused on proven terrorists, and action implemented with broad international support – the original Afghan model – is still the best way forward. Inadequately funded homeland security, plus unilateral overseas action against potential threats, action implemented by ad hoc coalitions of the rough and the ready – the Iraq model – visibly is not.[69]
- *Iraq*: A phased withdrawal of US and allied troops from Iraq is both right and necessary. We have to get out – not to cut and

run, but certainly to internationalize and pull back. The biggest danger – visible even in the Obama plan for withdrawal – is that large numbers of American troops will still remain in Iraq, and will stay there for far too long. We have to set dates for complete withdrawal. We have to pull the UN and all the regional powers, especially Islamic ones, into a negotiated settlement of the Iraqi insurgency; and we have to redirect the bulk of our diplomatic energies to a rapid and full settlement of the dispute between Israel and Palestine that so fuels contemporary Arab anti-Americanism. We need to stand full-square with those who argue that we can support the state of Israel without supporting its occupation of the West Bank.[70] We need to stand full-square with those who say that with more US and Israeli flexibility, the major problems of the region can be solved diplomatically rather than by force of arms;[71] and we need to stand full-square with those who argue that the route to peace in the Middle East lies through a focus on the achievement there of global development goals rather than of US (or even Israeli) military ones.[72] Talking to "terrorists" (certainly to Hamas and to Hezbollah) is, ironically, going to be a vital part of that diplomatic and economic effort.

8. Fully home or back to Afghanistan?

Whether the Obama administration should orchestrate the redeployment of US troops fully to home or partially to Afghanistan remains the key foreign policy issue left open by this war. Invading Afghanistan to take out the Taliban made perfect sense in 2001, and the President clearly thinks it does so again in 2009. But he, and we, would do well to pause and rethink the similarity of those two conditions. For the world created by the war in Iraq has changed the pattern of support for al-Qaeda. The Taliban have no monopoly of that any more. Taking them on with US military might, so long after the events of 9/11, runs the very great risk of generating a second Iraqi syndrome: *quagmire* on the ground, *mission-creep* as the problems deepen, larger and larger *antipathy* to the United States as civilian casualties grow and regional *destabilization* as the fragile political compact currently in place in

Pakistan collapses under the weight of the American presence. Afghanistan might very well become Obama's Iraq, and where is the progress or the safety in that? It is time, surely, not to take that risk but rather to learn the real lesson of Iraq, and to bring the troops home. All the troops home, all the troops home now.

Notes

1. Dick Cheney, remarks to the traveling press, December 20, 2005.
2. These contacts, discussions of safe havens, evidence of training, and requests to Iraq by al-Qaeda for WMD, were all listed in an open letter from the CIA Director, published October 7, 2002.
3. George W. Bush, when declaring the end of military operations from the deck of the USS *Abraham Lincoln*, May 1, 2003.
4. Fuller extracts of the speech can be found in David Coates and Joel Krieger, *Blair's War*, Cambridge, UK, Polity Press, 2004, pp. 31–2.
5. Perhaps even treason and betrayal! (The titles of books on this by Anne Coulter and David Limbaugh.) This is a very strong and angry theme in many right-wing critiques of pre-9/11 policy: that the US "slept" while being attacked, and that Clinton was asleep more than most. For some, that "sleeping" goes back to Teheran and the hostage crisis of 1979. For others it begins with Beirut and the slaughter of marines in 1983. For others, it starts with the killing of an American citizen on the *Achille Lauro* in 1985 or the bringing down of Pan Am 103 over Locker-bie in 1988. But wherever the story is said to begin, there is general agreement in these circles that things deteriorated dramatically in the 1990s: that the ball was dropped by the Clinton administration. The Democrats both failed to recognize the danger posed to the United States by bin Laden (in spite of being told repeatedly) and failed to kill him in 1998 when they could have done so.
6. Remarks at Whitehall Palace, November 19, 2003.
7. State of the Union Address, 2004.
8. Remarks at Whitehall Palace, November 19, 2003.
9. See, for example, Tom Tancredo, *In Mortal Danger*, Nashville, WND Books, 2006, p. 185.
10. Remarks at Whitehall Palace, November 19, 2003.
11. George W. Bush, in his State of the Union Address, 2006.
12. This, according to a senior Palestinian politician (quoted in the *Guardian*, October 7, 2005). In April 2004, George W. Bush spoke of "this belief,

this strong belief that freedom is not this country's gift to the world. Freedom is the Almighty's gift to every man and woman in this world. And as the greatest power on the face of the earth, we have an obligation to help the spread of freedom." Dick Cheney made a similar argument, that "we are created in the image and likeness of God, and He has planted in our hearts a yearning to be free," in his remarks at the 2006 Vilnius Conference, May 4, 2006.

13. Speech to the American Legion, August 31, 2006.
14. This definition is Bill O'Reilly's, on *Townhall.com*, September 7, 2006.
15. Representative Lincoln Diaz-Balart, speaking in the House of Representatives, January 30, 2005.
16. See his remarks at a rally for the troops, April 19, 2006.
17. President Bush, Address to the Nation, September 11, 2006.
18. The first and third of these by Dick Cheney, the second by Kenneth Adelmann, recalled in the *New York Times*, August 6, 2006.
19. Cited by Paul Krugman in the *New York Times*, July 17, 2006.
20. On Fox News, as reported in the *Financial Times*, June 27, 2005.
21. Defense Budget Testimony, February 4, 2004.
22. Quoted in the *Washington Post*, December 20, 2006.
23. Office of the Press Secretary, The White House, reported in the *Washington Post*, September 6, 2006.
24. This on NBC, reported in the *Guardian*, August 31, 2004.
25. "It is a dangerous illusion to suppose that another retreat by the civilized world would satisfy the appetite of the terrorists and get them to leave us alone. In fact such a retreat would convince the terrorists that free nations will change their policies, forsake our friends, abandon our interests whenever we are confronted with murder and blackmail. A precipitous withdrawal from Iraq would be a victory for the terrorists, an invitation to further violence against free nations, and a terrible blow to the future security of the United States of America" (Dick Cheney, to the American Enterprise Institute, November 21, 2005).
26. George W. Bush, speaking at Crawford, August 11, 2005.
27. Quoted in the *Washington Post*, August 30, 2006.
28. According to Senator Bill Frist, quoted in the *New York Times*, June 23, 2006.
29. Remarks at a Luncheon for Arizona Victory 2006, August 15, 2006.
30. Quoted in the *Washington Post*, August 30, 2006.
31. Cited in the *Nation*, March 6, 2009, p. 9.
32. The argument in this section draws heavily on the Report of the Select Committee on Intelligence on *Post-War Findings about Iraq's WMD*

Programs and Links to Terrorism and How They Compare with Pre-war Assessments, Report of the Senate Select Committee on Intelligence, September 2005; The 9/11 Commission Report Final Report of the National Commission on Terrorist Attacks Upon the United States, New York, W. W. Norton, 2005; *WMD in Iraq: Evidence and Implications*, The Carnegie Endowment for International Peace, Washington, DC, January 2004; Craig Whitney, *The WMD Mirage*, New York, Public Affairs, 2005; Richard Clarke, *Against All Enemies*, New York, Free Press, 2004; Eric Alterman and Mark Green, *The Book on Bush*, New York, Viking, 2004: and the sources listed in David Coates and Joel Krieger, *Blair's War*, Cambridge UK, Polity, 2004.

33. The veracity of many of the claims made in the February 2003 speech was challenged in the report of the Senate Intelligence Committee released in July 2004. (On this, see the *Financial Times*, July 14, 2004.)

34. This from David Kay, head of the Iraq Survey Group, at the end of its fruitless search for Iraqi WMD: "I was convinced and still am convinced that there were no stockpiles of weapons of mass destruction at the time of the war" (*Guardian*, March 3, 2004). As he put it to the Senate on January 28, 2004, "Let me begin by saying, we were almost all wrong, and I include myself there." The White House discretely abandoned the search for WMD in January 2005.

35. If any doubt remained, it was put to rest in 2008. The Joint Forces Command surveyed 600,000 captured Iraqi documents, and interviewed a string of captured Iraqi leaders, only to report that they could find no evidence of ties between Saddam Hussein's regime and al-Qaeda (CNN, March 11, 2008).

36. On the *lack* of a direct connection between Hussein and bin Laden, the evidence is now unambiguously clear. Indeed that evidence was reconfirmed by the Senate Intelligence Committee in September 2006: that "Saddam Hussein was distrustful of al-Qaeda and viewed Islamic extremists as a threat to his regime, refusing all requests from al-Qaeda to provide material or operational support." (*Postwar Findings about Iraq's WMD Programs and Links to Terrorism and How They Compare with Pre-war Assessments*, Report of the Senate Select Committee on Intelligence, September 2006, p. 105.)

37. "I have indicated that it was not in conformity with the UN charter. From our point of view and from the charter point of view it was illegal." Kofi Annan, on the legality of the invasion, September 15, 2004.

38. The documents on Rumsfeld's two visits to Iraq in 1983/4 were released in December 2003, and show the Reagan administration privately more

relaxed about Hussein's use of chemical weapons than their public statements suggested at the time. (On this, see the *New York Times*, December 22, 2003.)

39. Primarily in Richard Clarke's evidence to Senate in March 2004, and in his *Against All Enemies.*

40. See Bob Woodward, *Bush at War*, New York, Simon and Schuster, 2002, p. 49.

41. "The truth is that for reasons that have a lot to do with the U.S. government bureaucracy we settled on the one issue that everyone could agree on, which was weapons of mass destruction as the core reason" (Wolfowitz interview with *Vanity Fair*, Friday, May 30, 2003).

42. The call for military action to effect regime change in Baghdad was made in an open letter to President Clinton in January 1998 signed by, among others, Richard Armitage, John Bolton, Richard Perle, Donald Rumsfeld and Paul Wolfowitz – all big players in the formation of foreign policy under George W. Bush.

43. The arguments that Iraq had WMD, that Saddam Hussein and al-Qaeda were linked, and that Saddam Hussein was involved in the attacks of 9/11 were common currency on right-wing blog sites throughout the Bush years; reinforced by regular references to the veracity of one/all of these positions by media luminaries like Rush Limbaugh and Bill O'Reilly, and by opinion pieces in newspapers like the *Weekly Standard* and the *Wall Street Journal.* They were reinforced too by a pattern of *non-denial, deflection* and the attribution of *guilt by association* by senior administration figures. *Non-denial*: Vice President Cheney praised one such assertion of the linkage – by Stephen Hayes in *The Weekly Standard* – when interviewed on Tony Snow's radio show in January 2006, using as his defense the possible content of captured documents not yet analyzed. *Deflection*: Dick Cheney regularly responded to the argument that Saddam Hussein had no WMD by saying he could/ would have quickly have put them together but for the invasion. "I think he would, eventually, have been back in the business. . . . I don't think there was any question about his intent" was how he put it to Wolf Blitzer on CNN, June 23, 2005. And *guilt by association*: "We were not in Iraq on September 11th 2001, and the terrorists hit us anyway. The reality is that the terrorists were at war with our country long before the liberation of Iraq" (Dick Cheney to the American Enterprise Institute, 21 November, 2005). But we were not in lots of places on 9/11 – so why pick out Iraq?

44. As late as August 2006, George W. Bush was on record linking Hussein to Abu Musab al-Zarqawi, and in his 9/11 address in September 2006

described Saddam Hussein as a "clear threat," even when conceding that he "was not responsible for the 9/11 attacks." Dick Cheney regularly spoke of the attack on 9/11 and our response to it, and included in that list of responses the removal of Saddam Hussein from power, leaving an impression of a direct linkage between the two. The linkage was never spoken, always implied. (See, for example, his remarks at the 73rd National Convention of the Military Order of the Purple Heart, August 18, 2005, available on the Website of the Office of the Vice President.)

45. See, for example, the Vice President's address to the American Enterprise Institute, November 21, 2005.

46. Cited in the *Guardian*, September 26, 2006.

47. The attempt to discredit Joseph Wilson, after he reported that Iraq was not actively seeking uranium in Niger, by outing his wife Valerie Plame as a CIA agent, brought Lewis "Scooter" Libby, Dick Cheney's Chief of Staff, before a grand jury in October 2005.

48. We now have clear evidence that the Bush administration was less than fully honest with the American public on the causes for war. That evidence can be found in the June 2008 report of the Senate Intelligence Committee, showing time and again that the White House took vague and intelligence on Iraq and presented it as sound and incontrovertible fact. It can be found too in the memoirs of key participants, not least Scott McClellan's *What Happened: Inside the Bush White House and Washington's Culture of Deception*, New York, PublicAffairs, 2008.

49. Quoted in Paul Krugman, "Reign of Error," *New York Times*, July 28, 2006.

50. The first at a news conference, January 8, 2004; the second when interviewed by Barbara Walters of ABC News, September 2005; the third when interviewed by James Naughtie: see his *The Accidental American*, London, PublicAffairs, 2004, p. 121.

51. On NBC News, *Meet the Press*, September 10, 2006.

52. "It is true that much of the [pre-war] intelligence turned out to be wrong." George W. Bush, quoted in the *Financial Times*, December 15, 2005. Tony Blair conceded the same point in the House of Commons on October 13, 2004.

53. For details, see BBC News, *Bush's Iraq WMD joke backfires*, March 26, 2006.

54. Press Conference by the president, August 21, 2006.

55. Quoted in S. Ackerman and J. B. Judis, "The first casualty," *New Republic*, June 30, 2003.

56. Robert Appel, "Foreign Fighters in Iraq Are tied to Allies of U.S." *New York Times*, November 22, 2007.

57. There are now many official reports arguing this. The CIA's own internal think tank concluded in January 2005 that Iraq had now replaced Afghanistan as the training ground for a new generation of jihadist terrorists. (On this, see the *New York Times*, July 27, 2006.) The Center for Strategic and International Studies in Washington concluded in September 2005 that probably only 10 percent of insurgents were foreign, the vast majority of them radicalized by the invasion itself. (On this, see the *Guardian*, September 23, 2005.) For similar arguments from London, see the report of the House of Commons Foreign Affairs Committee, issued in July 2004, or the International Institute for Strategic Studies' report, issued in October 2004, that the invasion had "enhanced jihadist recruitment and intensified al-Qaeda's motivation" to mount operations, and left the terror network with as many as 18,000 new recruits (this, in the *Guardian*, October 20, 2004).

58. *The New York Times, The Washington Post* and the BBC all reported the existence of a National Intelligence Estimate, based on the analyses of the United States' sixteen intelligence agencies, arguing that the invasion had spawned a new generation of Islamic radicalism worldwide. (See the Websites of the three sources for September 24, 2006.)

59. Brookings, *Iraq Index*, November 20, 2008, p. 18.

60. Karen DeYoung, "What Defines a Killing as Sectarian?" *Washington Post*, September 25, 2007, p. A01.

61. Cited in the *New York Times*, March 24, 2008.

62. *The Financial Times*, October 12, 2006. This figure is large, but it is possible: the WHO reported that 150,000 Iraqis had met violent deaths in the first three years of the US occupation alone (source: NPR, January 9, 2008) – certainly a lot of death!

63. Robert Pallin and Heidi Garrett-Peltier, "The Wages of Peace," *Nation*, March 31, 2008, p. 13.

64. Bob Herbert, "The $2 Trillion Nightmare," *New York Times*, March 4, 2008.

65. This was the conclusion of a report commissioned by the UK's MoD Defence Academy, leaked to the BBC, September 27, 2006.

66. The official report into the events of 7/7 made it clear that the four bombers were motivated to act by UK involvement in the Iraq invasion. In November 2006, MI5 reported 30 terror plots being planned, 1,600 individuals and 200 networks under surveillance in the UK, with the UK as al-Qaeda's "number one target."

67. "...the federal government is spending more every three days to finance the war in Iraq than it has provided over the last three years to prop up

the security of all 361 US commercial seaports." Stephen Flynn, author of *America the Vulnerable*, cited in the *Washington Post*, July 18, 2005.

68. Dick Cheney referred to them accurately as "enemies who dwell in the shadows and recognize neither the laws of warfare nor standards of morality." (Remarks to the National Restaurant Association, September 12, 2005.) The novelty of this enemy, and its particular illusiveness, was a key part of many of his speeches – and quite properly so. The dispute here is not with the characterization of the problem, but with the nature of the Bush administration's response to it.

69. This argument is developed at length in chapters 7 and 8 of David Coates and Joel Krieger's *Blair's War*.

70. Most strikingly, John Mearsheimer and Stephen Walt, whose March 23, 2006 article in *The London Review of Books* brought a gale of abuse down upon them; but also Thomas Friedman (see, for example, his "War of Ideas: Part 4," *New York Times*, January 18, 2004).

71. Among them, Noam Chomsky, writing in the *Guardian*, June 23, 2006.

72. Most notably, ex-President Clinton, in his *Financial Times* interview of September 20, 2006.

CHAPTER 10

The Real Causes of the
Financial Meltdown

The Blue Sky Studios film *Ice Age* begins with an overactive squirrel trying to break open a nut. As those who have seen it will remember, what begins as a small crack in the ice quickly escalates into something entirely other, as the crack races its way through the entire ice mass. The nut remains unbroken, but not so the ice.

Likewise with the credit crunch of 2008: what began as a seemingly localized problem of overlending to cash-strapped house buyers in parts of the US housing market steadily escalated into the worst, and the most global, recession of our lifetime. Few of us saw the crisis coming until it arrived, and yet when it did arrive – in the last quarter of 2008 – it fundamentally transformed the lives and prospects of us all. One who did anticipate it, Martin Wolf – the most esteemed of contemporary financial journalists – rightly called the consequences of the US housing bubble "the mother of all meltdowns."[1]

- The credit crisis began in the *US housing market* in 2006 and 2007. After a decade in which house prices had effectively doubled[2] and in which many home owners had remortgaged their houses to sustain high levels of immediate consumption, two Bear Stearns hedge funds heavily engaged with subprime loans unexpectedly collapsed at the end of July 2007. Concern then spread rapidly through the entire US financial system about the widespread sale of such loans to house buyers on low incomes,[3] and about the associated danger of a foreclosure tsunami; and with good reason. In 2001 new subprime and home equity loans[4] had totaled $330 billion, just 15 percent of all new residential mortgages.[5] Five years later the equivalent figures were $1.4 *trillion* and 48 percent of all new residential mortgages.[6] This would not have mattered – outside the housing sector at least – had not these mortgages also been *securitized*. But they had. "Securitization is the process of aggregating similar financial instruments, such as loans or mortgages, into pools and selling investors securities that are backed by cash flows from these pools."[7] Securitization of mortgages had gone on apace in the United States since the early 1980s, which had been fine so long as the mortgages used as collateral had themselves been financially sound – taken out, that is, only by home owners able to meet their monthly payments. Securities collateralized by mortgages increased in the US financial system from $18.5 billion in 1995 to a staggering $507.9 billion in 2005.[8] The two dates were divided by what the proponents of easier loan terms called "the democratization of credit" and what the Federal Reserve Board more accurately called "a dramatic weakening of underwriting standards for US sub-prime mortgages."[9] That weakening was so dramatic that by November 2007 Merrill Lynch was obliged to write off $8 billion in losses on mortgage-backed securities; by mid-2008 US house prices were falling at 15 percent a year and the default rate even on second mortgages was rising dramatically; and by the end of 2008 one house in ten in the United States was either in or on the edge of foreclosure. Whatever else many of these new mortgages were, by 2008 they were *not* financially sound. There were more than 3.2 million house foreclosures in the United States in 2008 alone.

- This deepening foreclosure crisis spread rapidly through the entire *US banking and insurance system*, leaving key players unsure about their own viability and the viability of others, and bringing down a number of leading US financial institutions – household names that had hitherto seemed indestructible. The crisis spread in this fashion because too many financial institutions had spent the previous half decade gobbling up sizable numbers of the increasingly ubiquitous mortgage-backed securities that linked the US housing market to the rest of the credit-generating system, apparently unaware of (or simply indifferent to) the weakness of many of the mortgages on which those securities were based.[10] It spread because too many other and stronger institutions had succumbed to Treasury pressure in 2007 to bail out their weaker brethren,[11] and/or had taken advantage of that weakness to grow their market share by swallowing more cash-starved competitors. The foolish went first, the greedy second. The year 2008 witnessed first the forced sale, to Bank of America in July, of Countrywide Financial (the main private provider of subprime loans[12]) followed in September by the Treasury conservatorship of Fannie Mae and Freddie Mac[13] and the seizure by federal regulators of Washington Mutual, the nation's largest savings and loan institution. The year 2008 also witnessed the complete collapse of Bear Stearns in March 2008 (sold to J. P. Morgan Chase at a derisory $2 a share) and then, in a single terrifying week in September, the swallowing up of Merrill Lynch by Bank of America, the first of many Treasury bailouts of insurance giant AIG, and the allowed collapse of Lehman Brothers. It was the Lehman Brothers collapse that seemingly then broke the entire banking system's confidence in the viability of even the strongest financial institutions, and brought vital short-term lending between banks to a shuddering and initially complete halt.

- Nor was this simply an American financial crisis. It began here but it did not stop here. On the contrary, the global interconnections of the banking system and the scale of US trade indebtedness had already spread these toxic US-based mortgage-backed securities out into Europe and Asia, drying up credit there and bringing local banks to their knees. Indeed the first major subprime bank failure occurred not in the US but in the UK: with the collapse of the overambitious mortgage lender and Lehman Brothers collaborator *Northern Rock* in September 2007: a collapse that precipitated the first run on a private bank in the UK since the 1880s. Northern Rock was initially bailed out and then reluctantly nationalized by the UK government in February 2008. Indeed by December 2008, the UK central bank had lent the UK banking system an unprecedented £185 billion – only to find major UK banks (Barclays, HSB) and others still struggling to survive. Iceland's banks had by then required an $6 billion international bailout, the Irish government had taken control of the Anglo-Irish Bank, the German government had underwritten its entire banking system, the world's largest wealth management company UBS had lost $17 billion in 2008 alone (the largest loss in Swiss banking history) and the Belgian and Dutch governments had moved together to take effective control of the European financial giant, Fortis.

- The spreading financial crisis broke the confidence of banks in each other, and dried up the supply of credit from bank to bank, and from bank to consumer. What had begun as a financial problem in the housing market became a credit-shortage problem for firms and households alike. Across the US economy as a whole – in sector after sector – credit dried up, demand diminished, firms cut costs and labor, unemployment rose and job insecurity intensified. *A problem of Wall Street became a problem of Main Street*, a problem from which progressively there was no safe space to hide. The US GDP fell at an annualized rate of 6.2 percent in the last quarter of 2008, a year in which 2.6 million Americans lost their jobs; and 2009 opened with the prospect of at least a further job loss of a similar scale. The Federal Reserve spent 2008 cutting interest rates in a vain attempt to blunt the recession – the benchmark discount rate was cut from 6.25 percent in August 2007 to 3.75 percent in January 2008 and to 1 percent by November 2008 – yet the US economy still moved into recession in December 2007 and stayed there throughout 2008.

- By December 2008, falling US demand for internationally traded goods had also impacted adversely on the export-led industrial growth of newly industrializing economies, bringing the threat of mass unemployment to China, Latin America and the Asian south. This prompted the ILO to forecast a global unemployment spurt for 2009 of at least 51 million people, the

World Bank to forecast a global shrinkage in industrial output of maybe 15 percent in 2009 and the International Monetary Fund to forecast a shrinkage in the global economy of between 0.5 percent and 1.0 percent – which, if it occurs, will be the first such *global economic contraction* in 60 years.[14] Across the globe, stock values fell – and with them, the purchasing power of people's savings and retirement funds. The US Stock Market lost at least 25 percent of its value in the last quarter of 2008 alone; and there was one particular week in October 2008 when stock values plunged on the Shanghai exchange by 12.78 percent, on the Indian by 19.3 percent and in Russia by 21.12 percent. In the last quarter of 2008, the Japanese economy shrunk at an annual rate of 12.7 percent, the British at 3.3 percent and the German at 2.1 percent (the third, fourth and fifth largest economies in the advanced capitalist world).[15] Not surprisingly therefore, and across the G20 economies as a whole, government after government responded quickly to local signs of deepening recession by pumping money and guarantees into their banking systems, by cutting interest rates as aggressively as possible, and by dramatically boosting their own public spending. EU governments moved quickly on all three fronts in the last months of 2008, as did the Russian Government, the Japanese and the Chinese.[16] So too eventually did the Bush administration.[17]

- For one final casualty of this deepening and widening financial and housing crisis was the hitherto unquestioned faith in governing circles in the US in the superiority of unregulated markets and limited government spending. Suddenly all that was gone – it became yesterday's story – as the focus of public debate switched from deregulation and government retrenchment to bailouts and stimulus packages. An entire electorate was suddenly educated in a range of new things: the selfish bonus culture of Wall Street highfliers; the intricacies of interbank lending; and even the old-fashioned Keynesian notion that public spending has a role to play in correcting private market excess. The new president said as much in his Inaugural Address, telling American conservatives that "the ground had shifted beneath them," that "this crisis has reminded us that without a watchful eye, the market can spin out of control."[18] It was shades of FDR again, only this time with public spending on the truly grand scale: initially $30 billion to Bear Stearns and $85 billion to AIG, and eventually (September 2008) $700 *billion* to the entire US banking system to buy out "toxic" mortgage-based securities: plus $900 billion in short-term loans to the banking system from the Federal Reserve (October 2008) and an initial stimulus package (February 2009) of more than $789 billion to head off the recessionary consequences of bank failures and credit collapse.

Conservative blues

When in 2009 the incoming Obama administration picked up the responsibility for managing this deeply embedded crisis, a Republican Party shaken by loss of power was obliged to respond to the most interventionist-minded political leadership the US had seen since the mid-1960s. They did not respond well. Though the new president urged them not to return to the table pushing the discredited policies that, as he put it, "had brought us to this impasse in the first place,"[19] that was precisely what many of them continued to do. The Conservative opposition to Obama's mild Keynesianism ran broadly as follows.

1. The roots of this crisis lie, not in the market but in politics – in particular, in the politics of Fannie Mae and Freddie Mac – and the leadership of Barney Frank

Democrats in Congress are way too keen to point the finger of responsibility for the credit crisis at the greed and selfishness of the banking community, when in truth they ought to point the finger of responsibility at themselves. This is not Alan Greenspan's crisis. It is Barney Frank's. It was Barney Frank – and Democrats of his ilk – who systematically encouraged the two publicly underwritten mortgage giants to provide credit to social groups hitherto excluded from house ownership by their lack of adequate earning power.

Barney Frank quickly became the bogey man here. "The Dancing Queen,"
Rush Limbaugh calls him. It was he, after all, who in 2003 had said of
Fannie and Freddie: "I do not want the same kind of focus on safety and
soundness . . . I want to roll the dice a little bit more in this situation towards
subsidized housing."[20] *How those words would come back to haunt him!*

    The conservative case here is that "blaming greedy bankers, incompetent
rating agencies, or other actors in this unprecedented drama misses the
point – perhaps intentionally – that government policies created the incentives
for both a housing bubble and a reduction in the bank capital and home equity
that could have mitigated its effects." "We've been looking in the wrong place,"
Thomas Woods has recently written, "the current crisis was caused not by the
market but by the government's intervention in the market."[21]

- *After all it was Democrats, not Republicans, who saw political capital*
  in the spread of subprime loans to marginal groups – often African-
  American urban voters – and so had Fannie Mae and Freddie Mac
  systematically lowered the bar on income requirements for house
  purchase.[22]
- *It was the special status of Fannie and Freddie as government-*
  sponsored enterprises (GSEs) that encouraged banks and other private
  financial institutions to treat their mortgage-backed securities as the
  rock-solid basis on which to lend yet more money to home owners, so
  triggering "this artificial diversion of resources into mortgage lending
  [which] inflate[d] home prices," "divert[ed capital] from its most pro-
  ductive use into housing" and "create[ed] a short-term boom in hous-
  ing . . . an artificially created bubble."[23]
- *It was Democrats who blocked the 2005 attempt to bring Fannie Mae*
  and Freddie Mac under proper accounting control, so allowing "in
  2005, 2006 and 2007 a blizzard of terrible mortgage paper [to
  flutter] out of the Fannie and Freddie clouds, burying many of our
  oldest and most venerable institutions."[24]
- *And it was after the passing of the Community Reinvestment Act*
  under Jimmy Carter – a law that "opened banks to crushing discrimi-
  nation suits if they did not lend to minorities in numbers high enough
  to satisfy the authorities" – that "left-wing groups like ACORN
  blocked drive-up lanes and made business impossible for banks until
  they surrendered to demands that they make millions in loans they
  wouldn't otherwise have made."[25] *"Banks were morally pressured by*
  politicians," Pat Buchanan has written, "into making home loans to

folks who could not remotely qualify under standards set by decades of experience with mortgage defaults."[26]

Democrats may now find political capital in bewailing the adverse impact of the credit crisis on the American poor – spreading first foreclosures and then unemployment down the American income distribution – but it was actually they who laid the foundations for the crisis they now bewail, by the irresponsibility, fecklessness even, of the lending policies they forced on a reluctant financial industry. Ann Coulter, as always, put the case in its least adorned way.[27]

> From the "Community Reinvestment Act" that pressured banks into affirmative-action lending, to those "government sponsored enterprises" Fannie Mae and Freddie Mac – who bought up all the resulting sub-prime loans and repackaged them as "investment grade" securities – the greasy thumb-prints of government were all over this fiasco from beginning to end.

2. The scale and importance of bank deregulation as a cause of this crisis is entirely exaggerated

The counterpoint to that argument is the speed and ease with which conservative commentators on our present crisis move to deny the role of bank deregulation in its genesis. There are conservative voices out there decrying the inadequacy of regulatory practice – building the case that the regulations were there but were inadequately enforced. John McCain in particular, at the height of the crisis in 2008, called for the dismissal of the SEC chairman on precisely that ground.[28] *There are even conservatives willing to admit that the regulatory structure around the banking industry was, and now is, too weak: not least because of the complexity of the new financial products developed within the industry, and because of the increasingly dense network of relationships between different kinds of financial institutions. But they then point the finger of responsibility back to the Democratic-controlled Senate which passed the Gramm-Leach-Bliley Act in 1999, and to the personal greed and inappropriate lending practices of a few rogue traders.*

The more normal route, however, for conservatives keen to protect the autonomy of the financial sector is quite simply to deny that the industry is, or has been, deregulated, and then to turn the criticism on its head – pointing to the way in which regulation distorts the market and leaves consumers vulnerable to crises generated by those market distortions. "Capital punishment" is how in 2006 the AEI's Peter Wallison described the drift in business regulation since Sarbanes-Oxley: "regulatory burdens that cumulatively are taking the already heavy US regulatory structure over the edge."[29] "The three overriding facts" of our present circumstances, according to CATO's David Henderson, "are (1) we have not had a period of light regulation, (2) deregulation didn't fail and (3) regulations make things worse."[30] On this argument, the recent bank failures have been the product of excessive regulation rather than of deregulation — and not just the regulation of banks — there is even conservative scholarship arguing that the overregulation of land use was an additional source of the house price inflation that eventually brought the system of subprime loans crashing to the ground.[31]

- *One aspect of the regulatory structure in particular often mentioned by critics of the politicization of Fannie and Freddie[32] is the parallel dysfunctional interest rate policy of the Federal Reserve. Post 9/11, that policy was initially "excessively loose," bringing interest rates down so low (down to 1 percent in mid-2003 to mid-2004) as to trigger "overinvestment in housing and other capital-intensive industries."[33] It then tightened, bringing interest rates up, leaving more and more people unable to pay the mortgages that low interest rates had made possible. Bad financial management, that is, and not excessive financial deregulation, then stands alongside political interference with the market as the other cause célèbre of the 2008 crisis.*

- *The libertarian critique is slightly otherwise: not the volume of regulation so much as its agenda and partial nature. "The problem . . . is not regulation or the lack thereof," Thomas Woods has written, "the problem is the system itself, a system that . . . artificially encourages indebtedness, excessive leverage, and reckless money management in general." Banks are regulated. They ought to be entirely deregulated, and treated like all other businesses: because, as things stand now ". . . with regard to the housing market, the point is that lenders were doing exactly what the federal government and the central bank wanted them to do. Saying that more government oversight was needed misses the point. More and riskier loans are what the government wanted . . . the American dream extended to more and more people."[34]*

3. Government spending will not get us out of this crisis.
It will simply make matters worse, as it did in the 1930s

All that ground-clearing then leaves conservative opponents of government intervention able to argue for free market solutions to the present serious downturn in the US economy. Some recognize the need for a stimulus but disagree with the Obama administration about its content. Others – not least Karl Rove – question the need for a stimulus at all, arguing that intervention must make things worse. This is Karl Rove in the Wall Street Journal *in February 2009:*[35]

> *The Democratic stimulus will slow recovery, but not stop it. Recessions don't last forever and, if history is a guide, sometime late this year or early next the economy will rebound on its own. When that happens, Democrats will argue that their untargeted permanent spending actually revived the economy.*

The free market solution contains a number of distinct threads.

- *At its core is a straightforward denial of the economic literacy of John Maynard Keynes. It is not possible, they say, to spend your way out of recession.*[36] *Governments do not create money, they appropriate it. Spending by governments has to be financed. It can only be financed by either borrowing or taxation – both of which crowd out privately generated investment and demand. Printing money only produces inflation. Borrowing money slows down investment. Taxation reduces levels of personal consumption. "Government spending cannot cause prosperity; it can only reallocate resources from one person or activity to another. Prosperity – economic expansion – can be achieved only by increasing total production, not by simply moving it around."*[37] *Governments do not solve economic crises. They make them worse.*
- *The proof, so the argument runs, is there in the experience of the 1930s. Liberals like to hail FDR as a role model for the Obama administration. What they are less keen to do is to admit that the New Deal did not solve the Great Depression. It actually extended it. There are conservative commentators out there arguing that Roosevelt actually created the Depression – turning a recession already en route to recovery into a decade of economic disaster. There are others arguing,*

more moderately, that his policies simply accentuated it, pointing to the return of higher unemployment to the US in 1937 to demonstrate that the New Deal experiment failed. "According to research by economists at UCLA," the Cato Institute tell us, "New Deal policies extended the Depression by seven years."[38]

- *Instead of hailing the bailouts and the stimulus packages as routes to renewed prosperity, their critics treat them as further evidence of a government-led rake's progress. What we face is not a return to sustained economic growth. What we face is a hugely inflated public spending deficit. That deficit will have to be financed. The burden of its financing will fall on future generations – "fiscal child abuse" is what CATO's Chris Edwards called it[39] – and the scale of that burden threatens us as a nation with the possibility of total insolvency. The US may well go bust because of this government largesse; and even if it does not, the tax burden created by debt repayment will throttle the very economic growth that the debt's acquisition was meant to prevent.*

- *And then, of course, there are those who go the further inch. Government spending is not only ineffective in moments of economic crisis such as these. It is also profoundly un-American. We are, we are told, by virtue of all this government intervention now being moved inexorably onto the slippery slope to socialism.[40] Indeed, for certain conservative commentators, getting to socialism is Barack Obama's ultimate goal. Rush Limbaugh, as we saw in Chapter 2, regularly tells his radio audience that Obama "wants to move [the country] far left. He wants the government to be as large as it can. He wants power. He wants to punish success. He wants to try to make everybody as equal and the same as possible." And because he does "I shamelessly say 'No, I want him to fail'. If his agenda is a far-left collectivism – some people say socialism – as a conservative heartfelt, deeply, why should I want socialism to succeed?"[41]*

4. So what we do not need is more Democratic Party "pork"

For at least the following three reasons; that much of this spending simply protects the feckless behavior of others; that it sends public money where public money should not go; and that so many of the proposals packaged inside the various stimulus plans are only there because Democratic Party constituencies and lobbyists have to be serviced, regardless of the value to the rest of the economy of the services demanded.

- *The moral hazard argument is everywhere in the conservative case against government intervention. Bailing out those who make economic mistakes penalizes those who don't. It penalizes the very people whose entrepreneurship deserves our full attention and reward. "As a cardinal principle, the federal government should not intervene to save firms from the consequences of bad business decisions."[42] Sometimes that argument is used in conservative circles to make the case against bank bailouts,[43] and against federal aid to high-spending state governors; but more normally it is used to make the case against sending tax-dollars to car companies that cannot compete and to house buyers who cannot pay. Yes, some of the mortgage-selling practices were predatory. But so too were the appetites of house buyers who signed mortgage deals which their incomes could never have hoped to support. Bailing out feckless consumers effectively taxes those many more responsible home buyers who restricted their sights to houses they knew were within their purchasing capacity. And of course the Big Three car makers want a slice of the action; but they need it only because of past management decisions to make cars that people now no longer want to buy. Bailing them out will simply delay the inevitable, wasting tax payers' money to prop up companies that ought properly to be left to fail – a classic case of CEO corporate welfare. Far better therefore to inflict modest pain now to avoid greater pain later.[44]*
- *In any case, so many of the items to be funded in Democratic Party designed stimulus packages ought not to be funded, and the Republicans have suddenly become a party opposed to waste. No bridges to nowhere for them any more. The green lobby is opposed to economic growth; funding green initiatives is simply throwing money at the moon. Extending unemployment insurance just slows the rate at which the unemployed seek and find new private-sector employment:[45] it is an unwarranted transfer of resources from the hard-pressed working poor to the idle. Extra Medicaid funding only postpones and deepens the entitlement crisis that is the real barrier to economic growth. Even enhanced education spending, we are occasionally told, will bring no immediate economic boost.[46] If Democrats genuinely want to boost the economy while servicing legitimate public goals, let the bulk of the*

spending part of their stimulus packages go directly to the military.[47] *That way, we will all get a really potent "bang" for our buck.*

- But Democrats won't do that, so the conservative argument runs. Their claims for the job-creating capacities of their stimulus packages are based on very *"loose assumptions about multiplier effects and inexact rules of thumb about job creation."*[48] This is not surprising, since in truth the packages themselves are really only a cover for the Democrats' partisan medium and long-term agenda: designed to shore up their political base by rewarding their friends and punishing their enemies. Democratic Party–initiated stimulus packages do not produce economic growth but they do produce a feeding frenzy for the progressive lobby. They act as cover for programs that otherwise would never make it out of committee. Stimulus packages serve the needs of teachers unions, proabortion advocacy groups and antipoverty lobbyists. They serve their interests, but not the interests of Americans as a whole: which is why not a single Republican in the House of Representatives voted for the $819 billion stimulus package (H.R. 1) passed by the Democratic Party majority in the House in January 2009 or for the eventual compromise package passed in February 2009. Not a single one!

5. What we need are larger and more permanent tax cuts

What does serve the needs of the American people, by directly countering the recessionary features of the present economic downturn, are tax cuts: tax cuts made permanent; tax cuts made substantial; and tax cuts that are matched down the road, dollar for dollar, by an equivalent reduction in government programs. Republican lawmakers saw in the first stimulus package of the Obama years an opportunity to plant their flag again on the firm ground of their core principles. These, for Representative Paul D. Rynan (R-Wis) at least, were *"fiscal conservatism and economic liberty . . . the tallest pole in our tent to which the Bush administration had taken the axe. Now we're building it back,"*[49] he said, by pushing for a stimulus package entirely based on tax cuts. His party chairman put a similar argument in this way:[50]

> The fastest way to help families is by letting them keep more of the money they earn. Individual empowerment: that's how you stimulate the economy. . . . when families keep the money, they spend it, save it or invest it. And the private sector economy benefits when families and businesses buy consumer goods or invest in

*it for the future. But when Washington spends the money, some of it may flow
into the economy, but all too often, much gets wasted.*

*The tax cuts must be permanent; because only permanent tax cuts can hope
to change the long-term behavior of American investors and consumers. Tax
cuts must be substantial, on both corporations and households, because only
substantial tax cuts can give spenders the confidence to reignite the demand
side of the US economy; and tax cuts must be matched by equivalent reductions in government spending, to avoid the deficit-creating habits of the Bush
administration from whose fiscal irresponsibility many core Republicans now
wish clearly to distance themselves.*[51] *No Obama. No Bush. Back to an earlier
era of fiscal conservatism and enhanced individual consumer liberty. Back to
Ronald Reagan.*[52]

A liberal response

So how should liberals respond to that? They should respond by
conceding that, as usual with conservative arguments, there are significant strands of truth in part of what is on offer – but only in part,
so that in consequence, yet again, the total conservative response is
less valuable than the strongest of its individual elements. We need to
remember that, in this case perhaps more than in many others, it
always takes two to tango. Public and private institutions definitely
interacted here – neither danced alone – so by putting the full weight
of responsibility for the housing debacle on public sector actors to the
exclusion of all else, the broad conservative argument misleads us in
two important ways. It ignores, sometimes entirely, the central role
played by private institutions in this story; and it mis-specifies, by
overstating, the particular contribution of public sector players. There
are public sector dimensions to the causal story here, but in conservative hands those public sector–based causes are given far too much
weight. We need a better balance: this one.

1. To blame Barney Frank for our current impasse
   is like blaming Noah for the flood

Let us be absolutely clear at the outset: there is nothing reprehensible
in elected politicians being concerned with the housing market and

with housing finance. In fact it would be reprehensible if they were not. Houses are a vital physical element in the quality of life of all of us. Buying them is the biggest single purchase that most of us make. The financing of housing has huge social as well as economic ramifications. So politics should take precedence here. The only question it is legitimate to ask is whether the present housing crisis is the product of political intervention of an inappropriate kind, particularly intervention by Barney Frank. The answer to that question has to be "No."

- The timing of the stages of the crisis does not fit the vulgar "Barney Frank did it" thesis. In fact political oversight in the years preceding the collapse of the housing bubble was predominantly in the hands of Republican lawmakers, not Democratic ones. Republicans controlled the House from 1994 to 2006, the Senate from 2002 to 2006 and the White House throughout the entire housing bubble crisis. Barney Frank was an important player through that period too – as the ranking *minority* member on the House Finance Committee – but he was not in a leadership position in Congress until January 2007, only months before the closure of the first hedge funds brought down by the emerging housing crisis. The explosion in US house prices was a post-1995 phenomenon. Average house prices in 1995 were only slightly higher than they had been in the 1950s, and house ownership rates were similarly stable, not rising.[53] The housing bubble occurred after 1995. Its expansion coincided with the rise of *Republican* political power, not Democratic.
- So it is simply wrong to assert that Barney Frank caused this crisis, or to imply that his 2003 remarks fixed housing policy. They did not. It is more accurate to say that Barney Frank and the Democrats *inherited* a crisis in whose development they had played but one consistent and major role. Theirs had been, and remains, a strong voice arguing for the rights of the lower middle class to own their own homes. But spreading home ownership down the income ladder was not a policy goal that Barney Frank invented or that the Democratic Party monopolized. It was a policy goal that the Clinton and the Bush administrations shared. It was a *bipartisan policy* pursued through the terms of reference that successive administrations gave to

Fannie Mae and Freddie Mac; terms of reference that both these Treasury-backed private mortgage companies implemented until 2001 with notable caution. We need to remember that subprime and home equity line loans made up only 15 percent of all new residential mortgages in 2001. By 2006 they made up 48 percent.[54] It was the explosion of subprime and home equity lending *after* 2001 that we have to explain.

2. If political finger-pointing is of any value here, let's point it in the right direction

US housing policy is made by many people and many institutions. It is also made over a long period of time. There are indeed powerful voices lobbying for the better and more generous funding of social housing, and those voices have used the Community Reinvestment Act, and the powers of the Department of Housing and Urban Development, to press their case. But that pressure has been neither as irresponsible nor as one-dimensional as the critics of the funding of generous housing often imply.

- Certainly there is no evidence that the main lobby group in play here wanted the banks to meet their obligations under the Community Reinvestment Act by giving subprime loans to people who would inevitably later default. On the contrary, ACORN pressed regularly for "quality fixed-rate loans based on documentation of what borrowers really could pay" and was an early leading critic of Lehmann Brothers for the lax standards they tolerated in the mortgages they bought and securitized.[55] "During the 1990s enforcement under the reinvestment act was strong, prime lending to low-income communities increased and it was done safely. In 2000 a Federal Reserve report found that lending under the act was generally profitable and not overly risky."[56] Moreover after 2000, as indeed before, "bad subprime loans were predominantly made by firms not covered by the act. According to recent Fed data, 75 percent of higher-priced loans made during the peak years of the subprime boom were made by independent mortgage firms and bank affiliates not covered by the act."[57] No less an authority than the president of the San Francisco Federal Reserve is on record as rejecting the "tendency to conflate the current problems in the subprime market with CRA-motivated lending." The CRA, Janet Yellen insisted, "has increased the volume of responsible lending to low- and moderate-income households,"[58] not decreased it. And well she might, for the evidence in this case is very clear.[59]

- It is true that Clinton's Secretary of Housing, Andrew Cuomo, was one of those pushing Fannie Mae and Freddie Mac to increase the percentage of their mortgages serving low and moderate income families;[60] but his was not the only voice in the Clinton administration. Warnings on the dangers of predatory lending were given – not least by both a Treasury task force and Treasury Secretary Lawrence Summers in 1999 and again in 2000 – and they were heeded. Both the Urban Institute and the American Enterprise Institute have made clear Fannie Mae and Freddie Mac's systematic *underperformance* on low-income mortgages throughout the 1990s.[61] HUD in 1996 required that 12 percent of all mortgage purchases by the GSEs were to be "special affordable loans," typically made to borrowers with income less than 60 percent of their area's median income; and that figure was only increased to 20 percent while Clinton remained in office. It would be set at 28 percent by 2008. The Cuomo years witnessed the beginning of the lowering of standards inside the GSEs, but when Clinton left office, Fannie and Freddie were still only marginal players in the subprime market.

- If political oversight then went wrong, it went wrong in a serious way only after 2000. For it was the second Bush administration that created the lethal cocktail: a commitment to social housing mixed with a partisan enthusiasm for financial deregulation. Both elements of the cocktail had been there in the Clinton years, but in less acute form. It was the Bush administration that announced plans in 2004, at the height of the subprime loan explosion, "to sharply weaken CRA regulations, pulling small and mid-sized banks out from under the law's toughest standards."[62] It was the Bush administration's HUD that agreed to "give Fannie Mae and Freddie Mac credit for buying subprime mortgage-backed securities to meet their affordable housing goals."[63] Only after 2000 did Fannie Mae fall victim to lax internal accounting standards and the whiff of corruption, with its Clinton-appointed head forced to resign. It was his successor – the unfortunately named and Bush-appointed Daniel H. Mudd – who then made the fatal decision to aggressively expand the number of subprime loans that Fannie Mae underwrote, primarily through his agreement with Countrywide Financial.[64] He made that decision despite internal warnings from his own chief credit officer (in March 2005) that "the combination of these risks may be difficult for subprime borrowers to understand," and that "rating agencies may not be properly assessing the risks in these securities."[65] "Between 2005 and 2008, Fannie purchased or guaranteed at least $270 billion in loans to risky borrowers, more than three times as much as in all its earlier years combined."[66] And Fannie Mae did so because its new management team was by then operating in an all-pervasive governing culture that actively prized deregulation. Leaders of the four federal agencies overseeing the banking industry even gathered for a photo-shoot in 2003, posing behind a stack of paper wrapped in red tape, and holding in their hands garden shears and – in one case – a chain saw. Literally, a chain saw, held by the man whose office oversaw the internal accounting practices of Country-wide Financial![67]

3. The main drivers of the subprime loan crisis were private sector actors, not public ones

Even that change of policy by the Bush administration occurred only *after* smaller private mortgage companies had got themselves into financial difficulties doing the same. Fannie Mae and Freddie Mac came into this market late,[68] and came to be dominant players there only *after* fully private banks and associated hedge funds ran into liquidity difficulties. All of which serves to remind us that the initial drivers of the flow of subprime loans were not public or semipublic institutions. They were private ones.

- "The subprime loan boom was led by investment banks and mortgage brokers, not by government sponsored enterprises. Fannie and Freddie became unhinged in the middle of the decade only when they tried to play catch up."[69] After all, "Fannie and Freddie were [legally] barred from making subprime, alt-A, and jumbo loan business, so these other institutions moved in, expanding these markets"[70] by lowering the underwriting standards previously prevalent within them. Fannie Mae's criteria for mortgages to be packaged into securities had originally been strong ones: "10–20 percent down payments, housing debt payments no higher than 28 percent of gross income, and total debt payments restricted to 36 percent of gross income";[71] criteria that banks then passed on as terms to their mortgage customers. But from the late 1990s "new nonbank mortgage lenders began aggressively offering 'Alt-A' and subprime mortgages to households with bad credit history, no or minuscule down payments, and quite high debt-to-income ratios."[72] The result was a kind of mortgage Gresham's Law: bad lending practices began to drive out good ones.[73] "In 1990 only 4 percent of home loans allowed down payments of 5 percent or less: in 2007 . . . the median down payment for first-time buyers was just 2 percent." Worst still, "by 2006 nine out of every ten new subprime mortgages came with adjustable interest rates that typically jumped upwards after two years – the riskiest loans for the riskiest borrowers."[74]
- Such subprime loans were the brainchild of private mortgage companies keen to capture a larger and larger share of a financial market that in the midst of the house price explosion looked like a sure fire route to greater and greater profits. *Countrywide Financial* was the key private bank playing that role in the US. *Northern Rock* was its equivalent in the UK. Both had strong links to major triple-A rated financial institutions – Countrywide to Fannie Mae, Northern Rock to Lehman Brothers – and Countrywide at least worked hard to resist public regulation. When pressured to change its lending practices by the Office of the Comptroller of the Currency, it abruptly changed its regulator, opting instead for the less strident Office of Thrift Supervision. Three of the OTC's lightly regulated responsibilities failed during the subprime crisis: IndyMac Bancorp,

Washington Mutual, and Downey Savings and Loans (not to mention AIG FP, the hedge fund that brought AIG to its knees). That cannot have been accidental, as the rapid expansion of private mortgage providers increased their share of the mortgage market by 10 percent between 2000 and 2005 (that of the GSE's declined by 7 percent).[75]

- Well might Countrywide have resisted close supervision of its lending practices because lightly regulated predatory lending was very profitable before 2008, and made a lot of money for a lot of people. Adjustable rate mortgages, Alt-A mortgages, low/no down-payment mortgages, interest-only mortgages and negative-amortization mortgages proliferated because those developing them were able to take a fee at each stage of the transaction. These were fees taken before the inevitable toll of defaulters emerged to cloud the horizon, but they were also fees that shrunk as a proportion of the money loaned as competition between brokers intensified. Maintaining fee income then required increasing the volume of loans made, and so necessitating their extension, via ever easier underwriting standards, to less and less financially secure borrowers.[76] The risk of those mortgages then spread through the financial system because an "originate and distribute" business model was rapidly replacing the "originate and hold" way of mortgage finance that had prevailed in the staid housing markets of the immediate postwar period. More and more now it was a case of "make a loan, pocket the fee, bundle the mortgage with others and sell the securitized package to another institution to assume the risk."[77] And not just subprime loans – equity loans too: loans taken out to spend on home improvements, debt reduction and other consumer goods. We need to remember that, in 6 of the 8 years between 1999 and 2006, less than 40 percent of new loans were used to purchase an owner-occupied house. The rest were loans issued to refinance existing mortgages: as a mixture of predatory lending and ill-informed/naïve borrowing combined to persuade wider and wider sections of the American middle class that they would be wise to treat their house as a kind of personal ATM machine from which a seemingly endless flow of crisp bank notes could regularly be extracted without effort!

- So, as Mark Zandi has rightly observed, "*staid* was the last thing you could call mortgage lending during the housing boom. *Frenzied* might be a better term: and as the boom became a bubble, *out of control* would be even more appropriate." Out of control, and dominated by big financial institutions: "during the peak of the housing boom in 2005, the nation's 30 largest institutions accounted for half the loans originated . . . Countrywide topped the list, originating more than one million loans worth almost a quarter-trillion dollars that year."[78] It was Wall Street, with its apparently insatiable demand for mortgage-based securities, which drove the changes in the mortgage lending business. "Lenders now made their money solely on volume: the more loans they originated, the greater the profit."[79] What then developed with dizzying speed and complexity was a *shadow* banking system, one in which originating banks passed on mortgages to a mixed bag of investment banks, hedge funds, money-market funds and insurance companies, who in their turn protected themselves against risk by deploying increasingly obscure and complex derivatives such as collateralized debt obligations and credit default swaps. This shadow banking system was genuinely global in nature, one lubricated (and directed toward the US) by the sheer size of dollar debt held internationally because of the scale and persistence of the US trade deficit. In the first decade of the new century, what Zandi called "a self-reinforcing cycle" developed: American consumers flush with easy access to cheap credit bought heavily whatever the rest of the world was happy to sell, and the dollars sent overseas quickly returned as investments in US-based financial instruments, especially mortgage-based securities, in a flow of imported capital that brought interest rates down even lower in the US, making credit here cheaper still. "Cheap and easy credit spurred more home purchases and still more borrowing and spending. The cycle was complete."[80]

4. Lubricating the cycle with greed

There are cultural variations between national economic systems, and much of that variation has deep historical and institutional roots.[81]

Capitalisms which rely on stock markets rather than banks for their externally generated investment funds are vulnerable to a culture of short-term profit taking in a way that more bank-led capitalisms are not; and capitalisms with weak labor movements are prone to salary excess at the top of corporations on a scale which more socially democratic capitalisms would never tolerate. As the most stock-market dependent and least labor influenced capitalist system in the modern world, the men (and it is invariably men) who head the big US corporations have long overpaid themselves, relative to their counterparts elsewhere: and certainly since the Reagan era they have really piled on the compensation excess. The ratio of average CEO salary to the average wages of those they employed widened from 70:1 to possibly 300:1 in the three decades preceding the 2008 crash – levels of income inequality and corporate greed not seen in the US since the 1920s and levels that were (and remain) far larger than any generated elsewhere in the advanced capitalist world. That compensation excess made its own contribution to the way American financial institutions walked blindly into the crisis of 2008.

- In the post-Reagan years, corporate leaders paid themselves handsomely, and none did so with greater gusto than the corporate leaders of the United States' major financial institutions. Henry Paulson reportedly earned $30 million the year he left Goldman Sachs to head the Treasury, and his salary was not exceptional. Goldman Sachs' CEO earned $68.5 million in 2007 alone. The compensation packages for the CEOs of *failed* companies are even more striking. Angelo Mozilo walked away from Countrywide Financial with a reported $132 million; Stan O'Neal left Merrill Lynch with $162 million; and Richard Fuld took $34.4 million as Lehman Brothers collapsed beneath him. Merrill Lynch paid $209 million in cash and stock as bonuses to senior executives in the year (2008) in which the company lost $27 billion and its independence, and AIG followed that with a $165 million bonus pay out to its senior executives in 2009 (money paid for from taxpayer provider bail out funds). Well might the new president brand these payments "shameful" and Congress demand their return. Shameful seems the least of it in an economy in free fall and with unemployment soaring.

- What corporate leaders initiated corporate minions then
  followed. The housing bubble was built on the predatory lending practices of brokers dependent for their affluent lifestyle on
  fees and bonuses linked to the number and value of the mortgages they sold. Subprime loans proliferated in the easy money
  culture of post-2001 America because creating them, packag-
  ing them and selling them on all yielded "handsome fees to the
  many loan bundlers, securitization packagers and securitization repackagers that formed a gauntlet of fee-paying opportunity between the initial borrower and ultimate investor."[82]
  Short-term profit-seeking and individual salary excess was not
  marginal to this crisis. It was core; which is why the current
  outrage against Wall Street largesse, from both conservative and
  liberal populists, is so well-founded. Bankers and mortgage
  brokers took those fees from money contributed by the rest of
  us, and they completely overheated the housing market in
  order to do so. Their greed brought the rest of us down.[83]

5. This is not to deny that Fannie Mae and Freddie Mac remain part of the problem: it is simply to insist that they constitute only part of that problem

The financing of housing markets is always difficult. To buy a house,
people need to borrow long-term. The institutions lending them the
money have to borrow short. Institutions that borrow short and lend
long are inevitably unstable, able to survive only so long as long-term
rates are higher than short-term ones, and rates in general remain
stable over time. Historically, both the US and UK addressed the pre-
cariousness of such institutions in two ways. They insisted that only
specialist financial institutions service the housing market (savings
and loans in the US, building societies in the UK), and that those
institutions provide mortgages only on rigorous terms (requiring a
certain percentage of deposit, and lent only to people with appropriate
levels of income). They also set up strong barriers between mortgage
providers (and the housing market they financed) and the rest of the
banking system. The US went one stage further, and created a public
institution, the FNMA (Fannie Mae) to underwrite those mortgages.

(The United States, that is, has had a secondary mortgage market since the 1930s.) The problems we now face derive from the deconstruction of that historical settlement: the increasing tolerance, across wider and wider sections of the house financing system, of lower and lower accounting standards; and the removal of the firewalls that had hitherto isolated the mortgage market from the rest of the credit-providing system. That deconstruction took the following route.

- Fannie Mae was privatized in 1968, and an equivalent private institution, the FHLMC (Freddie Mac), was created alongside it in 1970 to extend the underwriting to a wider set of house mortgages. Fannie Mae and Freddie Mac functioned thereafter as private mortgage underwriters with implicit Treasury guarantees of their viability. This was never an ideal arrangement because it effectively enabled them to privatize their profits while socializing their losses.[84] The status of Fannie and Freddie as GSEs gave them market advantage over other institutions in the business of financing housing while leaving them free to lobby extensively, as they regularly did on a *very* grand and bipartisan scale, against any tighter regulation of their lending practices. The trade-off after 1992 was a GSE willingness to pursue federal targets for low-income housing and to take up the slack as private mortgage providers ran into the problem of falling house prices and rising foreclosures. There were clearly deficiencies in the GSEs' internal accounting practices in the years straddling the millennium, and even a whiff of illegality and corruption that forced resignations at the top; but even so, the GSEs remained minor players in the underwriting of subprime mortgages until very late in the story. It was only in 2007, as confidence in mortgage-backed securities waned, that investors increasingly switched to MBS issued by Fannie Mae and Freddie Mac. The two GSEs then became responsible for 84 percent of all MBS issuance in the first quarter of 2008, but their share of that market had only been 33 percent as recently as the peak of the housing boom in 2006.[85] Pulled then between their responsibility to their shareholders and their deal with federal government, neither GSE had the capacity to withstand the housing crisis as it deepened. By March 2008 the total credit outstanding on the books of the two GSEs was equivalent to the entire publicly held debt of the US Government. Defaulting on that scale would have brought the entire house down, which is presumably why it was not allowed to happen.

- Yet this special status of Fannie Mae and Freddie Mac, problematic as it is, was not the main weakness in what has now turned out to be a fundamentally dysfunctional US house-financing system. The main weakness was the diminishing adequacy over time of the firewalls that divided housing finance as a system from the rest of the credit-creating world. It was the systematic erosion of these firewalls that laid the foundations for the contemporary crisis;[86] and they were removed in two ways – one formal, one not. The formal way was the passing of a string of legislative acts from the Depository Institutions Deregulatory and Monetary Control Act of 1980 through the Alternative Mortgage Transaction Parity Act of 1982 to the Gramm-Leach-Bliley Act of 1999. This was legislation introduced largely at the behest of Wall Street lobbyists[87] that cumulatively facilitated the lowering of underwriting standards and ultimately ended the 1933 Glass-Steagall separation of commercial and investment banks.[88] The informal way, ultimately far more potent, was the failure by any part of the US regulatory system to stop the spread of subprime mortgage-backed securities out of the housing market into the rest of the financial system. As Mark Zandi put it, "lost in the rapid wholesale rush to securitization . . . was the notion that someone – anyone – should ensure that individual loans are made responsibly, to responsible borrowers."[89]

- There were regulatory agencies in place overseeing parts of the mortgage market throughout the build up to the credit crisis, but in truth there were too many of them – "too many cooks" as Zandi puts it – impossible to coordinate, with half of the mortgage providers regulated at federal level and half at the level of the states.[90] There were sins of omission and sins of commission by the existing regulatory structure in that rush to securitization: sins of *omission*, in moments such as the hastily passed Commodity Futures Modernization Act in 2000, a moment when the newly emerging derivatives market could have been regulated but was not; and sins of *commission*, when the credit-rating agencies in particular, overwhelmed by the volume of new mortgage-based products, failed in their key responsibility of differentiating sound financial products from toxic ones.[91] The resulting lemming-like rush to profits by leading financial institutions traditionally unconnected to the housing market induced them to buy large quantities of mortgages bundled up in packages whose viability neither they nor the credit rating agencies on which they relied were able to assess accurately. It was that rush to profits that led them and us, as we now know, into a veritable financial minefield of securitized disaster.

6. The roots of this crisis do indeed lie in a failure of regulation and control

The excesses of Countrywide Financial cannot simply be dismissed by the deployment of the "bad apple" theory, attractive as that theory is to those who would leave unchanged the regulatory structure surrounding banking in the US. Countrywide Financial was a bad apple, but it was not alone in its predatory practices and its corrosive impact. Apples left to rot in the sun of cheap money and inadequate husbandry do so in abundance, and they certainly did so on this occasion.

- As we have just seen, the regulatory structure established around American banking in the wake of the Great Depression was systematically loosened under both the Clinton and second Bush administrations. Republicans are right to point here to the role played in that deregulatory trajectory by members of the Clinton administration who are now key architects of Obama's economic policy, and to the far too cozy relationships between Wall Street lobbyists and certain Democratic (as well as Republican) Senators.[92] Poachers have turned gamekeepers here, and we are right to be wary of the turn. Alan Greenspan too is a figure straddling both Democratic and Republican administrations; and he, at least, has had the grace partially to concede the apparent error of some of his ways. It is hard to think that financial deregulation was not a key element in this story when the former Fed chairman is on the record, conceding a flaw in his general deregulatory stance – a concession made to Henry Waxman no less. The conversation between them ran as follows.[93]

> *Waxman:* You had the authority to prevent irresponsible lending practices that led to the subprime loan crisis. You were advised to do so by many. Do you feel that your ideology pushed you to make decisions you wish you had not made?
>
> *Greenspan:* Yes, I've found a flaw. I don't know how significant or permanent it is. But I've been very distressed by that fact.
>
> *Waxman:* Were you wrong?
>
> *Greenspan:* Partially.

- Alan Greenspan did voice alarm – late in the day (2005) – about the funding and practices of Fannie Mae and Freddie Mac;[94] and yet he remained to the end of his tenure at the Fed reluctant to tighten controls on the flow and distribution of the new financial products spreading with such speed through the US (and then global) banking system. "The Fed could have weighed in on the side of tighter regulation and disclosure standards for highly complex and risky over-the-counter derivatives . . . but Greenspan repeatedly testified that he believed derivatives improved market liquidity and needed no regulation."[95] Yet it was the development of those new derivatives that went one stage further than simply removing the wall between the housing market and the rest of the credit system. It was those products that pushed the weaknesses of housing finance into the very core of American (and eventually global) financial networks. Mortgage-backed securities were not new of course. They can be traced back to the 1970s.[96] What was new was their scale. What was new was the fragility of the subprime mortgages packaged within them. What was new was how far they spread through the entire financial world under the light touch of Greenspan's regulatory regime and philosophy, and how poorly the credit-rating agencies responded to that spread.

To complete the mix we need add only two other pieces of public policy: one definitely bipartisan, one possibly not. The bipartisan bit was the commitment to the granting of tax relief on mortgage interest – a huge middle-class tax subsidy, enshrined in the 1986 Tax Reform Act, which built into the whole US housing finance system a propensity to inflate demand.[97] Because of it, people earning enough to get a mortgage (a growing proportion of the population as accounting standards fell) were able to get a bigger mortgage than they might otherwise have acquired, because tax relief on the interest on that mortgage effectively turned the federal government into a subordinate co-purchaser. And the decision to extend that tax relief to second mortgages meant that vast swathes of the US middle class got tax relief on their equity lines of credit too, with the federal government effectively giving them tax relief on whatever they chose to spend that line of credit on (rarely home improvements!). Then add to the mix the Fed's interest rate policy – bringing rates lower and lower after 2001 to stimulate the economic growth that helped reelect George W. Bush in 2004 – and you have all the ingredients for a classical overheated housing market: with prices escalating in a seemingly unending spiral that brought more and more speculative capital in to fuel the spiral still further.

7. Eating a three-layered cake

Financial crises are like layered cakes. To grasp them in their totality, you have to cut your way through every level.

- The top level of this one is, as is hopefully now clear, the *American housing market* with its high levels of tax subsidization and securitization. Each national housing finance system has its own history, of course, and the US is no exception. The US housing finance system has always been distinct. It was distinct in the 1930s for its development of 30-year fixed rate fully amortized mortgages. It is distinct now for the proliferation of the types of mortgages it tolerates; and it is distinct in this fashion, as we noted earlier, because that toleration rests on a far higher securitization of mortgage finance than is common elsewhere in the advanced industrial world.[98] In layman's language, US institutions providing mortgages used to keep those mortgages on their books. In most industrial countries they still do. In the US (and these days, the UK too), by contrast, most of the mortgages now being provided – including the dodgy ones – are packaged and sold on, to become the assets on which further lending can be based. They are even sold on to financial institutions abroad, in economies whose housing finance is not similarly highly securitized![99] The crisis of 2008 has shown that Martin Wolf was right: "America's housing solution is not a good one to follow."[100] "The key promise of securitization – that it would make the financial system more robust by spreading risk more widely – turned out to be a lie. Banks used securitization to increase their risk, not reduce it, and in the process they made the economy more, not less, vulnerable to financial disruption."[101]

- The middle level is clearly the *inadequacy of the regulatory structures* governing financial institutions in the United States. Excessive securitization is not just a feature of the housing market. US banks too used to make loans to businesses and customers, and keep those loans on their books: patient capital that meant banks and clients swam or sank together. "However in the past decade, this financial model has changed radically." Banks now "sell their credit risk to other investment groups, either by direct loan sales or by repackaging loans into bonds." And they do this because they can: "regulatory reform has allowed the banks to reduce the amount of capital that they need to hold against the danger that borrowers default."[102] Undercapitalized financial institutions are, of course, an accident waiting to happen. All they need is the complacency that comes with a prolonged period of sustained economic growth, easy profit-taking and – in this case – a supply of housing which, though growing, could not keep pace with the supply of money being thrown at it. The crisis of 2008 obliges us to recognize the importance of adequate financial regulation, and to demand its reimposition. Indeed a list of unlikely characters – from Nigel Lawson to Hank Paulson – is already on record saying so.[103]

- But the bottom level is something else entirely: the *all-pervasiveness of debt* in the current US economic model – not just housing debt but also general consumer debt, government debt and international debt. Of the latter three, government debt is the one most often discussed and criticized, and yet it is the least troublesome of the lot. Public sector deficits rise and fall with the scale of government spending and the size of tax revenues. Well-directed public spending has generated, and will again generate the economic growth and tax flows that can take the public sector back into surplus. No, it is the other two debts that underpin this financial crisis. It is the scale of US overseas indebtedness – anchored in the growing lack of domestic competitiveness of US-based manufacturing industry – that has flooded the global financial system with unwanted dollars, dollars whose reinvestment in US financial institutions both inflated the supply of credit available for house purchase and ensured that a housing collapse here would race out (tsunami-like) into the wider global economy. And it is the scale of personal indebtedness in the United States – anchored in the stagnation of real wages for the bulk of American workers since the mid 1970s – that made subprime loans so attractive to so many Americans, and yet made it so difficult to pay off when their "teaser" period was over.[104] The immediate crisis requires an immediate response, directed at the top two layers of the cake, but to avoid its repetition over the long term public policy will also need to do something fundamental about the internal and external dependence of US living standards on our collective ability to borrow.

In this last regard, it is worth remembering that there have been not one, but two periods of prolonged economic growth since World War II: the first from 1948 to 1973, the second from 1992 (with a brief dip in 2002) to 2008. In the first of those economic booms, the internal deal underpinning growth was a union-negotiated productivity-wages pact – rising productivity and *rising wages* going together in a social contract that gave the long postwar boom a strong internal base. The second time round the internal deal was different. It was one imposed by an overconfident business class on a seriously weakened labor movement, one combining rising productivity with *rising income inequality*. For the vast majority of working Americans, earnings/hour stagnated during this second boom – rising only briefly in the late 1990s before stabilizing again. Since 1992 growth has rested on a Faustian contract between Main Street and Wall Street. Wall Street has been awash with money, and keen to lend. Main Street has been financially pressed, and keen to borrow. The second postwar boom rested not on rising wages but on credit, on money borrowed from Wall Street by US consumers, and borrowed by Wall Street in significant measure from financial sources abroad. Houses built on sand invariably fall over. The year 2008 brought the fall.

The immediate credit crisis clearly requires a regulatory fix. But equally clearly, the long-term weakness of the US economy requires a resetting of the underlying social contract. Currently we are debt soaked. We have never been so debt soaked; and we will have periodic credit crises until we dry out. We need to return to a world in which rising productivity and rising wages go together, so that people buy commodities today out of wages they earn today, not out of wages they might earn tomorrow and which they bring forward only by borrowing at high rates of interest. We need to return to a world in which the bulk of what we buy we also build here. The underlying requirement now is one of reconfiguring investment in the United States so that good jobs return to America, and of reconfiguring the tax code so that good wages return to the middle class. The lesson of 2008 is that we need a *new deal* as well as a new *bailout*. Does anyone in Washington realize that? I do hope so.

The role of government

Government spending is part of the solution, not part of the problem, and to argue otherwise is to compound the crisis, not to solve it. Part of the problem of federal economic leadership in the contemporary United States is that, for the last eight years at least, responsibility for it has lain with an administration ideologically opposed to its extensive use. People looked at FEMA under Brown, or the TARP rescue package under Paulson, and decided that federal action was inevitably flawed. But it is only flawed if left in the hands of those uncomfortable with its deployment. TARP under Henry Poulson's leadership was indeed "Goldman Sachs' socialism":[105] money handed over to banks and other lending institutions with inadequate oversight, lack of tight terms of reference for its use, and available for executives to raid for their own considerable bonuses. All that was regrettable and reprehensible, but it was also amendable. Government spending doesn't have to be that inept. It depends on the quality of the hands that guide it.

Those hands were effective the last time this was tried on a grand scale, namely in the 1930s. One of the least impressive parts of the conservative counter-case is the trashing some commentators have given of FDR's record in the 1930s. True, unemployment did not vanish from the US economy until full-time mobilization was achieved after 1941. But unemployment did come down, and job creation was sustained, almost without a break from 1933 until the outbreak of World War II. The US unemployment rate was 25 percent in 1933. It was down 10 points by 1940; and it only spiked – and then only temporarily – when FDR succumbed in 1937 to his generation's conservative arguments against public spending and briefly tried to balance the budget. The arguments used by contemporary conservatives on fiscal restraint in the face of recession intensified that recession when briefly put into practice in 1937; which makes it all the more ironic, and misleading, for fiscal conservatives now to point to FDR as evidence for their case. When FDR spent, unemployment fell. When he did not, it rose. When unemployment is massive, government spending is like that. It is a good thing.

So the current trashing of Keynesian economics by supply-side conservatives has to be challenged as entirely misguided. Government spending does not crowd out private spending when private spending has stalled. What government spending does, if properly directed, is trigger again private sector employment, wages, demand and growth. Keynesian critics these days treat government and private spending as dollar for dollar equivalents. They are not. Government spending in a stagnant economy has a multiplier effect. Print a dollar, give it to someone lacking a wage, they will spend it, it becomes income for the person receiving it, who then spends it on. The extra revenue generated, if large enough, sustains a flow of taxation back to the government that more than compensates for the original dollar. There is no "generational theft" here. Properly targeted public spending leaves future generations not with debt but with better roads, schools, housing and hospitals. The trick is to properly target it – to spent it, that is, where the "bang for the buck" is greatest – spend it where it is least likely to be saved and most likely to be passed on. We have tables telling us where the bang is biggest: we need to follow those tables!

What do those tables tell us? They tell us that a government dollar spent on food stamps ends up generating $1.73 of extra demand in the economy; on unemployment benefits $1.64; on infrastructure $1.59; and on aid to states $1.36. They also tell us, by contrast, that making the Bush tax cuts permanent would add only 29 cents for every dollar surrendered, that a cut in corporation tax yields only 30 cents for each dollar, and that making dividend and capital gains tax cuts permanent yields only 37 cents for each dollar.[106] So which kind of stimulus package is likely to generate the biggest immediate boost to an economy in recession: tax cuts and public spending aimed at the poor and at infrastructure or one aimed at the rich and the large corporations? This is not rocket science! It is really quite straightforward: or at least it is straightforward if ideology and class interests are not allowed to get in the way.

It is now clear what we need. We need to let the logic of the argument that has been developed here guide the design of policy. We need to roll back through the stages, going from the surface to the roots of this problem. This is no time for inactivity because of moral hazard. Everyone is touched by this crisis: house owners who cannot pay their mortgage; house owners who can but who see their house values driven down by the foreclosures of others; house owners whose job security is threatened or lost (and with it, their homes) by the impact of bad mortgages on the flow of credit in the wider financial system; and house owners who see the quality of their local communities undermined by failing businesses and shrinking local tax revenues.

- At the very least, policy must bring relief to those facing immediate foreclosure on their primary residence, with the choice being between schemes that restructure mortgage packages and those that bring public bodies in as co-buyers. The Obama administration favor the first, using Fannie and Freddie to socialize the cost; but going that route does leave public policy vulnerable to the charge that it discriminates against those whose financial prudence makes assistance unnecessary. Sharing the cost of mortgage borrowing, and taking a slice of any subsequent capital gain, turns the US federal government into a major house owner – something liberals probably fear – but it may yet turn out to be the better short-term fix.[107]

- Longer term, tighter regulation is clearly required to recreate – in a new climate of complex financial products – a strong firewall dividing the housing market from the rest of the financial system. If that can be done by moving back toward Glass-Steagall, with general banking excluded from either direct or indirect linkages to housing finance, all well and good; but that is unlikely. That horse bolted long ago, and it is unlikely ever again to be re-stabled: which is why the tight public regulation (or even full nationalization) of Fannie and Freddie, with a public monopoly on mortgage underwriting for primary residences, must be in the mix for longer-term solutions. So too must be a larger program of public housing, and the incremental removal of tax relief on first and second mortgages.

- But in the end the ability of people to buy their houses turns on the level of their earnings. Housing finance will remain problematic, for the bottom third of the US population, until general wages rise again and income inequality significantly diminishes. A stable housing market in the US, as elsewhere, requires more than an adequate supply of houses and a stable financial system to lubricate their purchase, though it clearly needs both of those. It also needs a generalized rise and distribution in the capacity of people needing houses to buy them without the risk of default. American housing will not be stable and shared until American prosperity is stable and shared. There are big things, way beyond housing, that need to be done.

Notes

1. Martin Wolf, "America's economy risks the mother of all meltdowns," *Financial Times*, February 20, 2008.

2. Average US house prices hardly rose in real terms from 1945 to 1995 (taking 1949 prices as 100, prices in 1995 were 105). They then doubled in a decade. From 1999 to July 2006, when they peaked, the house price index rose 155 percent. From July 2006 to January 2009 it fell 25 percent.

3. The term "subprime loan" covers a lot of different mortgage products, all characterized by their high default potential because their terms of payment either intensify over time or are higher than it is prudent for people on a certain income to acquire.

4. It is worth remembering that home equity loans grew by 43 percent in 2004–7, as total home loans rose only by 30 percent (*Financial Times*, June 9, 2008, p. 1).

5. In 1994 subprime loans had been less than 5 percent of total mortgage loans, at $35 billion. (Edward M. Gramlich, *Subprime Mortgages: America's Latest Boom and Bust*, Washington, DC, Urban Institute Press, 2007, p. 6.)

6. "The frenzied lending hit its peak in 2006. Of the $3 trillion in loans extended to all mortgage borrowers that year, $615 billion were sub-prime, $475 billion were alt-A, and $395 billion were jumbo ARMs. An incredible $250 billion in the riskiest stated-income, no-down-payment sub-prime ARM loans were originated" (M. Zandi, *Financial Shock*, Upper Saddle River, NJ, Pearson Education, 2009, p. 43).

7. GAO, *Housing Government-Sponsored Enterprises: A New Oversight Structure is Needed*, April 21, 2005. Securitization of mortgages first grew significantly in the late 1970s and early 1980s, triggered by Saving and Loan institutions. Securitization enables banks to increase their lending, and to increase their own earnings from the transaction fees involved. It takes mortgages off their books and into the portfolios of institutions interested in long-term lending, not least pension funds. The pension funds get their income stream from the monthly payments of individual mortgage holders, and since the mortgages are packaged, the impact on their income flows of individual mortgage default is significantly diminished. The impact of one defaulter on a mortgage is covered by the continuing mortgage payments of the rest. The problem only arises if the number of defaults rises – which of course is exactly what began to happen on the grand scale after 2006!

8. Ronald Utt, *The Subprime Mortgage Market collapse: A Primer on the Causes and Possible Solutions*, The Heritage Foundation Backgrounder, No. 2127, April 22, 2008, p. 2.

9. Cited by Robert Fanney in an Associated Press piece issued October 24, 2008.

10. For the scale of their growth, see Chris Giles, "Into the Storm," *Financial Times*, November 14, 2007, p. 8.

11. A little known network of Federal Home Loan Banks – a network including Citibank, Bank of America and Washington Mutual – had, at the behest of the US Treasury – lent heavily in 2007 to maintain the viability of a number of subprime loan providers. The FHLB pumped $746 billion into such institutions in the third quarter of 2007. The figure for the second quarter had been virtually zero. (For details, see the *Financial Times*, December 12, 2007, p. 2.)

12. In 2006 Countrywide Financial was the largest single mortgage lender in the United States. In 2005 it had accounted for 8 percent of all new private asset-backed securities *globally*! (Herman Schwartz and Leonard Seabrooke, "Varieties of Residential Capitalism in the International Political Economy," *Comparative European Politics*, vol. 6, 2008, p. 254.)

13. Fannie Mae had been set up in 1938 and Freddie Mac in 1970, to underwrite mortgages issued by the Federal Housing Authority and the Veterans Administration (Fannie) and by the Savings and Loans Industry (Freddie), with a Treasury-provided credit line of $2.25 billion set in the 1970s when Fannie had only $15 billion in outstanding debt. Both government-sponsored enterprises (GSEs) buy millions of dollars of mortgages each month from commercial lenders, and either retain some of those in their own portfolios or sell on to other financial institutions (pension funds, insurance companies and investment banks) in packages of mortgage-backed securities. Fannie May and Freddie Mac operate in a "secondary mortgage market." You can't get a mortgage from them. You get your mortgage from a bank or a broker, who then sells the mortgage on to Fannie or Freddie. They pool those mortgages into pass-through securities, and either hold them or sell them on to other investors. Either way, the GSE bears the default risk of the mortgage. Traditionally, Freddie always sold on most of its mortgages while Fannie Mae held on to most of its. By September 2007 Fannie and Freddie owned $1.5 trillion of mortgages and guaranteed a further $3.7 trillion, roughly 50 percent of all outstanding US mortgage debt. Owned by shareholders but chartered by Congress, operating under terms of reference set by HUD (The Department of Housing and Urban Development) and regulated by the Office of Federal Housing Enterprises Oversight, the two GSEs were always highly leveraged: their net worth in 2008 was reportedly only $114 billion.

14. It also induced the Obama administration to the view that instability caused by global recession now outranked terrorism as the greatest

single threat to US national security: this from Dennis Blair, the Obama national security director, to Congress, February 12, 2009.

15. Details in the *Washington Post*, February 18, 2009, p. A01.

16. Big numbers too, as far as public spending goes: $586 billion by the Chinese, $50.8 billion by the Japanese, $26 billion by the French, even $15.7 billion by the Germans.

17. It was not an easy or smooth ideological journey for Republicans to take. George Bush's initial response to the unease about foreclosures had been to play the *moral hazard* card, saying "it's not the government's job to bail out speculators or those who made the decision to buy a home they knew they could never afford" (cited in the *Financial Times*, September 12, 2007, p. 3). He later changed his mind: but that did not stop other leading Republicans denouncing his administration's September 2008 bailout proposals as "financial socialism" (this from Jim Bunning of Kentucky, cited in the same paper, September 24, 2008, p. 3).

18. Barack Obama, January 20, 2009.

19. The President, speaking in Virginia, February 5, 2009.

20. At a House Financial Services Committee meeting, September 2003.

21. Thomas E. Woods Jr, *Meltdown*, Washington, DC, Regnery Publishing, 2009, p. 2.

22. "Okay we just went back in time to the news archives of the *New York Times*, September 30, 1999, and learned everything we know about the mortgage industry. Fannie Mae, Freddie Mac make loans to people who can't afford them. Expand home ownership for millions of people. Reducing down payment requirements. All the things that led to all this." *The Rush Limbaugh Show*, transcript February 24, 2009.

23. Woods, *Meltdown*, pp. 14 and 16 (quoting Ron Paul).

24. Kevin Hassett, *How the Democrats Created the Financial Crisis*, Bloomberg News, September 22, 2008.

25. Woods, *Meltdown*, pp. 17 and 21.

26. Pat Buchanan, *Systemic Failure,* Human Events Website, posted March 20, 2009.

27. Ann Coulter, "Surviving Obama's New New Deal," at Ann_Coulter@ HumanEventsOnline.com, February 6, 2009.

28. Mccain said SEC officials "had kept in place trading rules that let speculators and hedge funds turn our markets into a casino" (quoted in the *Financial Times*, September 19, 2008, p. 6).

29. Posted on the AEI Website, November 4, 2006.

30. David Henderson, *Are We Ailing from Too Much Deregulation?* Cato Policy Report, vol. XXX, no. 6, November/December 2008, p. 8.

31. See for example Wendell Cox, *How Smart Growth Exacerbated the International Financial Crisis*, Heritage Foundation Web memo No. 1906, April 29, 2008.

32. Though not by David Henderson. (See his coauthored *Greenspan's Monetary Policy in Retrospect: Discretion or Rules?* Cato Briefing Paper No. 109, November 3, 2008.)

33. See for example the testimony of Richard Vedder to a Joint Economic Committee of Congress, October 30, 2008.

34. Woods, *Meltdown*, p. 28.

35. February 12, 2009.

36. The Cato Institute brought together the signatures of over 200 economists to make that point, in an advert in the *Wall Street Journal*, January 2009.

37. Robert A. Book, *The Fallacy of Health Care Reform as Economic Stimulus*, Heritage Foundation Web memo No 2231, January 16, 2009, p. 1.

38. Daniel J. Mitchell, *Spending is Not Stimulus*, Cato Institute Tax and Budget Bulletin, no. 53, February 2009, p. 2.; also Woods, *Meltdown*, pp. 100–7.

39. Chris Edwards, *10 Reasons to Oppose a Stimulus Package for the States*, Cato Institute Tax and Budget Bulletin No. 51, December 2008.

40. For example, Rich Lowry in *National Review*: on the stimulus package, "in just six months, America will have moved from free market capitalism to quasi-socialism." (Quoted with approval by the Family Research Council, on their Website, February 11, 2009.)

41. From the transcript of Rush Limbaugh's radio program, January 27, 2009; and his interview with Sean Hannity, January 21, 2009. Rush Limbaugh characterized the 2009 Obama stimulus plan as "the most irresponsible confiscation of wealth and power from you, the American people, in our nation's history" (January 29, 2009); as a "socialist stimulus package" (February 9); as a "a war on achievement" (February 11) and "on prosperity" (January 30); and as a "full scale war on capitalism" (February 11, 2009).

42. Stuart M. Butler, *Time to End the TARP Bailout Program*, Heritage Foundation Web memo No. 2174, December 15, 2008, p. 1.

43. Ibid.; and Arnold Kling, *Main Street vs Wall Street*, Cato Website, October 3, 2008.

44. David Brookes, "Bailout to Nowhere," *New York Times*, November 14, 2008.

45. James Sherk and Karen Campbell, *Extending Unemployment Insurance: No Economic Stimulus*, Report of the Heritage Center for Data Analysis, November 18, 2008.

46. For details of this claim, see Heritage Foundation Backgrounder No. 2233, January 26, 2009.

47. For the case, see Heritage Foundation Web memo No 2243, January 26, 2009.

48. Curtis Dubay et al., *Economic Stimulus Pushed by Flawed Jobs Analysis*, The Heritage Foundation Web memo No 2252, January 28, 2009, p. 2.

49. Cited in the *Washington Post*, February 9, 2009, p. A01.

50. RNC Chairman Michael Steele's Weekly Republican Address, Saturday, February 7, 2009.

51. David Walker has written of President George W. Bush as "likely to go down as one of the most – if not the most – fiscally irresponsible presidents in US history" for combining "guns, butter and tax cuts all at once." ("America cannot spend its way to prosperity," *Financial Times* January 15, 2009, p. 9.)

52. Grover Norquist, "Republicans cannot spend their way out of crisis," *Financial Times*, October 2, 2008, p. 9.

53. For details, see Zandi, *Financial Shock*, p. 48.

54. Utt, *The Subprime Mortgage Market collapse*, p. 11.

55. Eileen Markey, "ACORN led Financial Sector with Warnings on Lending," *City Limits* 661, October 27, 2008.

56. Michael S. Barr and Gene Sperling, "Poor Homeowners, Good Loans," *New York Times*, October 18, 2008.

57. Ibid.

58. Quoted in Robert Gordon, "Did Liberals Cause the Sub-Prime Crisis?" *The American Prospect*: Website only, April 7, 2008.

59. "The blame-the-CRA theory says that the subprime mess was caused by weak-hearted lenders pushed by misguided bureaucrats into making loans to poor people and minorities who can't repay them. Nothing could be further from the truth. First, subprime mortgages that are now defaulting in droves were made mostly by unregulated mortgage bankers with no CRA obligations or oversight. Second, the Alt-A mortgages that are a major part of the crisis were made mostly to middle-and upper-income white borrowers who didn't want to verify income or wanted a bigger loan than a prime lender would offer. Third, loans made by banks to fulfill CRA obligations, even those to very low-income homebuyers, perform quite well. Fourth, the only category of mortgages in which the foreclosure and default rates are not going up is the FHA program, a program that makes loans almost exclusively to low- and moderate-income Americans, many of them African-American and Latino. The bottom line is that it was the design of subprime mortgages, not the selection of borrowers, which caused

them to default in massive numbers" (Alan Wilson, *Consumer Law and Policy Blog*, September 23, 2008).

60. For a particularly censorious report on Cuomo's role here, see Wayne Barrett, "Andrew Cuomo and Fannie and Freddie," *Village Voice*, August 5, 2008.

61. "The GSE's guidelines, designed to identify creditworthy applicants, are more likely to disqualify borrowers with low incomes, limited wealth and poor credit histories; applicants with those characteristics are disproportionately minorities" (Urban League report, 1997, cited in Peter J. Wallison, *Cause and Effect: Government Policies and the Financial Crisis*, AEI, November 2008, p. 5); "Fannie and Freddie's supposed commitment to affordable and low-income housing are almost entirely pretense" (Wallison, *Serving Two Masters Yet Out of Control – Fannie Mae and Freddie Mac*, Washington, DC, AEI Press, 2000, p. 152).

62. Gordon, "Did Liberals Cause the Sub-Prime Crisis?"

63. Wilson, *Consumer Law and Policy Blog*.

64. For details, see Charles Duhrigg, "Pressured to take more risk, Fannie hits a tipping point," *New York Times*, October 5, 2008.

65. Adolfo Marzoi, quoted in the *Washington Post*, December 9, 2009, p. D01.

66. Duhrigg, "Pressured to take more risk, Fannie hits a tipping point."

67. Details are in *The Washington Post*, November 23, 2008, p. A01. "Representatives of four of the five government agencies responsible for financial supervision used tree shears to attack a stack of paper representing bank regulations. The fifth representative, James Gilleran of the Office of Thrift Supervision, wielded a chainsaw." (Paul Krugman, "Blindly into the Bubble," *New York Times*, December 21, 2007.)

68. The evidence for this is in Luci Ellis, *The Housing Meltdown: Why Did It Happen in the United States*, BIS Working Papers No. 259, Basel, Switzerland, Bank of International Settlements, September 2008, p. 14, including this: "arrears rates on the GSE's single-family home portfolio has risen a great deal recently, but this only started in the second half of 2007 . . . Likewise, the increase in arrears rates on FHA mortgages has been fairly mild."

69. Barr and Sperling, "Poor Homeowners, Good Loans," p. 2.

70. Zandi, *Financial Shock*, p. 42.

71. Herman Schwartz, "Housing, Global Finance, and American Hegemony: Building Conservative Politics One Brick at a Time," *Comparative European Politics*, vol. 6, 2008, p. 275.

72. Ibid., p. 275.

73. Zandi, *Financial Shock*, p. 103. On the lowering of underwriting standards, see also Ellis, *The Housing Meltdown*, p. 6, including this: "First and

perhaps most importantly, requirements for documentation of incomes and assets became progressively laxer . . . amongst securitized subprime loans, the share of 2001 originations that were 'low doc' stood at around 30%. For the 2006 cohort, the share increased to more than half."

74. Max Fraser, "The House Folds," *Nation*, December 15, 2008, p. 31.

75. Utt, *The Subprime Mortgage Market Collapse*, p. 8.

76. For chapter and verse on this, see Richard Bitner, *Confessions of a Subprime Lender*, New York, Wiley, 2008, pp. 143–9.

77. Kenneth Jost, "Financial Crisis: Did Lax Regulation Cause a Credit Meltdown?" *CQ Researcher*, May 9, 2008, p. 16 of 33.

78. Zandi, *Financial Shock*, pp. 95 and 100.

79. Fraser, "The House Folds," p. 31.

80. Zandi, *Financial Shock*, p. 80.

81. See David Coates, *Models of Capitalism: Growth and Stagnation in the Modern Era*, Cambridge, UK, Polity Press, 2000.

82. Utt, *The Subprime Mortgage Market Collapse*, p. 12.

83. For this argument in more detail, see John Bellamy Foster and Fred Magdoff, *The Great Financial Crisis*, New York, Monthly Review Press, 2009, p. 137.

84. Peter Wallison has been particularly critical of this, and has called for full privatization in a series of prescient publications that include *Serving Two Masters*, and (with Thomas H. Stanton and Bert Ely) *Privatizing Fannie Mae, Freddie Mac and the Federal Home Loan Banks*, Washington, DC, The AEI Press, 2004.

85. *The Financial Times*, June 4, 2008, p. 9.

86. "Mortgage networks on both sides of the Atlantic were relatively short and disconnected from other financial networks prior to the early 1980s, as lending institutions would issue a mortgage, collect payments and, in effect, file the mortgage away until the principal was paid. With MBS, a set of close interconnections between Anglo-American mortgage networks and the multiple networks of the capital and derivatives markets have been formed. Mortgage networks have been significantly lengthened, such that they typically embrace the residential suburb, high street and a financial center on the other side of the globe." (Paul Langley, "Securitising Suburbia," *Competition and Change*, vol. 10, no. 3, September 2006, p. 289.)

87. "In the two years before Glass-Steagall was repealed in 1999, financial service industries gave $58 million to congressional campaigns, $87 million to political parties, and spent $163 million lobbying Washington" (*Economists for Obama*, September 15, 2008, at http://econ4obama.blogspot.com).

88. Though the importance of this act is a matter of disagreement among analysts of the crisis, it is worth noting that no less a player than Margaret Thatcher's finance minister has recently called for a "return, in all major financial centers, to the separation of commercial banking from investment banking" (Nigel Lawson, "Capitalism needs a revived Glass-Steagall," *Financial Times*, March 16, 2009, p. 9).

89. Zandi, *Financial Shock*, p. 126.

90. Ibid., p. 145.

91. The role of credit rating agencies in this developing tragedy has yet to be fully told. But for an example of how the sheer volume of these mortgage-backed securities overwhelmed the credit-rating agencies assessing them, read Roger Lowenstein, "Triple-A Failure" in Michael Lewis (editor), *Panic: The Story of Modern Financial Insanity*, New York, W. W. Norton and Co., 2009, pp. 316–29. On the conflicts of interest endemic to rating agencies, see Jerome S. Fons and Frank Partnoy, "Rated F for Failure," *New York Times*, March 16, 2009.

92. The AIG bonus scandal certainly tarnished Senator Chris Dodd, to that point a major player in the bail out saga that followed the September 2008 financial crash.

93. At a Congressional hearing, cited in Edmund L. Andrews, "Greenspan Concedes Error on Regulation," *New York Times*, October 24, 2008.

94. If Fannie and Freddie "continue to grow, continue to have the low capital that they have, continue to engage in the dynamic hedging of their portfolios, which they need to do for interest risk aversion, they potentially create ever-growing potential systemic risk down the road. We are placing the total financial system of the future at a substantial risk" (This to Congress, quoted in Kevin Hassett, *How the Democrats Created the Financial Crisis*, Bloomberg.com, September 22, 2008).

95. Robert Kuttner, "The Bubble Economy," *The American Prospect*, September 24, 2007. p. 4 of 6.

96. After the privatization of Fannie Mae in 1968, "investment bankers invented a daisy chain known as 'securitization'. Through securitization, a mortgage broker could originate a loan, sell it to a mortgage banker, who could then sell it to an investment bank like Salamon Brothers, who in turn would package the mortgage into securities. These were then evaluated and coded (for a fee) by private bond-rating agencies according to their supposed risk, and sold off to hedge funds or pension funds" (ibid., p. 3 of 6).

97. The US is virtually unique among advanced industrial countries in giving this tax subsidy to home owners. For details, see Ellis, *The Housing Meltdown*, p. 17.

98. Schwartz and Seabrooke have recently offered a four-fold typology of housing markets depending on the degree of owner occupation, as against renting, going on in each; and the degree to which each is subject to high levels of mortgage debt relative to GDP and to high levels of mortgage securitization – four boxes, "liberal market," "corporatist-market," "statist-developmentalist" and "familial". The "liberal market" is the highest scorer on their criteria: the box includes the US, UK, Canada, Norway and New Zealand (pp. 243–4). The US secondary mortgage market is the biggest in the world, containing $5.37 *trillion* of securitized mortgage loans in 2005, and an additional $4.48 trillion held as "whole loans" – secondary market sales which are not securitized. Most European countries now have some SSM, largely concentrated in the UK, but the total EU volume was only €244.6 *billion* in 2006. Australia is next, with $126 billion (HUD, *Mortgage Securitization: Lessons for Emerging Markets*, July 2007, p. 4).

99. For details, see Richard K. Green and Susan M. Wachter, "The American Mortgage in Historical and International Context," *Journal of European Perspectives*, vol. 19, no. 4, Fall 2005, pp. 93–114.

100. *Financial Times*, September 10, 2008, p. 9.

101. Paul Krugman, "The Market Mystique," *New York Times*, March 27, 2009.

102. Gillian Tett and Paul. J. Davies, "Out of the Shadows: How banking's hidden system broke down," *Financial Times*, December 17, 2007, p. 8.

103. For Henry Paulson, see his "Reform the architecture of regulation," *Financial Times*, March 18, 2009, p. 9.

104. For details on the class distribution of debt, see Foster and Magdoff, *The Great Financial Crisis*, pp. 31–8. "At the bubble's peak, subprime borrowers were devoting an astonishing 35 percent of their after-tax income to paying off mortgage and other debt, a recipe for disaster once house prices began to fall and homes could no longer be used as collateral for more borrowing" (Fraser, "The House Folds," p. 33).

105. William Grieber, "Goldman Sachs' socialism," *Nation*, October 13, 2008, p. 5.

106. The key source here is again Mark Zandi, at Moody's Economy.com. For these figures, see his *The Economic Impact of the American Recovery and Reinvestment Act*, Moody's Economy, January 21, 2009. For the debate around multipliers, see John Cogan et al., *New Keynesian Versus old Keynesian Government spending Multipliers*, NBER Working paper 14782, March 2009.

107. See Charles Calamoris, *The Subprime Turmoil*, October 2, 2008, pp. 3–4. See also Marty Feldstein, "How to shore up America's crumbling housing market," *Financial Times*, May 27, 2008.

Select Bibliography

For a full list of sources and suggestions or further reading, go to
http://answeringbackdavidcoates.blogspot.com

Aaronovitz, Stanley. *Just around the Corner: The Paradox of the Jobless Recovery.* Philadelphia, PA: Temple University Press, 2005.

Alterman, Eric. *Why We're Liberals.* New York: Viking, 2008.

Altman, Nancy. *The Battle for Social Security.* Hoboken, NJ: Wiley, 2005.

Baker, Dean and Weisbrot, Mark. *Social Security: The Phony Crisis.* Chicago, IL: University of Chicago Press, 1999.

Balmer, Randall. *Thy Kingdom Come.* New York: Basic Books, 2006.

Bartlett, Bruce. *Impostor, How George W. Bush Bankrupted America and Betrayed the Reagan Legacy.* New York: Doubleday, 2006.

Beck, Roy. *The Case against Immigration.* New York: W. W. Norton, 1996.

Bernstein, Jared. *Common Sense for a Fair Economy.* San Francisco, CA: Berrett-Koehler Publishers, 2006.

Borjas, George. *Heaven's Door: Immigration Policy and the American Economy.* Princeton, NJ: Princeton University Press, 1999.

Buchanan, Pat. *The Death of the West.* New York: Thomas Dunne Books, 2002.

—. *Where the Right Went Wrong.* New York: Thomas Dunne Books, 2004.

Cannon, Michael and Tanner, Michael. *Healthy Competition.* Washington, DC: Cato Institute, 2005.

Carville, James and Begala, Paul. *Take it Back: A Battle Plan for Democratic Victory.* New York: Simon and Schuster, 2006.

Cline, William R. *The United States as a Debtor Nation*. Washington, DC: Institute for International Economics, 2005.

Coates, David and Siavelis, Peter. *Getting Immigration Right: What Every American Needs to Know*. Dulles, VA: Potomac Books, 2009.

Cogan, John, Hubbard, R. Glenn and Kessler, Daniel P. *Healthy, Wealthy and Wise*. Washington, DC: The AEI Press, 2005.

Danziger, Sheldon et al. (editors). *Confronting Poverty*. Cambridge, MA: Harvard University Press, 1994.

Darby, Michael (editor). *Reducing Poverty in America*. Thousand Oaks, CA: Sage, 1996.

DeParle, Jason. *American Dream*. New York: Penguin, 2004.

D'Souza, Dinesh. *What's So Great about America*. Washington, DC: Regnery Publishing Inc., 2002.

Duignan, Peter and Gann, Lewis. *The Debate in the United States over Immigration*. Stanford, CA: Hoover Institution Press, 1998.

Ferrara, Peter J. and Tanner, Michael. *A New Deal for Social Security*. Washington, DC: Cato Institute, 1998.

Forbes, Steve. *Flat Tax Revolution*. Washington, DC: Regnery Publishing Inc., 2005.

Foster, John Bellamy and Magdoff, Fred. *The Great Financial Crisis*. New York: Monthly Review Press, 2009.

Frank, Thomas. *What's the Matter with Kansas?* New York: Henry Holt, 2004.

Galbraith, James K. *Created Unequal*. New York: The Free Press, 1998.

Ghilarducci, Teresa. *When I'm Sixty-Four: The Plot against Pensions and the Plan to Save Them*. Princeton, NJ: Princeton University Press, 2008.

Greeley, Andrew and Hout, Michael. *The Truth about Conservative Christians*. Chicago, IL: University of Chicago Press, 2006.

Hacker, Jacob. *The Great Risk Shift*. Oxford: Oxford University Press, 2006.

Hays, Sharon. *Flat Broke with Children*. New York: Oxford University Press, 2003.

Hayworth, J. D. *Whatever It Takes: Illegal Immigration, Border Security and the War on Terror*. Washington, DC: Regnery Publishing Inc., 2006.

Howard, Christopher. *The Welfare State Nobody Knows*. Princeton, NJ: Princeton University Press, 2007.

Hunter, James Davison and Wolfe, Alan. *Is There a Culture War?* Washington, DC: Brookings Institution, 2006.

Huntington, Samuel. *Who Are We? The Challenge to America's National Identity*. New York: Simon and Schuster, 2004.

Hutton, Will. *A Declaration of Independence*. New York: W. W. Norton, 2003.

Kimball, Charles. *When Religion Becomes Evil*. San Francisco, CA: Harper Collins, 2002.

Kochan, Thomas A. *Restoring the American Dream*. Cambridge, MA: The MIT Press, 2006.

Kotlikoff, Laurence and Burns, Scott. *The Coming Generational Storm*. Cambridge, MA: MIT Press, 2004.

Krugman, Paul. *The Conscience of a Liberal*. New York: W. W. Norton, 2007.

Kuttner, Robert. *The Squandering of America*. New York: Alfred A. Knopf, 2007.

Lakoff, George. *Don't Think of an Elephant: Know Your Values and Frame the Debate*. River Junction, VT: Chelsea Green Publishing, 2004.

Lardner, James and Smith, David A. (editors). *Inequality Matters*. New York: The Free Press, 2005.

Lindsay, James and Singer, Aubrey. *Changing Faces: Immigrants and Diversity in the Twenty-First Century*. Washington, DC: Brookings Institution, 2003.

Massey, Douglas. *Return of the "L" Word*. Princeton, NJ: Princeton University Press, 2000.

McGovern, George. *Social Security and the Golden Age*. Golden, CO: Fulcrum Publishing, 2005.

Mishel, Lawrence, Bernstein, Jared and Allegretto, Sylvia. *The State of Working America*. Ithaca, NY: ILR Press, 2005.

Mogensen, Vernon (editor). *Worker Safety under Siege*. New York: M. E. Sharpe, 2006.

Morone, James and Jacobs, Lawrence (editors). *Healthy, Wealthy and Fair*. New York: Oxford University Press, 2004.

Murray, Charles. *Losing Ground*. New York: Basic Books, 1984.

—. *In Our Hands*. Washington, DC: AEI Press, 2006.

Myers, David and Scanzoni, Letha Dawson. *What God Has Put Together: The Christian Case for Gay Marriage*. New York: HarperCollins, 2005.

OECD. *Towards High Performing Health Systems*. Paris, 2004.

O'Reilly, Bill. *Culture Warrior*. New York: Broadway Books, 2006.

Philips, Kevin. *American Theocracy*. New York: Viking, 2006.

Pierson, Paul (editor). *The New Politics of the Welfare State*. Oxford: Oxford University Press, 2001.

Podesta, John. *The Power of Progress*. New York: Crown Publishers, 2008.

Pontusson, Jonas. *Inequality and Prosperity*. New York: The Century Foundation Press, 2005.

Preble, Christopher (director). *Exiting Iraq: Why the US Must End the Military Occupation and Renew the War against Al Qaeda*. Washington, DC: The Cato Institute, 2004.

Press, Bill. *How the Republicans Stole Christmas*. New York: Doubleday, 2005.

Rainwater, Lee and Smeeding, Timothy. *Poor Kids in a Rich Country*. New York: Russell Sage Foundation, 2003.

Raunch, Jonathan. *Gay Marriage: Why It Is Good for Gays, Good for Straights, and Good for America.* Time Books: Henry Holt and Company, 2004.

Reich, Robert. *Reason: Why Liberals Will Win the Battle for America.* New York: Vintage Books, 2004.

—. *Supercapitalism.* New York: Alfred A. Knopf, 2007.

Rifkin, Jeremy. *The European Dream: How Europe's Vision of the Future is Quietly Eclipsing the American Dream.* London: Penguin, 2005.

Ryscavage, Paul. *Income Inequality in America: An Analysis of Trends.* New York: M. E. Sharpe, 1999.

Sager, Ryan. *The Elephant in the Room.* Hoboken, NJ: John Wiley, 2006.

Savage, Michael. *Liberalism is a Mental Disorder.* New York: Nelson Current, 2003.

Schwarz, John and Volgy, Thomas. *The Forgotten Americans; Thirty Million Working Poor in the Land of Opportunity.* New York: W. W. Norton, 1993.

Shipler, David. *The Working Poor: Invisible in America.* New York: Alfred A. Knopf, 2004.

Skocpol, Theda. *The Missing Middle.* New York: W.W. Norton, 2000.

Starr, Paul. *Freedom's Power: The True Force of Liberalism.* New York: Basic Books, 2007.

Tancredo, Tom. *In Mortal Danger.* Nashville, TN: WND Books, 2006.

Tanner, Michael. *The End of Welfare.* Washington, DC: Cato Institute, 1996.

—. *Leviathan on the Right.* Washington, DC: Cato Institute, 2007.

Wakefield, Dan. *The Hijacking of Jesus.* New York: Nation Books, 2006.

Wellington Haase, Leif. *A New Deal for Health.* New York: The Century Foundation Press, 2005.

Willis, Clint and Hardcastle, Nate (editors). *Jesus is Not a Republican.* New York: Thunder's Mouth Press, 2005.

Wolff, Edward N. *Top Heavy: The Increasing Inequality of Wealth in America and What Can Be Done about It.* New York: The New Press, 2002.

—. *What Has Happened to the Quality of Life in the Advanced Industrial Nations?* Northampton, MA: Edward Elgar, 2004.

Wolfson, Evan. *Why Marriage Matters.* New York: Simon and Schuster, 2004.

Woods, Thomas E. Jr. *Meltdown.* Washington, DC: Regnery Publishing Inc., 2009.

Woodward, Bob. *Bush at War.* New York: Simon and Schuster, 2003.

—. *Plan of Attack.* New York: Simon and Schuster, 2004.

—. *State of Denial.* New York: Simon and Schuster, 2006.

Zandi, Mark. *Financial Shock.* Upper Saddle River, NJ: Pearson Education, 2009.

Index

9/11 176, 201, 205, 209, 212, 414, 215, 216, 219, 238

Aaron, Henry 97–8
abortion 50, 177–8, 181, 186–8, 191
Abu Graib 176, 200
accounting standards 253
ACORN 245
activist judges 17, 18, 22
adverse selection 123
affirmative action 68
AFDC (Aid to Families with Dependent Children) 63, 70
Afghanistan 203, 215, 216, 22–3
African-Americans 6, 47, 66, 67, 77, 98, 101, 146, 151, 157, 186, 236
agribusiness 44, 145–6, 160–1, 165
AIDS 177, 183
AIG 51, 232, 235, 249, 251
alcoholism 185
Al-Qaeda 23, 145, 202, 203, 205, 206, 208, 211, 213, 215–16, 222
Al Zarquawi 202
American Enterprise Institute (AEI) 246
American Family Association 173

American Option Plan 35–6
Americans for Tax Reform 51
amnesty 147–8
Anglo-Irish Bank 233
Anglo-Saxon culture 151, 174
Annan, Kofi 211, 225
anti-communism 180
anti feminism 178–9, 188–9
anti-Semitism 206, 219
appeasement 209
Asia-Pacific triangle 138
axis of evil 203

baby boomers 86, 87, 159
Bachelet, Michelle 99
Baker, Dean 104, 105
Balkanization 144, 151
Balmer, Randall 180, 190
bank bailouts 241
Bank of America 232
banking system 237
Barclays 233
Bartlett, Bruce 133
Bauer, Gary 182, 198
Bear Stearns 230–1, 232, 235
Beck, Roy 155

Bible, the 174, 175, 178, 182,
184, 192
big government 50–1
Bin Laden, Osama 23, 201, 212
Bismarck, Otto von 57, 103
Black Death, the 153
Blair, Tony 123, 206, 213, 214, 216
Bloomberg, Michael 149
blowback 218–20
Bob Jones University 180
Bootz, Neal 37, 48
border fence 139, 140, 162
border patrol 139, 147
Borjas, George 156
Bosworth, Barry 103
Bracero program 139, 163
Brookings Institute 103
Brown, Gordon 123
Buchanan, Pat 20, 147, 148, 152, 161,
166, 167, 175, 236–7
Building Societies (UK) 252
Burtless, Gary 103
Bush, George W. 2, 11, 18–19, 20,
24–5, 27, 35, 37, 85–90, 95, 99,
108, 120, 132, 140, 148, 150–1,
203, 204–6, 208, 210, 212–14,
216, 218, 223, 226–7, 243

Campaign for Working Families 173
Canada 118, 125, 127, 187
Cannon, Michael 114
Carlton, Allan 102
capitalism, models of 251
car companies 241
Carter, President Jimmy 61, 181,
198, 236
Cato Institute 53, 63, 64, 74, 82,
87, 88, 89, 90, 91, 98, 109, 111,
114, 116, 120–1, 134, 149, 166,
238, 240
Center for American Progress 128
Center for Moral Clarity 173
Century Foundation 128
CEO salaries 46–7, 50–1, 75

charity illusion 64, 70–2
Cheney, Vice President Dick 23,
203, 206, 210, 213, 214, 224,
226–7, 229
child care 74, 76
child pornography 189
child tax credit 35
children in poverty 60, 62, 64, 66, 188
Chile 89, 99
China 74, 89, 99, 223
Christ, Jesus 175, 176, 180, 191
Christian Center 192
Christian Coalition of America 173,
179, 180
Christian Left 191–2
Christian Right 2, 4, 63, 172, 173,
179, 181, 206
church-state separation 174, 181
Churchill, Ward 15
Civil War pensions 103
Clinton Administration 41, 124, 203,
244, 246, 255
Clinton, Hillary 129, 154
collaterized debt obligations 250
Columbus, Christopher 152
Commodity Futures Modernization
Act 254
Commonwealth Fund 107
Community Reinvestment Act,
the 236, 246
Compassionate Conservatism 20, 26
compound interest 89, 93, 97
Concerned Women for America 174,
178, 195
condoms 177
conservatism, dominance of 1–2
Conservative Political Action
Conference 14
Conservative views on:
US economy 139–42
financial meltdown 235–43
gay marriage 176–7
health care 108–14
immigration 41–8

social questions 174–80
Social Security 86–90
taxes 35–41
war with Iraq 202–10
welfare 58–64
contraception 187
Contract with America 62
cost-shifting 119
Costa Rico 118
Coulter, Ann 13, 23, 26, 27, 28, 30, 223, 237
Countrywide Financial 232, 237, 245, 247, 248, 249, 250, 251, 255, 265
Crane, Edward 89, 97
credit crunch 230
credit default swaps 250
credit rating agencies 255, 256
crime, causes of 144, 176, 183
Crouse, Janice Shaw 178
crowding out 38
Cuba 118
culture war 26, 179
Cuomo, Andrew 246
cycles of credit 250
cycles of deprivation 47–8, 77

Dartmouth College 109
death penalty 178
debt: 258–9
  governmental 259
  international 250, 259
  personal 259–60
defensive medicine 119
defined benefits 93
defined contributions 93
democratic dialogue 27–8
demographic change 86, 98, 117
dependency 71, 88, 141
deregulation 237, 246, 247, 254, 256
derivatives 254, 256
Devil, the 175, 193
Discovery Institute 173

disease 145, 153
divorce 184, 185
Dobson, James 173, 178, 189
domestic violence 73, 82–3, 189
Downey Savings and Loans 249
Dukakis, Michael 162

Economic Policy Institute 128
Edwards, Chris 240
Egypt 219
elections 2, 3, 11, 18, 19, 21
Ellis Island 138
employer-financed health insurance 106, 110, 115
employer-financed pensions 93
enlightenment project 23, 182
entitlement crisis 241
environmental degradation 189
Epistles, the 184
estate tax 35
Ethics and Public Policy Center 173
euthanasia 178
Evangelical Christians 173, 174

Fairness Doctrine 32
Falwell, Jerry 173, 195, 196
family planning 177
Family Research Council 173
Fannie Mae 232, 235–6, 237, 238, 245, 246, 247, 248, 251, 253, 262, 263, 265
FDR 23, 60–1, 69, 90, 235, 239, 260
Federal Communication Commission 32
Federal Emergency Management Agency (FEMA) 72, 261
Federal Employees Health Benefit Program 128
Federal Reserve 231, 233, 235, 238
fee-setting 119
fee taking 249, 251
Ferrera, Peter 84, 90
Fidelity 95
financial meltdown 230–63

Finland 117
firewalls 251–2, 254, 263
fiscal child abuse 240
fiscal conservatives 242
fiscal responsibility summit 86
flat tax 39, 48
flawed conservatism 18
Focus on the Family 173, 178
Food and Drug Administration
    (FDA) 111
food insecurity 65
food stamps 70
foreclosures 231, 237
Fortis 233
Fox News 14, 18, 32
framing, importance of 7, 22, 114,
    152, 220
France 24, 25
France, Anatole 25
Frank, Barney 235–6, 243–4
Franklin, Ben 151
Freddie Mac 232, 235–6, 237, 238,
    245, 246, 247, 248, 251, 262,
    263, 265
Free Congress Foundation 173
freedom of conscience 182
French fries 25
Friedman, Milton 111
Fukuyama, Francis 142
Fuld, Richard 251
fundamentalism 27, 174, 184
    danger of 181–2
    Islamic 182, 202, 209, 211, 215–16,
    218, 219

Galbraith, James 72, 83
gay bashing 186
gay marriage 151, 177, 184–6
General Motors 94
genocide 189
German immigrants 150, 151
Germany 57, 76, 103, 123, 151, 234
gift exhaustion 71
Gingrich, Newt 62

Glass-Steagall 254, 263
God 175, 179, 192–3, 206, 224
Goldman Sachs 251
Goldman Sachs' socialism 260
Gospels, the 184
Government-Sponsored Enterprise
    (GSE) 236, 246, 249, 253
Graham, Reverend Franklin 179–80,
    195
Gramm-Leach-Bliley Act 237, 254
Great Depression 2, 28, 43, 259–60,
    255
Great Moving Left Show 10, 11
Great Moving Right Show 10, 11
Greece 118
Greenspan, Alan 235, 255–6, 271
Gresham's Law 248
Guantanamo Bay 220
guest-worker system 140
Gulf War, the first 202
Guns, Germs and Steel 152
Gutierrez, Carlos 159

Hacker, Jacob 102
Hagel, Senator Chuck 139, 141
Hamas 222
Hannity, Sean 3, 37
Hayworth, J. D. 143
health care system 4, 5, 22, 57,
    106–31
Health Savings Accounts 111, 113
Henderson, David 238
Heritage Foundation, The 48, 63, 91,
    142, 145, 148, 166
Hewitt Associates 95
Hezbollah 222
high wage dynamic 74
Hispanic Americans 47, 66
Hitler 193
Holy War 193–4
Homeland Security 219–20, 221
homophobia 180, 190
homosexuality 26, 177, 180, 184–6
Hong Kong 118

Hong Kong and Shanghai Bank
(HSB) 234
House Finance Committee 244
house prices 230, 231, 238, 244
Housing and Urban Development,
Department of (HUD) 245, 246
housing market 230, 244, 251, 257
Howard, Christopher 79
Hussein, Saddam 23, 202, 203, 206,
207, 211, 213, 215, 216

IBM 94
illegitimacy rates 45
immigration 4, 20, 25, 27, 138–65
incarceration rates 67, 77, 158
income tax 36–7
IndyMac Bancorp 248
inequality 5, 6, 45–7, 75, 78, 104,
259–60
infidelity 177, 184
intelligence, reliability of 213
interest rates 238, 257
Internal Revenue Service (IRS) 26
International Labor Organization
(ILO) 233
International Monetary Fund
(IMF) 234
investment banks 248
IQ 59
Iran 203, 211, 214
Iraq 2, 23, 201–24
Iraq Body Count 217
Islam 179, 180
Islamic fundamentalism 182, 202,
209, 211, 215–16, 218, 219
Islamofascism 205, 206
Israel 179–80, 203, 206, 209, 211,
219, 222

Japan 50, 58, 234
Jefferson, Thomas 22
Jihad 193, 216
Jim Crow 186
Jindal, Bobby 29

J. P. Morgan Chase 232
judges 17, 18, 22

Katrina, Hurricane 23, 68–9, 176
Kay, David 225
Kennedy, Senator Edward 39, 129
Kennedy, President John F. 190
Keynesian economics 100, 234, 235,
239, 260–1
Kimball, Charles 194
Kobach, Kris 145
Krugman, Paul 45, 127

labor market regulation 26, 44–5, 50–1
Labour Party, British 4
LaHaye, Beverley 174, 178
Lancet, The 217
Lawson, Nigel 258, 271
Lazarus, Emma 138
Lehman Brothers 232, 245, 249, 251
level playing field 4
Liberal Republicans 20, 147
liberal voice 2, 5, 15
Libya 208
Limbaugh, Rush 11, 13, 14, 22, 27,
40–1, 131, 147, 148, 209, 226,
236, 240, 266, 267
Lincoln, Abraham 40
Lockheed, Martin 94
London, bombings in 218

Madrid, bombings in 218
Main Street 233
managed care 119, 125
mandates 128–9
market forces 5, 40
markets
deregulation of 237, 246, 247,
254, 256
financial 234–5
health care and 111–13, 116,
121–4, 130–1
inequality and 101–2
unregulated 5, 6, 43–4, 48, 75

marriage 63, 177, 184–6
Martinez, Senator Mel 139, 141
Martinique 118
mass media 176
McCain, Senator John 19, 111, 237, 266
McClelland, Scott 214
McGovern, George 90
Medicaid 108, 109, 110, 113, 116, 120, 124, 146, 241
Medicare 109, 110, 112–13, 116, 120, 124, 126, 129
Medicare prescription drug coverage 112, 120
Mercer 94
Merkel, Angela 123
Merrill Lynch 231, 232, 251
Mexican drug cartels 144, 145, 153
Mexican immigration 141, 143, 144, 145–6, 155, 156–7
Mexican mafia 149
Mexico 114, 115
Meyer, Joyce 175
military Keynesianism 44, 48
minimum wage 26, 45, 49
Ministry of International Trade and Industry (MITI) 44, 50
moral agenda 189–91
moral hazard 241, 262, 266
Moral Majority, The 173
Morris, Charles 122, 128, 135
mortgage brokers 248, 249, 251
mortgage tax relief 257
mortgage-backed securities 232, 233, 256
mortgages 230, 231
    second mortgages 231, 245, 249
    subprime: 236, 245, 248, 251, 253, 264
Motorola 94
Mozilo, Angelo 251
Mudd, Donald H. 247
multiplier effect 261
Murray, Charles 72, 73, 80, 83

narrative, political 7–8
National Academy of Sciences 154
National Opinion Research Center 192
National Strategy for Combating Terrorism 208
Native-Americans 151
New Deal 2, 21, 57, 63, 69, 90, 173, 179, 239–40, 260
New Testament, the 184
neo-cons 213, 214
Nixon, Richard 91
Norquist, Grover 91
North American Free Trade Agreement (NAFTA) 160
North Korea 203, 210
Northern Rock 249
Norway 65, 118

Obama, Barack 4, 11, 12, 14, 27, 77, 86, 108, 129, 196, 210, 234, 235, 240, 243, 251
Obama administration 2, 4, 11, 34, 36, 110, 129, 131, 201, 221–3, 239, 262–3
Occupational Health and Safety Agency (OHSA) 44
OECD 66, 117
Office of Thrift Supervision 248
O'Neal, Stan 251
O'Reilly, Bill 13, 26, 39, 226
Orshansky, Mollie 64

Pacific Research Institute 112
Pakistan 211, 212
Palestine 180, 203, 215, 219, 222
Palin, Sarah 19
patient capital 258
Paulson, Henry 251, 258, 260
pay-as-you-go (PAYG) schemes 98–9
payroll taxes 43, 87
Pence, Representative Mike 140, 149
Pension Benefit Guaranty Corporation 94

Pentagon 44, 50
Perot, Ross 159
Personal Responsibility and Work
   Opportunity Reconciliation
   Act 58, 73
planned parenthood 187
Pledge of Allegiance 21
political parties 1–2
pork 44, 50, 240–2
poverty 47, 58–61, 68, 101, 115
Powell, Colin 203, 210, 214
privatization 88, 94–6
productivity 98, 259–60
pro-life 177
proposition-8 151, 177
public transport 65

racism 68, 180
RAND Corporation, The 110, 123
Raunch, Jonathan 185
Reagan, Ronald 61, 72, 79, 91, 184,
   243
recession 230, 233
"Reconquista, La" 144, 152, 166
Rector, Robert 60, 61, 62
regime change 194
Reich, Robert 10
remittances 150
rendition 220
Research and Development
   (R&D) 50
Rice, Condoleezza 209, 210, 214
right to choose 186–8
Rising Tides 40, 45, 47
Robertson, Pat 173, 179
Roe v Wade 18, 177, 180, 186
rogue states 202
rogue traders 237
Roman Catholicism 151, 172,
   174, 180
Roosevelt, Franklin Delano 23,
   60–1, 69, 90, 235, 239, 260
Rottweilers, Republican 13
Rove, Karl 27, 239

Rumsfeld, Donald 206, 211, 215
rush to war 210
Russett, Tim 214
Ryan, Paul 242

Sarbanes-Oxley 238
Satan 175, 183
Saudi Arabia 211, 212, 219
Savage, Michael 13, 20, 23, 111–12,
   125, 141, 142, 145, 146, 148,
   154, 157, 159–60
saving, rate of 87–8
savings accounts 86, 88, 89, 93, 113
savings and loans 232, 252
Schlesinger, Mark 127
schooling 176
second great migration 141
second mortgages 231, 245, 249
secondary mortgage markets 252
Securities and Exchange
   Commission (SEC) 237
securitization 231, 249, 250, 257,
   258, 264
selective literalism 192
Sermon on the Mount, the 191
sexual abstinence 187
sexual harrassment 189
sexual orientation 184, 191
sexual violence 185
sexually-transmitted diseases 187
shadow banking system 250
single-payer system 112, 126, 127
skills 142–3
small businesses 115
Smith, Adam 39
Snow, John 40
social contract 259–60
social mobility 47, 59
Social Security 57, 70, 85–102, 121
social wage 36
socialism 17, 18, 22, 109, 111–12,
   126, 240, 266, 267
soft Marxism 30
Solow, Robert 83

Southern Baptists 172, 181
Sowell, Thomas 83
State Child Health Insurance
    Program (SCHIP) 129
state pensions 104
starving the beast 38
Steele, Michael 29, 242–3
Stiglitz, Joseph 217
stimulus packages 19, 235, 241
stock market 234
stock values 234
subprime mortgages 236, 245, 248,
    251, 253, 264
Summers, Lawrence 246
surge 208
Sweden 42, 64, 76, 118, 217
Switzerland 118
Syria 208, 213

Taliban 212
Tancredo, Tom 148, 168
Tanner, Michael 64, 72, 74, 80, 84,
    89, 90, 114, 133
Tawney, R. H. 3, 4
taxation 5, 25, 34–41, 75, 78, 240
Tebbit, Norman 67
teenage pregnancies 176, 182,
    185
Temporary Assistance for Needy
    Families (TANF) 63
terrorism 145, 162, 205, 208
Terry, Randall 181
Thatcher, Margaret 11, 67
think tanks 7
Third Way 123
Thompson, Fred 85
toxic forces 185
toxic mortgages 232
Toyota 125
trade policy 10, 49
trade unions 39, 74, 93, 147, 242
Traditional Values Coalition 173,
    175, 178
Treasury, US 246

trickle-down economics 34, 43, 45,
    143, 191
trickle-up economics 48–50
triple trench 125
Trojan Horse 20
Truman, Harry 124
Trust Fund, Social Security 87, 88,
    91–3, 100
Turkey 114

UBS 233
undercapitalization 258
underclass 61
underwriting standards 231
unemployment 149
United Airlines 94
United Nations (UN) 210, 211,
    213, 220
UN Declaration of Human Rights,
    The 130
UNICEF 66
United Kingdom (UK) 47, 118
universal health care 115
Urban Institute 246

values 100, 174, 179, 182, 206–7, 219
Verizon 94
Vietnam 209
vouchers 113, 120, 121

wages 46–7, 75, 93, 98, 145–6, 155,
    156–7, 259, 263
Wall Street 92, 95, 233, 250
Wallison, Peter 238, 269
war of choice 210–12
War on Poverty 57, 60, 61, 69,
    72, 124
Washington Mutual 232, 249
water boarding 220
Waxman, Henry 256
Weapons of Mass Destruction
    (WMD) 202, 204, 210–11,
    214, 221
Weisbrot, Mark 104, 105

welfare 57–64, 69–78
Welfare Reform Act (1996) 58
Wellington-Haas, Leif 126, 128
Wilson, Alan 268–9
Wolf, Martin 230, 257
Wolfowitz, Paul 206, 212, 226
Woods, Thomas 236, 238

World Bank 234
World Trade Center 203

Yellen, Janet 246
young workers 86, 88, 115

Zandi, Mark 250, 254

WITHDRAWN

JUL 2 5 2022

By: _____